MYTH EDUCATION:
A Guide to Gods, Goddesses, and Other Supernatural Beings

By David Fletcher

Foreword by Arthur George
Afterword by Dr. Karl E.H. Seigfried

Myth Education: A Guide to Gods, Goddesses, and Other Supernatural Beings

Copyright © 2017 David Fletcher

Published by *Onus Books*

Printed by Lightning Source International

Cover design: Philip Mitri

Trade paperback ISBN: 978-0-9935102-3-6

OB 14/24

*For Kris who has
the heart of Kuan Yin,
the strength of Freyja,
and the passion of Oya.*

Praise for the book:

"Myth Education is exactly what the title implies, a great introduction to our knowledge of mythology around the world. David Fletcher does a great job of introducing us to the stories that cultures across the globe have created to explain their origins, their culture and the world they lived in. He draws out the fascinating comparisons and contrasts as these myths are borrowed from other cultures and adapted to new situations. It's a book that anyone interested in the stories we tell ourselves should have on their shelves."

–Ed Brayton, author at *Dispatches from the Culture Wars*, recipient of the Friend of Darwin award from the National Center for Science Education, co-founder of Michigan Citizens for Science

"David Fletcher has written an entertaining yet substantive introduction to most of the world's mythologies and their principal deities and heroes that surely will be welcomed by students of myth."

–Arthur George, mythologist and author of *The Mythology of Eden*

"I wish, though, that I had had access to a copy of David Fletcher's wonderful new tome, 'Myth Education: A Guide to Gods, Goddesses, and Other Supernatural Beings.' In it, he does an outstanding job of introducing those new to the field to major figures from a multitude of the world's mythologies, but at the same time includes enough detail and breadth to provide new insight even to the most seasoned mythographers.... Fletcher's writing is pithy, insightful, and not infrequently causes an eruption of laughter via his footnotes. Adding to the joy of reading are the wonderful illustrations throughout the book, from a variety of artists who are all masters of their craft. In fact, the only criticism I have about this book is that it's too damn short. I'm putting my copy snugly next to Hamilton and Campbell on my bookshelf, and I think they will fully approve of their new company."

–Dr. Caleb Lack, author of *Critical Thinking, Science, and Pseudoscience: Why You Can't Trust Your Brain*

"Mythology still permeates through society, whether in popular culture or in the religions and beliefs that many hold. The sheer volume of gods and goddesses that fill the cultural spaces in society is staggering. Fletcher goes some way to detailing these many deities, and in a manner that fuses the ancient with the modern. His narrative voice joins these divine constellations of dots with often acerbic wit. With some fabulously striking artwork, this book is a superb anthology that will take pride of place on my bookshelf."

–Jonathan MS Pearce, author of *The Little Book of Unholy Questions* and *The Curse of the Maya*

About the author:

Dave Fletcher is a mythographer, instructor, father, and husband. He began teaching courses on mythology in 2008, more or less by accident. Since that time, he has developed an unhealthy obsession with the mythologies of the world. A former podcaster, radio host, actor, and custodian, Dave identifies as a polyatheist and hopes to educate as many people as possible about all the gods and goddesses of the world that are worth not believing in.

Author's Note

How to use this text: You may read this book any way you want. Not that you need my permission, but you do have it. If you want to read it cover to cover, you are more than welcome to do so. If you'd rather flip through and read about whatever deity catches your fancy at that moment, you can do that too. The goal is for each piece to stand on its own but also for reading them in order to build off each other for a richer, fuller picture of the mythic landscape of each culture. The introductions to each chapter should help orient you to the cultures and their source material but you can read the chapters in any order you choose.

The chapters are arranged chronologically by the date of the earliest recorded forms of each culture's myths. Egypt's *Pyramid Texts* date to roughly 2400 BCE; the Mesopotamian creation tale *Enuma Elish* dates to approximately 1800 BCE; the Chinese *Shanhaijing* was written around 400 BCE; the Japanese *Kojiki* in 711 CE; relatively reliable Celtic accounts go back to the *Book of Invasions* around 1000 CE; the Norse *Prose Edda* was composed around 1220 CE; Indigenous American stories such as the Quiche Mayan *Popol Vuh* were recorded in Central America in the 1500s with serious scholarship into the mythologies of peoples indigenous to the Americas starting closer to 1900. It is only in the last century or so that the outside world has taken notice of African myths and has begun setting those very ancient stories down on paper. Of course, this order does not reflect the chronology of the inception of these cultures, but ordering them this way puts the emphasis on the received mythology which is, after all, what we have to work with.

At the beginning of each profile, you'll see some of the basic details such as additional names, what pantheon they come from, the names of their spouse(s)/lovers, siblings, parents, and offspring, as well as what they are "deity of" and some of the symbols they are most closely associated with. These are not exhaustive lists and, given the nature of myth, very few of the details there included should be taken as gospel. Because translation is not an exact science, you will find many of the characters' names rendered into English differently from one source to another and so I've given a sampling of the most common versions. The information in the fields is ordered either with the most common first or, when commonalities are not so common, in simple alphabetical order. When it comes to parents, I have listed (when applicable) the mother before the father. That runs in opposition to the way these things are traditionally catalogued and does so intentionally. When men start squeezing babies out of their bodies (which, of course, does happen in mythology) they can get top billing; in the meantime, I will err on the side of crediting women as the more important part of the birthing process.

Perhaps surprisingly, the most frustrating field of the basic information, but also the one people tend to be most interested in, is what the deities are "deity of." I blame the Greeks for that. Because the study of mythology in the west has so heavily been influenced by the Greeks (and Romans), we tend to think of gods and goddesses in Greco-Roman categories. Geraldine Pinch addressed this issue in *Egyptian Myth: A Very Short Introduction* saying:

> It has been traditional for scholars who study polytheistic systems to classify deities as being the gods or goddesses of some natural phenomenon or particular area of responsibility. [. . .] Such labels are useful for us but may not correspond with the way that these deities were seen by their original worshippers. For the Egyptians, deities were first and foremost possessors of power. They could all be prayed to about anything, but there was some degree of specialization.

Though speaking specifically about the Egyptians, Pinch's point is (to one extent or another) true of most polytheistic cultures. While I have tried to satisfy the thirst for Greco-Roman categorizations of deities, I also want you to bear in mind that such labels do tend to be an oversimplification.

Speaking of the Greeks and Romans, you will notice while rifling through this book that many diverse cultures are addressed but neither the Greeks nor the Romans are included. This is largely because there is no shortage of texts on the figures of "classical" mythology. From children's books to scholarly texts to pop culture, the Greeks and Romans have dominated the landscape for centuries. This book is less of an attempt to even the score and more of an effort to present some of the figures that are not as well known to the general populace. And because I hate Zeus.

CONTENTS

AFRICAN MYTHOLOGY 271

AFTERWORD: MYTHOLOGY MATTERS BY KARL E.H. SEIGFRIED 318

Foreword

When I started studying mythology many years ago—this was long before the Internet—I longed for a handy reference book with bite-sized summaries of most world bodies of myth and their principal mythological figures, together with illustrations of the deities and heroes. Back then, I never dreamed that I would be a published mythologist writing the Foreword for just such a book.

Dave Fletcher is a veteran mythologist, having earned his cred by teaching mythology over many years to creative students at an art college. This experience has given him an acute sensitivity for what material beginning students of mythology need to hear about, as well as for what kinds of questions such students tend to have. This book answers these needs. For most bodies of world myth, Dave first summarizes the mythology of the culture complex in question, and then describes the main characteristics and deeds of the principal mythological figures. Rather than reproduce ancient depictions of these figures (which would not be possible for some of them anyway), Dave has enlisted contemporary artists (many of them his former students to whom he taught the corresponding myths) to draw illustrations of these figures that depict their salient characteristics and which can resonate with the modern reader, perhaps better than the ancient renderings. Dave plans another similar volume that will cover additional material not included here for reasons of space, such as Indian mythology.

These days, one can always access the Internet to read entries about particular mythological figures. In my experience, however, with the exception of classical myths, the Internet material is not consistently well written, is often unreliable, and is not always authored by competent, experienced mythologists. The entries in this book, however, demonstrate a deep familiarity with the subject matter that has enabled Dave to be selective in what material to present and how to present it. He also writes in an easy and non-technical style. And he does not shy away from retaining some of the edgy, potentially offensive details in the myths (e.g., unconventional sex, graphic violence, cannibalism) that we usually do not hear about, which earns the book at least a PG-13 rating. (Rather than offer any spoilers, however, I'll keep this Foreword to a G.)

A particularly valuable aspect of Dave's book is his choice to pay considerable attention to lesser-known bodies of mythology (such as Chinese, Japanese, and African), while leaving aside the well-trodden path of classical (Greek and Roman) myth because it is so well known. (As I mentioned, good summaries of classical myths are available on the Internet, as well as in other books.) For this reason, the book can be useful even for more knowledgeable readers. Everyone has their own favorite bodies of myth and areas of expertise, but no one can master the details of them all. (Joseph Campbell came very close, however!) It is especially interesting to see how many familiar mythological motifs play out, say, in Chinese and African myths. For example, Fletcher relates how the African epic hero Mwindo fits many facets of the Hero's Journey but with many twists: he is born of a (tribal) royal lineage, and miraculously (from the palm of his mother's hand). Once Mwindo is born, the king tries to kill him, and he must flee. (His mother put him in a drum and set it adrift in the sea.) As an adult, he is killed but resurrects. He was known as a great teacher. Is this starting to sound familiar? Another example is the Chinese primeval flood myth, in which the Chinese culture hero Yu, rather than build a boat to ride out the flood, one-ups Noah by stopping the flood itself.

So, while I am no longer the college student who once craved for a book such as this, and even though my library of mythology books is overflowing, this one will have a welcome spot on my shelf, and it won't just be gathering dust.

Arthur George
Author, *The Mythology of Eden*
Blog: www.mythologymatters.wordpress.com

Introduction

This text is meant to serve as an introduction to those new to the study of mythology, a refresher to those who haven't studied it in a while, and an enhancer to those already obsessed with the mythic figures of the world. If your knowledge of myth only goes as far as Marvel's *Thor* or if you've recently published your own translation of the *Poetic Edda*, my hope is that this book will serve to both entertain and inform.

Famed mythographer Joseph Campbell once wrote that "myths don't count if they're just hitting your rational faculties—they have to hit the heart. You have to absorb them and adjust them and make them your life." While I don't subscribe to all of Campbell's ideas (and certainly he can be accused of adjusting myths a little too liberally at times), his sentiment here is an important one. Studying mythology purely for its intellectual value is to ignore the very reason why these figures and stories have been passed down for centuries. As a modern audience, we can learn a great deal of anthropological, psychological, and philosophical value by looking at the myths of ancient peoples, but we would do well to remember their most important function: entertainment. These stories are entertaining. At times, they can be touching or horrifying, inspiring or just silly. But it was the collective experience of listening to these tales that not only passed the time, but drew people together. Before there were fandoms that brought people together over a shared appreciation for a television show or book series, there were mythologies.

Just as the poets and skalds and bards and shamans of old adapted their stories for their time and audience, I have tried here to present the figures of myth through a modern lens while still not losing sight of what they originally meant. I believe it is possible (and even necessary) to be critical of those things that deserve critique while still celebrating the character and spirit of their original context.

Defining Mythology

The terms *myth* and *mythology* get tossed around a lot, but their colloquial usage can be quite different from how we use them within the context of this book. For example, *MythBusters* was one of the greatest television programs of all time: it saved lives, taught people to think in terms of the scientific method and to challenge unproven claims, and showed us all how neat things look when caught

3

on high speed camera. One thing they failed to do on *MythBusters* was to ever actually take on a myth. The way they use the term on *MythBusters*, and in fact, the way we hear it most often in our daily lives, a *myth* is a popular idea that is not based on evidence. The ideas that it is easy to shoot fish in a barrel, that you can't fly a lead balloon, or that you can make your muscle car more aerodynamic by rotating the body 180 degrees are all myths. Or, to put it another way: they are bullshit.

The myths we are talking about in this book are not bullshit. Maybe. I mean, probably, yes, they are largely untrue tales in a literal sense, but *myth* and *mythology* in this context are more than just that. In my years of teaching courses on mythology I've developed a working definition. It's not a definition that you'll find in a dictionary and certainly there is plenty about it that most (if not all) other mythographers would disagree with, but for my purposes in class and the purposes of this book it should do just fine.

Mythology *is the set of stories (myths) that a particular culture believes to be true and which that culture uses as a means of understanding both themselves and the world around them.*

That's the basic definition but it needs to be teased out a bit for clarity.

"The set of stories" that makes up a mythology is a big tent. A big, porous tent that allows room for all sorts of things. No mythology, not even something like Christianity or Islam, can be condensed into a single book. Yes, many mythologies have a single text (Bible, Koran, Book of Mormon, Dianetics etc.) as the core of their beliefs, but it would be lunacy to suggest that any one text collects the complete and total history and variety of philosophy of a single person, let alone a complex and mutable culture. If the Bible were truly the last word on Christian belief, there would be no need for the enormous industry of people writing devotionals, philosophy papers, and even novels. There is more to Christianity than the one book. That's true for every culture. Especially when you account for the fact that in the history of the world only a fraction of the mythic tales that have been told and believed have even been written down. We know Homer's version of *The Iliad* because it was written down but that does not make it the only version. It doesn't even necessarily make it the best or most definitive version, just the one that made it down to us through the ages—the *received* form of the myth. The received mythology is all we have to work with. There are times when we can look at the received versions of stories and characters and make educated guesses about what they may have looked like in older, unpreserved forms, but such analysis can often prove difficult, if not impossible. The one thing

4

we know for certain is that we don't, and likely never will, have a full, comprehensive insight into the evolution of these mythologies. Stories change over time as they are transmitted orally. They change intentionally or unintentionally when they are translated for new audiences. We can often say what the most popular or most significant version of a myth is, but that doesn't make it the only one. It is not a closed set, it is a wide open one.

Myths are culturally specific. The myths of the Greeks are not the same as the myths of the Egyptians. That's fairly obvious but what's less obvious, perhaps, is that even when one culture draws their myths from another culture, they are not the same. The Romans took a lot of their myths from the Greeks but they made them Roman. And not just the facile stuff like "Zeus" becoming "Jupiter," but the tone, the intention, the meaning of the stories change and become distinctly Roman. Figures from one culture are syncretized with another to form something new that may or may not end up being greater than the sum of its parts. To complicate things even further, cultures change internally and with them so do the myths. The stories told and the gods worshipped in northern Egypt in 4000 BCE are not the exact same ones as those of southern Egypt in 4000 BCE, or those in northern or southern Egypt in 2000 BCE or in 40 BCE or in 2017 CE. To understand the myths you need to know the culture they are coming out of, and in order to understand the culture you need to know their myths. They are as inextricably linked as they are ever changing.

Truth is an elusive beast, so when I say that these people believe these stories to be "true," it's a loaded statement. "True" does not mean the same thing to every culture at every time or to every person within them. Take modern Christians for example: some believe the Bible is literally true, right down to how the sun revolves around a flat earth. Others believe that it is metaphorically or spiritually true—some of your more liberal Christians will even say that it doesn't matter if Jesus was an actual historical man or not because the truth of the teachings is all that matters. And then, between the two extremes, you have those who believe parts are literally true (Jesus was fully and historically god and man) whereas other parts are metaphorically true (the world wasn't created in seven twenty-four-hour periods but was created by a single, benevolent god). This is true of virtually every other culture's relationship with their myths as well. Did Erik the Red believe that each peal of thunder came from Thor or did he believe that the tales of the gods were meant to show us how to live? Some Egyptians may have believed that the sun was rolled over the horizon each morning by a dung beetle whereas others didn't take it quite as literally. Truth comes in many forms. And, importantly, this definition of mythology does not say anything about the actual truth value of these beliefs, only that it has some degree of perceived truth value by the believer. So, when I call Christianity, Islam, Hinduism or any other belief system a "mythology," I am not calling it either true or untrue, just saying that the believer finds a degree of truth in it. "Myth" is not a pejorative.

Myths serve the function of helping people understand the workings of the universe as well as their own inner workings. We are largely talking about pre-scientific cultures who did not have, for example, a knowledge of plate tectonics or the Earth's molten core to explain earthquakes and volcanoes. They didn't have medical diagnoses to explain why people had seizures or why some people were attracted to the opposite sex, whereas others were attracted to members of their own sex. So, we use myths. They explain not only why the sun rose in the sky this morning, but also what, if anything, we need to do to help make sure it does again tomorrow. Some myths serve clearer functions and offer better explanations than others but they all reveal something about the way the people telling or the people hearing the stories perceived the world.

Content Warning

Mythology is filled with numerous acts of horrific violence and mutilation, cannibalism, unconventional sex acts as well as nonconsensual sex acts like rape, incest, and bestiality. It is an unavoidable fact that the mythologies of the world showcase some seriously messed up stuff and dancing around them or covering them up is disingenuous to a real study of the characters, stories, and the people who believed them. The myths are presented here, warts and all, but not without judgement. The atrocities committed in myths and those committed in the name of mythic figures are still atrocities and are not given a pass simply because they are "of their time" or "they couldn't have known better" or any nonsense like that.

Along with that, it probably bears stating that mythology is not for children. Or rather, it contains material that many may find unsuitable for their children to consume. While there are many sanitized versions of myths designed for the consumption of children and those with milder sensibilities, this is not that kind of text. Parental discretion is advised.

"Anubis feeding the heart of an unworthy soul to Ammit" by Darian Papineau

Egyptian Mythology

The received Egyptian mythology took an exceptionally long time for us to receive. This thing that we refer to monolithically as "Ancient Egypt" covers a timeframe of nearly 5,000 years. Even if we trim off the predynastic period (roughly 5000–3100 BCE) and stop at the Ptolemaic period (beginning with Alexander's conquest in 332 BCE) we're talking about a very long stretch of time. Even though the Egyptians were responsible for one of the earliest forms of writing in history, and that they did plenty of it, we have not had a very clear understanding of their myths for most of modern history. Until the early 1800's CE when the brilliant linguist Jean-Francois Champollion got his hands on the so-called Rosetta Stone, the written language of the ancient Egyptians was virtually undecipherable. The idiosyncratic hieroglyphs had long since represented a dead, forgotten language. Indeed, until Champollion, we had only hazy and not terribly well-researched Greek and Roman accounts of Egyptian mythology to go by. It was enough to fascinate would-be world conquerors like Alexander, Julius Caesar, and Napoleon, but they weren't exactly rife with reliable information.

In unencrypting the hieroglyphic system, the modern world was finally let in on the secrets of Egyptian myth, the most significant pieces of which were found in crypts. True, there were other written sources that provided some information on their myths, but the most comprehensive and well-preserved sources are the funerary texts. These are called generally "Akh Makers" because the texts help instruct post-death people on how to attain immortality in the form of an *akh*. The earliest written religious texts known on Earth are what we call the Pyramid Texts. These are texts found in pyramids, specifically dating back to the 5th and 6th dynasties of the Old Kingdom (c. 2381 – 2181 BCE). There aren't a lot of narrative pieces in the Pyramid Texts, but they do give us the earliest depictions and references to many of the gods of Egypt. Next came the Coffin Texts, which started cropping up in the First Intermediate Period and on into the Middle Kingdom (c. 2134 – 2040 BCE). The Coffin Texts notably feature the first known human-made maps—though they only mapped the afterlife realm and so, they weren't a huge help to living travelers. Finally, the most comprehensive Akh Maker text is this thing we now call *The Book of the Dead*.

First, it is important to note that *The Book of the Dead* is not a book. Not only was it, of course, written on papyrus scrolls, but there was also no single, standardized version. What we call *The Book of the Dead* is made up of over 200 pieces of writing (often called "spells" or "orations" because they were meant to be spoken by the dead) that have been found in various gravesites and were cobbled together to create a composite. Original versions varied in length, largely dependent on how much someone was willing to pay. Wealthy Egyptians could be buried with a personalized scroll, containing their own name, and upwards of 150 spells. A less privileged person may be buried with a scroll containing blank spots for the name, and as few as only three or four of the most essential pieces. No matter how short or long the scroll was, the goal was to help the dead on their journey into their new life. A more accurate title would be *Spells of Emerging into Daytime*, but that's not nearly as sexy sounding as *The Book of the Dead*. As important as it was for the dead, so that they could avoid the various trips and traps they encountered on the way into their new life, it is, quite honestly, a tedious read for a modern audience. Along with the occasional interesting mythic tidbit, the saving grace is the gorgeous original art included on each scroll. If, however, you found yourself dead and emerging into daytime (as the dead are wont to do), you would do well to have as many of those spells on you as you could afford.

"Maat" by Annamarie Borowiak

Maat

a.k.a.: Ma'at, Ma'et

Pantheon: Egyptian

Spouse/Lover: Thoth

Parents: Ra

Deity of: truth, justice, balance, *maat*

Symbols: *baat* (Feather of *Maat*), sun disk, birds

If the greatest fear of the ancient Egyptians was chaos, their highest goal was its counter-point: *maat*.

Maat was a broad concept that loosely translates to order, balance, or justice. It was the guiding principle of Egyptian life. *Maat* not only compelled humans to act justly and avoid rocking the proverbial boat too much, but it also created a mindset that led the Egyptians to take an orderly view of the universe. It was this concept that allowed them to look at the heavens and create a 365-day calendar based on what they observed. It was *maat* that told them what to expect from their most important geographical feature: the Nile.

Whether it was the relative predictability of the Nile that led them to the concept of *maat*, or the concept of *maat* that led them to understand and appreciate the dependability of the Nile, is a bit of a chicken-and-egg scenario. Whichever came first, the two were doubtlessly related. Their calendar was built around the fact that, each year, the Nile would flood for four months ("The Inundation," they called it) and provide nutrient-rich soil for crops to grow in over the next four months ("The Emergence"), and then the next four months (they simply called it "Summer") would be spent harvesting and preparing for the cycle to begin again. When the regularly scheduled flooding of the Nile was too little, too much, too long, or too short, it was an indication that something was amiss with *maat* and needed to be corrected. Pray harder, work harder, listen closer to your leader, or replace your leader—something was required to get the universe back to its natural order.

The concept of *maat* governed not just the stars and the seasons, but also human behavior. After death, the Egyptians believed their hearts would be judged against the "Feather of *Maat*" (simply called a *baat*). If they were found to have lived a just life, their heart would balance with the feather on the scales of justice. They would then proceed into the afterlife, which was essentially the same as the pre-death life, but without any of the bad mixed in. The afterlife was simply a more orderly version of life. If, however, they had caused trouble and disrupted the universal harmony, they were dealt the harsh and eternal punishment of having their heart consumed.

Maat was also depicted as a goddess. Though her depictions are almost identical to the goddess Isis, the clearest difference between the two women is that Isis is most often depicted with the throne glyph on top of her head, whereas Maat bears either an ostrich feather or the sun disk on hers. Maat and Ra standing side-by-side with Isis and Horus would be like one of those games where you have to spot the differences between the two seemingly identical pictures.

Ra

a.k.a.: Re, Pre, Ra-Horakhty
Pantheon: Egyptian
Spouse/Lovers: Bastet, Hathor, Sekhmet, Mut
Siblings: Apep, Serket, Sobek, Thoth
Parents: None
Offspring: Bastet, Hathor, Maat, Serket, Shu, Tefnut
Deity of: sun
Symbols: sun disk, falcon, cobra

"Hail to the sun god! He's a fun god! Ra! Ra! Ra!" ~ Ancient Heliopolitan Prayer[1]

Ra's importance in the Egyptian pantheon is almost without rival. He was not only the primary sun deity for much of the land for much of its history, but he was often believed to have been the first god to rule Earth, and acted as pharaoh over the gods themselves. His daily/nightly activity required not only moving the sun across the sky, but re-invigorating it so it could be reborn each morning. Without Ra's work, the Egyptians would be sunless and that generally leads to trouble in the worlds of myth.

Given the significance of Ra's role, it is all the more surprising to learn that humanity was less than respectful to him while he sat upon his earthly throne. Like all pharaohs after him, Ra was both god and human and so, as time passed, his body grew old and frail, and his subjects took to mocking him for his droopy skin,

---

[1] Not really.

"Ra" by Madeleine Graumlich

sad shuffling walk, and his old man stink. While respecting one's elders is important, it is even more important when one's elder also happens to be a temperamental deity. Offended by their jeers and disrespect, Ra turned an angry eye on humanity. The Eye of Ra, the literal manifestation of his glare, became the vicious goddess Sekhmet, who dealt out harsh justice on humanity until finally being quelled by Ra himself.

After that incident, the goddess Isis decided that it was time for Ra to abdicate his throne, whether he wanted to or not. Isis created a venomous serpent and hid it along the path that Ra used for his daily shambling walks. When Ra shuffled by, the serpent struck out and bit Ra, knocking the lord of the gods to the ground. In horrible pain from the venom, Ra cried out for help. Luckily, Isis was not-so-coincidentally nearby and rushed over to help. As a goddess of healing versed in both medicine and magic, she told Ra she could end his suffering—for a price. For her magic to work, she needed him to tell her his true name. The true name of Ra was a word so powerful that any who knew it would be endowed with abilities to rival Ra himself. The pain was so excruciating, though, that Ra agreed to give her the forbidden knowledge with one caveat: she could only ever tell one other person. Isis cured Ra, who then felt compelled to step down from his earthly throne and turned it over to Isis' husband Osiris. Rather than keeping the name and its power to herself, Isis passed it on to her only begotten son, the falcon-headed Horus. Horus became pharaoh after Osiris and, indeed, each human pharaoh that followed was taken to be the manifestation of Horus himself. The power of Ra thus coursed through the veins of the pharaohs from the First Dynasty's Menes all the way to Cleopatra.

Ra was not the only sun god of Egypt, nor was he the first sun god of Egypt, but he was eventually all the sun gods of Egypt. More or less. Somewhere along the line, an astute Egyptian observed that their sky was filled with an array of sun gods but there remained only one sun. And so, the solar deities were mashed together into one god with a variety of aspects and titles. The Ra-Horus merged two falcon-headed gods and was the early morning manifestation of the sun because Horus was a young man. Ra-Atum brought the elder creator god Atum into the patchwork quilt of the solar god, and was the evening sun quite literally walking off into the sunset of life. Amun, who like Ra was a near monotheistic god who ruled over the other gods (considered to be largely aspects of himself), was also stirred in, giving us Amun-Ra.

"Osiris" by Christopher Kraklau

Osiris

a.k.a.: Asiri, Ausar, Ausir, Onnophris, Wenenefer, Wsjr
Pantheon: Egyptian
Spouse/Lovers: Isis, Nephthys
Siblings: Isis, Nephthys, Seth, Horus the Elder
Parents: Nut and Geb
Offspring: Horus, Anubis
Deity of: afterlife, death, life, resurrection, fertility
Symbols: crook and flail, *atef* crown, *djed* pillar, green skin, mummy wrappings

In *Star Wars*, Obi-wan Kenobi tells Darth Vader that "If you strike me down, I shall become more powerful than you can possibly imagine." And then Vader strikes him down and Old Ben becomes a translucent blue spirit who intermittently talks to Luke and Yoda. Apparently, Darth Vader does not have much of an imagination. That aside, the old Jedi's parting words could more appropriately have been spoken by the Egyptian god Osiris.

As the first son of the illicit union between the earth and the sky, Osiris was a very powerful figure, even in life. After the sun god Ra abdicated his throne[1] as the direct ruler of Earth, Osiris became the next pharaoh. When Osiris and his sister/wife Isis took power, humans were little better off than animals. The story goes that humanity was so stumped as to the workings of the world that they couldn't figure out what there was to eat aside from one another. Given that most other creatures in the animal kingdom are smart enough to figure out how to eat things other than their own immediate families, it seems that the human flock Osiris inherited was possibly the stupidest of all animals -- an honor that we can still lay claim to from time to time. One is left to wonder what Ra did as pharaoh if he couldn't even be bothered to educate his subjects beyond cannibalistic cuisine. Apparently, education was low on Ra's list of priorities.

The power couple of Osiris and Isis raised humanity up from the world of beasts and made them the paragon of animals. They offered the Promethean gift of enlightenment, as well as teaching the skills to make life not only livable, but enjoyable, rich, and full. First, they taught farming, and food preparation, then they

---

[1] Not entirely a decision of his own making. Isis engineered a set of circumstances that helped convince Ra it was time for him to retire.

established an orderly government and laws, and lastly, they introduced the arts. Their efforts were a roaring success and Osiris and his wife were beloved by all.

Except Seth.

Seth hated his brother Osiris. It may have been because Osiris got to be pharaoh instead of Seth. It may have been because Osiris impregnated their mutual sister/Seth's wife Nephthys. It may have been because Seth was jealous that Osiris was a handsome man with lush green skin and Seth had the head of some kind of anteater. The simple truth is: myths are often light on character motivation. All we can say for certain is that Seth hated Osiris because Seth hated Osiris.

While sibling rivalry is common, Seth dialed it up to the more extreme level of fratricide. There are differing accounts as to how Seth killed Osiris, but one way or another Osiris ended up ensconced in an ornate box (just as every pharaoh after him would be). When Isis found the corpse of her beloved, Osiris received a reprieve from his death sentence just long enough for he and his wife to have sex one last time. Isis turned into a bird and flapped the breath of life back into Osiris and then, apparently still in the form of a bird, she had sex with him and became pregnant. It was the final act of fertility for this fertility god. But more indignities were still to come.

As Isis was transporting the body of Osiris to its final resting place, Seth managed to sneak up, tear his brother's body into more than a dozen pieces and scatter those pieces up and down the Nile. His hope was that his friends, the Nile crocodiles, would eat Osiris thus barring him from moving forward into the afterlife. Luckily for Osiris, the Nile crocs were turned off by the green hue of the dead pharaoh's body and refrained from eating it. Unluckily for Osiris, the Nile was also populated by fish who did eat part of Osiris' body. Luckily for Osiris, they only ate one piece. Unluckily for Osiris, it was his genitals. Losing one's genitalia would be unfortunate for most, but a fertility god facing the sweet hereafter without his staff of life was a catastrophic prospect. Ever the healer, Isis remedied the situation by crafting Osiris a new set of equipment out of gold. Anubis, Osiris' son via Nephthys, took the pieces (both green and gold), pieced them back together, and embalmed his father, creating the first mummy and, arguably, the inspiration for both Frankenstein and jigsaw puzzles.

Struck down, torn apart, and stitched back together, Osiris became far more powerful in death than he had been in life. Rather than simply being a pharaoh/fertility god, Osiris became lord of the dead and was personally responsible for reinvigorating each dead person so that they too could enjoy the post-death life due them.

"Isis" by Amanda Zylstra

Isis

a.k.a.: Aset, Iset
Pantheon: Egyptian
Spouse: Osiris
Siblings: Osiris, Nephthys, Seth, Horus the elder
Parents: Nut and Geb
Offspring: Horus, Ammit, Bastet
Deity of: health and healing, marriage, wisdom
Symbols: throne, sun disk, cobra, birds (kite, sparrow and vulture)

The word "Isis" does not conjure up the same images and ideas today as it did for the ancient Egyptians. Isis was one of the most powerful, beloved, and popular goddesses in history. And she certainly wouldn't have stood for any of this ISIS/ISIL bullshit.

Her name was synonymous with healing and magic. The Egyptians may well have been the first people to consider natural causes for illness and to look for cures other than casting out demons or making sacrifices to unhappy gods. As a hybrid of what the best medical science (such as it was at the time) and magic had to offer, Isis was invoked by apothecaries and healers as they mixed their potions or applied their salves. Popular depictions showed her nursing her sickly son Horus to health and, legend has it, even the great Roman poet Ovid prayed to Isis for help as his wife was dying from a botched abortion. Because she knew the secrets of healing, Isis often used it as leverage to get what she wanted.

When the elder sun god Ra held the throne of both Heaven and Earth, Isis sent a venomous snake to attack him. As Ra lay dying, Isis offered to help him if, and only if, he revealed to her his true name—and with that knowledge, his power. He gave in to her demands, she healed him, and then passed the power of Ra down to her own son (who coincidentally had a falcon-head just like Ra's). The snake incident also led Ra to turn his earthly throne over to Isis' husband Osiris. Both her husband and their son gained enormous power and status – and all it took was a little attempted regicide – or was it deicide?

Osiris assumed the role of the pharaoh, but Isis remained his partner and most trusted advisor. The two of them raised humanity from a pack of cannibalistic morons by teaching them how to farm, harvest, and prepare food. They also established the first government, laws, and gave humanity the arts. Like a pair of Egyptian Prometheuses (Promethei?), they brought culture and elevated

19

humans above the other animals. When Osiris went out into the world to educate those people who lived beyond the limits of Kemet[1], Isis was left in charge and the people flourished under her rule. Given such a potent female leader at the core of their mythology, it is not surprising that the Egyptians actually had powerful female leaders like Hatshepsut and Cleopatra. Isis, like her real-life counterparts, was just as respected and effective as any male leader.

Even after her beloved husband was killed by their mutual brother Seth (yes, incest was totally cool if you were a god, a pharaoh, or a Lannister), she dedicated herself to recovering his body so that he could have a proper burial. A feat which she accomplished not once, but twice. The second time she had to find pieces of Osiris scattered across the Nile while also caring for the child whom she had conceived (in the form of a bird) after forcing the breath of life back into Osiris for one last act of fertility. When the gods failed to recover Osiris' little green obelisk, it fell to Isis to craft him a set of golden genitalia, making it possible for him to imbue both the dead and the sun with vital energy each night. When her son's claim to the throne was disputed by Seth, Isis stood firm and was a key figure each step of the way toward the eventual reign of Horus. This included advocating for her son, harpooning her brother, and even acting as the Hand Goddess by helping to collect Horus' semen in an ultimately successful Hail Mary attempt to dominate Seth. More on that to come. No pun intended.

Isis was such a beloved figure that her worship was picked up by the Romans after they found their way to Egypt (and to a lesser extent, by the Greeks before them). Altars to Isis could be found throughout the Roman Empire. By the time Rome turned Christian, Isis was still popular and, rather than forbidding her worship and tearing down her shrines, they found a creative work-around and simply changed their depictions of the pagan goddess into depictions of the Virgin Mother. Got a statue of Isis nursing the baby Horus? No problem! Now it's Mary suckling baby Jesus! The remnants of the Isis/Mary fusion can still be found in modern Catholicism—the sick and suffering pray to Mary, not because of Biblical accounts of Mary healing people[2] but because Isis was a goddess of healing. Even the sun disk that often adorned her head was easy to morph into a shiny Christian halo.

---

[1] The Egyptian name for Egypt. Literally meaning "the Dark Land," it is a reference to the nutrient-rich soil along the banks of the Nile where a majority of Egyptian people lived.
[2] There aren't any, just in case you were thinking of looking.

Seth

a.k.a.: Set, Setesh, Sutekh, Suty
Pantheon: Egyptian
Spouse: Nephthys
Siblings: Nephthys, Osiris, Isis, Horus the elder
Parents: Nut and Geb
Offspring: Anubis
Deity of: *isfet*, chaos, storms, desert
Symbols: *was* scepter, Set-animal

Seth is such an incredibly unique figure that I am forced to qualify the word "unique." He is so singular in his appearance that we literally do not know what type of animal his head was meant to represent. Modern versions often move him toward the canine realm but it's quite clear that the Egyptians did not think of him as a dog-headed god. They had dog-headed gods, they knew how to depict dogs and did so often—Seth was not a dog. With his long, blunted ears and slightly floppy-looking elongated snout, about the closest approximation to an animal found in our near Egypt is an African anteater. Whatever he was intended to be, by the time the Greeks came along it wasn't readily apparent, and so they just referred to it as a "Set [or Seth]-animal." A contributing factor to the mystery of the Set-animal is that actual depictions of Seth are relatively rare.

Seth was an agent of chaos and, as such, the Egyptians were dubious about drawing his attention. Along with chaotic animals like hippos and crocodiles, Seth was often alluded to more than directly shown so as not to risk invoking his presence. Depicting Seth was comparable to looking into a mirror in a dark room and saying, "Bloody Mary" three times – it probably won't do anything, but why risk it?

"Seth" by David Stokes

Seth embodied many of the greatest fears of the ancient Egyptians. The most important concept for the Egyptians was the idea of maat, a harmonious, orderly, and ultimately just view of the world. As a god of *isfit* (unbalance or chaos), Seth was completely antithetical to the very structure of Egyptian society. Seth was also associated with storms—which were not, as one might imagine, a welcome gift of water to the desert dwelling people. Instead, storms were troublesome; they threw off the natural balance of the Nile and were feared and loathed. Conversely, Seth represented the desert and its many dangers. Basically, if there was a natural phenomenon that the Egyptians didn't like, they associated it with Seth. In the story of *The Contendings of Horus and Seth*, wherein nephew Horus vies with Uncle Seth for the throne vacated by Osiris (when Seth killed him), Seth is described as being both excessively loud and prone to homosexual activity[1] both of which were considered taboo in Egypt because they were 'disorderly.' And if that was all he was, if Seth were nothing more than the manifestation of chaos, the enemy of good gods, and a loud-talking bisexual, he would make for a good boogeyman, but ultimately not much else.

What makes Seth such an interesting character is that he was so much more than a villain. Yes, he killed his brother Osiris and battled, mutilated, and attempted to rape his nephew Horus, but there was more to Seth than that. Because history is written by the victors, it is easy to overlook the fact that Seth was the primary god of Upper Egypt for a time, with temples, worshippers, prayers, and sacrifices being offered up to him. Perhaps his worship grew independently of characters like Osiris and Horus with whom he was later linked—what we do know is that he came to represent southern Egypt when the conflict between Upper and Lower Egypt was converted from history to myth. Historically, some time around 3000 BCE the legendary pharaoh Menes united the two lands, but mythologically Horus and Seth created the peace. Though Seth was the inevitable loser in *The Contendings*, afterwards he held on to one of the most important jobs of any god: the nightly protection of the sun.

Why a figure of chaos who seemed hellbent on disrupting the order of the universe was entrusted with protecting the sun from other chaotic forces (most prominently, the Apep serpent who wanted to eat the sun) boggles the mind. Or

---

[1] The "homosexual activity" Seth partakes in is not really homosexual at all, since it's not about attraction, it's simply a show of dominance over his opponent. It's about power, not about sex. That being said, the Egyptians regarded it as taboo largely because it was two males rather than the fact that it was rape. Which just goes to show that the Egyptians had some skewed ideas from time to time.

rather, it does if we look at the characters as we would with a narrative piece. But mythology does not always follow the rules of storytelling, it twists cause and effect, and defies a strict linear interpretation. The answer to why Seth was entrusted with such an important task may simply be that it was a remnant of another tradition (perhaps from southern Egypt) where Seth was more revered. Perhaps it was a political move to appease Seth (or his worshippers) after the culture shifted and lifted Horus to prominence. It could also be that, as Seth says in *The Contendings*, he was the only god powerful enough for the task. He may have been a jerk, but even Seth acknowledged the importance of the sun and did what only he could do to keep it safe. Because of this job, Seth was closely associated with the sun god Ra (or perhaps because he's closely associated with Ra, he was said to have this job). Ra was the only god who defended Seth's right to the throne over Horus', but since Ra had veto power over the other gods it was enough to keep the fight raging for years or even decades.

Seth was sometimes regarded as the father or pseudo-father to two very important gods. Some traditions hold that Seth and his sister/wife Nephthys were the parents of the dog-headed god of embalming, Anubis. The more common tale said, rather, that Nephthys got Osiris (brother to both her and Seth) drunk and got him to impregnate her. Which may be a contributing factor to why Seth disliked Osiris so much. Whatever origin is assigned to Anubis, it was clear where the black dog's allegiances were. After Seth had killed Osiris and mutilated his corpse, Anubis not only knit the pieces back together, but stood guard at the tomb expressly to prevent Seth from desecrating Osiris yet again. There's even a story of Seth, in the guise of a cheetah, being skinned alive by Anubis for attempting to sneak into the burial site. Another origin tale linked Seth to the creation of the god Thoth. In some accounts, Thoth was made manifest when Horus' sperm crawled out of Seth's ears. Given that Thoth was a god of wisdom, the moon, mathematics, and record keeping, and that he generally played an active role in *The Contendings* long before the scene where this would occur, it seems odd to link him to Seth or to the talking-ear-sperm event. But logic is not always the top priority in myth.

Despite often being cast as the villain, Seth was nonetheless a crucial part of the Egyptian worldview. Without the machinations of Seth, Osiris wouldn't have become the lord of the dead; without Seth's usurpation, Horus (and in turn, every earthly pharaoh after him) wouldn't have secured an airtight claim to the throne; and without Seth's nightly battle with the Apep serpent, the sun wouldn't have risen afresh each day. Perhaps a little chaos is necessary to keep the balance.

"Horus" by Caitlin Rausch

Horus

a.k.a.: Horus the younger, Harpokrates, Hor, Ra-Horakhty
Pantheon: Egyptian
Spouse/Lover: Hathor
Siblings: Anubis
Parents: Isis and Osiris
Offspring: Duamutef, Hapi, Imset, Qebehsenuef
Deity of: sky, kings and kingship, sun
Symbols: *wadjet* ("Eye of Horus"), falcon, sun disk

Part male ingénue, part action hero, Horus is the leading man of Egyptian myth. In fact, he was all the leading men in Egypt because every living pharaoh was believed to be an earthly form of Horus. Once the pharaoh died, they merged with his dead dad Osiris, but while they sat on the throne they were all Horus.

The young sun god's path to power was fraught with dangers from his very conception. He was born of the goddess Isis after her sexual liaison with her momentarily-undead husband Osiris. Whether it was the result of Isis having taken the form of the bird for said copulation, or because of his connection to the elder sun god Ra, or simply because he was the result of at least a couple of generations of inbreeding, Horus ended up with a falcon head. Isis hoped to protect her son from the evil machinations of her brother Seth, so she hid her newborn baby in a basket amongst the reeds of the Nile. If the idea of a baby being hidden in a basket in the Nile to prevent almost certain death at the hands of a wicked pharaoh sounds familiar, it may be because the biblical Moses had the same origin story. As did, more or less, Sargon of Akkad. Since they were all neighbors, it's not too surprising to see this story showing up among the Egyptians, the Hebrews, and the Akkadians.

Saved from death at the hands of his uncle, young Horus was still not in the clear. He was a sickly babe and had a poorly developed lower half, which may have been a nod to the pollutants in the pharaonic gene pool. Either his mother Isis or his wet-nurse Hathor offered the wee tot healing milk and young Horus grew healthy and strong. Once of age, Horus asserted his claim to the throne, leading to years, or even decades, of fighting between him and his usurper uncle Seth. The tale, known as *The Contendings of Horus and Seth* is one of the central parts of the Egyptian mythic cycle and reflects actual conflicts between Upper Egypt (the southern part, ruled and represented by Seth) and Lower Egypt (the northern part, ruled and represented by Horus). Historically, Menes was the Abraham Lincoln of Egypt—mythologically, it was Horus who took charge over both north and south and became the "Ruler of the Two Lands." Of course, since Menes was an embodiment of Horus, both can be said to be true at the same time. Because he unified Egypt, Horus was depicted with the crown of the two lands (a combination of the red crown of the north and the tall white crown of the south) atop his nifty bird-head. That's the easiest way to distinguish between Horus and the otherwise identical Ra—Horus wears the crown of the two lands, Ra is usually just rocking a solar disk with a serpent slung over it.

There are numerous accounts of *The Contendings*, each with a different contest or battle to determine who would sit upon the throne. In one, Horus and Seth became hippos and hung out at the bottom of the sea for three months to see who could hold their breath longer—in some versions Isis grew impatient and harpooned Seth, injuring though not killing him. In others, Isis grew impatient and harpooned Horus while trying to harpoon Seth. Either way, the hippo contest was aborted when an outraged Horus told his mom to butt out—sometimes by way of chopping off her head. In another story, the two held a boat race wherein Seth tried to cheat and ended up sinking both himself and Horus. At some point, all the stress got to be too much for Horus, so he went off to sulk in the wilderness. No one knew where he was and, strangely, Seth volunteered to look. Even more strangely, the other gods thought that sounded like a fine idea. Seth managed to track down Horus, but rather than bringing him back home, he snuck up while Horus was sleeping and plucked out both of his eyes. The blinded Horus stumbled back to civilization and his eyes were pieced back together by Thoth or Isis. One of the eyes shone more brightly than the other from that point on and thus they came to represent the sun and the moon. Horus wasn't the only one to suffer traumatic loss during *The Contendings*; Seth was temporarily robbed, not of his eyes, but of his testicles. Which was not the only time their fighting was vaguely or even overtly sexual.

In the most notorious version, Seth attempted to either seduce or outright rape his nephew. Horus knew enough to watch his back when Uncle Seth was around, and he avoided being penetrated by putting his hands behind his back to catch Seth's semen. Having not noticed, Seth believed himself to have dominated Horus, and left to have a good night's sleep. Horus flew off to ask his mother, Isis, for help. She began by chopping off her son's semen-soaked hand and tossing it into the Nile. Considering that he had chopped off her head previously, this seems only fair—and, besides, she caused a new one to grow in its place. Having realized that Seth was willing to go to any lengths to win, Isis came up with a way to prove Horus' dominance. She lent a hand and collected a jug of her own son's semen (yup, exactly the way you're thinking). Then, she spread it over a field of lettuce. When Seth awoke the next day, he ate his usual breakfast consisting of a field of lettuce (apparently, he needed a lot of roughage in his diet). When the gods were assembled, Seth announced that he had dominated his nephew and thus the kingdom was his. The other gods, who turned out to be super-homophobic for a culture with as much penis imagery lying around as the Egyptians had, spat on Horus for having been on the receiving end of Seth's sexual assault. Sadly, victim blaming is nothing new. When Horus asked for proof, Seth called out to his sperm.[1] His sperm cried out from the Nile and the other gods called shenanigans and heaped their scorn on Seth. Horus offered to call out to his sperm just to see and when he did, they responded from somewhere between Seth's throat and stomach. In some accounts, the sperm crawled out of Seth's ears to take roll. Whichever part of Seth's anatomy Horus' semen came from, it was obvious that it was Seth and not Horus who had been on the receiving end. As the politics of these things go, Horus then had an undisputed claim to his father's throne.

No matter which narrative elements are included in any particular account of *The Contendings*, the outcome is always the same: Horus wins. There was never a question about who would win, just variations on how Horus achieved victory. *The Contendings of Horus and Seth* is less of a story and more of a subgenre of Egyptian storytelling about how Horus became the Ruler of the Two Lands.

While it is easy to mistake Horus for Ra or Ra for Horus based on their appearances, there is an even more stymying issue between Horus and Horus. There were two (or three) characters named Horus who may or may not actually all have been the same character. Horus the Elder is said to have been born of Nut and Geb along with Osiris, Isis, Seth, and Nephthys, whereas Horus the Child is typically seen as the son of Osiris and Isis. Horus the Child is usually depicted with a human head, but the son of Isis and Osiris is shown with a falcon head when depicted as an adult. And then, to confuse matters further, Horus and a handful of other sky and solar deities were combined with Ra and/or Amun. Ra-Horus was the early morning sun which grew older throughout the day until, as Ra-Atum, it walked off into the horizon. In an attempt to streamline their bevy of sun gods, the Egyptians created a complex knot for modern folk to try to make sense of.

---

[1] This is apparently a thing that the gods can do. Maybe it works for people too. I invite you to give it a try and let us know.

"Anubis" by Tyler Space

29

Anubis

a.k.a.: Anpu, Inpw
Pantheon: Egyptian
Spouse/Lover: Anput
Siblings: Horus
Parents: Nephthys and Osiris; Nephthys and Seth; Ra
Offspring: Kebechet, Ammit
Deity of: mummification, embalming, burial, cemeteries, the dead
Symbols: black jackal, fetish, flail, *was* scepter

It is no secret that the Egyptians were a tad obsessed with death. They didn't build one of the Seven Wonders of the Ancient World to store grain, after all. From the step pyramid of Djoser in Saqqara to the Great Pyramids of Khufu, Khafre, and Menkaure in Giza, the Egyptians used a great deal of time, energy, and workforce to make sure their leaders made the journey to the afterlife in style. That included not just pyramids and other elaborate burial chambers, but the mummification process itself. If the pharaoh had a clean passage into the waking world beyond death, then the people could also be assured of continued safety into the undiscovered country. And no god was more closely associated with the passage into death than Anubis. Priests/embalmers would even wear Anubis masks while performing the mummification process and associated rituals and, for a time, he was the only god who could be depicted on non-royal caskets.

Anubis has long been identified as the jackal-headed Egyptian god of funerals, embalming, and the dead—the only problem with this is that there is no such thing as an Egyptian jackal. His head is actually that of an Egyptian wolf. Anubis is black in color not because Egyptian wolves have black fur (they don't) but because of the god's association with death. Anubis was sometimes depicted as a man with a canine head and other times shown as a full black dog. It was likely because wolves feed on carrion and can be found in the same type of out-of-the-way areas where you might bury your dead that they led to the inspiration for Anubis.

Like so many other gods, Anubis' parentage is inconsistent and complicated. At times, he was considered the only son of married siblings Seth and Nephthys, at other times he was the son of Osiris and Nephthys. If he was Seth's son that did not make him an ally of the god of chaos, rather both Anubis and his mother were squarely among the gods who sided with Osiris, Isis, and their son Horus when all the family drama went down. Viewing him as the son of Osiris certainly works in that both Osiris and Anubis were death gods and, in fact, Osiris became the first mummy when Anubis performed the first mummification ritual on him. It is said that Nephthys plied Osiris with alcohol and seduced him into sleeping with her in order to beget their puppy-baby—which seems an unnecessary complication since pharaohs were more than welcome to have multiple spouses, even multiple spouses that were part of their own immediate family. The tricky thing about Anubis being the offspring of Osiris (or Seth) is that the worship of Anubis predates the worship of Osiris (and Seth). What probably happened was the earlier death god Anubis was pushed into the background a bit when the worship of Osiris became more popular and Anubis was reassigned the role of son rather than predecessor. Regardless, Anubis seemed to take the demotion well and remained as faithful to his new master as one might expect of man's best friend.

Anubis played a huge role in Egyptian life (and death) but wasn't terribly active in their myths. He's a character who had a big job and was rarely seen doing anything but that job. He would escort the recently deceased to the land of the dead[1] and then oversee the all-important Weighing of the Heart ceremony. The Weighing of the Heart ceremony went a bit like this: the freshly dead in the form a *ba*[2] would make their way to the Hall of Double Justice where they would stand before forty-two judges and make a series of negative confessions (i.e. 'I have not taken a life,' 'I have not stolen from the dead,' 'I have not colluded with a foreign government' and so on), after which Anubis would place their heart[3] opposite the *baat* (or "Feather of *Maat*"). If the scales balanced, the *ba* moved on to the next

---

[1] In this way, the Greeks and Romans associated him with their messenger gods Hermes/ Mercury. The Romans even created a mash-up god called "Hermanubis." You can even find Roman statues of Hermanubis with a human, toga clad body and an uncomfortably realistic dog head.

[2] Often depicted as a human headed bird, the *ba* was the closest equivalent to the idea of a soul whereas the ka was the spark of life that returned to the creator at the time of death.

[3] As in other cultures, the heart rather than the brain was seen as the seat of the soul (or mind, or personality). Yes, the brain would be removed during the mummification process with a hook up the nose, but they saw it as essentially filler. Those weird gray noodles didn't serve any overt purpose and were often just discarded. The heart, though, was clearly linked to the life force – you could feel and hear it thumping away in life and then stop in death. It was so important that the heart alone was placed back inside the body cavity during the mummification process. The other important organs were put in jars, but the heart was too important even for that. It wasn't until much later that we worked out that thought happens in those weird gray noodles and that the heart is nothing more than a pump. A damned important pump, but still just a mechanical piece helping move blood throughout our systems.

room where Osiris would spray it with *ka* juice and create a completed spiritual form called an *akh*. As an *akh* they would live out the rest of eternity in relative ease and comfort. If, however, the scales were out of balance, Anubis would feed their heart to Ammit, the crocolionappotomus, and they would become one of the truly dead who shamble around, unthinking, and unfeeling, like zombies or GOP members of Congress.

When not embalming, shepherding the newly dead, or overseeing the Weighing ceremony, Anubis was a protector of the dead. Because so much of what we have of Egyptian culture and myth comes to us in the form of the Pyramid Texts, Coffin Texts, the so-called *Book of the Dead*, and other burial artifacts, we have no shortage of depictions of Anubis. Given the enormity and importance of his job, it is not surprising that Anubis seems to have been something of a workaholic who didn't have the time for much involvement in other mythic adventures.

It should be noted that Anubis was not the only 'jackal' god of Ancient Egypt. Wepwawet was a dog-headed god with lighter-colored hair and possibly began as a depiction of the pharaoh in war time. Because of the association with war, Wepwawet also became associated with death. He was called the "Opener of Ways" because he shepherded the dead to and through Duat, the realm of the dead. Eventually, it seems, the figure of Wepwawet was absorbed by Anubis.

Sekhmet

a.k.a.: Sakhmet, Sachmis, Nesert
Pantheon: Egyptian
Spouse/Lover: Ptah
Siblings: Bastet, Khonsu, Maat, Shu, Tefnut
Parents: Ra; Hut-Hern and Ra; Heru Sa-Aset
Offspring: Maahes, Nefertem
Deity of: fire, war, dance
Symbols: lioness, sun disk, cobra, red clothing

A living example of the expression "if looks could kill," Sekhmet is as vicious as a lioness. Not to be confused with the various cat-headed goddesses of Egypt, Sekhmet has rounded ears and features to match the terrifying power of a mama

"Sekhmet" by Malena Salinas

lion whose cubs are being threatened. Her most befitting origin story showcases her as the Eye of Ra—the physical embodiment of the angry look Ra turned toward humanity when they showed him disrespect. She was not the only goddess to act as the Eye of Ra, but she was the go-to choice when a bit of ultra-violence was called for. And she was good at her job. Sometimes, a little too good.

When Ra was mocked by his subjects because of his old, disheveled, human body, he got mad. He channeled that rage into a look and the look became Sekhmet. Sekhmet was unleashed upon the world to bring swift and brutal justice. While other gods were known to use floods to cull humanity, the Egyptians had a much more hands-on approach: Sekhmet started ripping their heads off and drinking their blood. And by gods, she loved it. So much so that when the gods saw that humanity had learned its lesson and they told her to stop, she refused. Ra himself stood in her path to stop her from her daily foray into massacre, and she shoved him to the ground. Ra was beaten up by his own eye. Since he couldn't physically stop her, he was forced to use guile to get the best of her.

As Sekhmet was resting from a hard day's slaughter, Ra ordered the remaining women of Heliopolis to brew up as much beer as possible, while he sent messengers to gather as much red dye as they could. Then, combining the beer and the dye, they dumped vats of red beer out into the streets. When Sekhmet woke up the next morning, she saw that the streets were literally running red with blood. Being a bloodthirsty goddess, this was the grandest feast she could have asked for. She lapped up as much as she could before she passed out. Like many who have had a little too much to drink, Sekhmet awoke the next morning with a deep desire to make some changes to her lifestyle. In some traditions, she was no longer Sekhmet at all, but the sweet, loving, milky, cow goddess Hathor. Considering that humanity was born from the tears of Ra and Sekhmet was the embodiment of the Eye of Ra, the story was ultimately about the mother killing her own children and then learning to be more loving and gentle.

Of all the goddesses, Sekhmet was perhaps the fiercest. She would ride into battle with the pharaoh and could perform both traditional and biological warfare. She was associated with medicine, but mostly to the extent that she created plagues which she used to assail the enemies of the pharaoh. Her strength and prowess were so respected that she was often depicted standing at the prow of the solar ship protecting the sun from its nightly attack by Apep, the sun-hungry serpent. The Egyptians also associated her with the all-too-familiar dangerous aspects of the sun, from drought to heatstroke. And, as if a lion-headed warrior woman wasn't fierce enough, she could also breathe fire. Cross Sekhmet at your own risk.

"Hathor" by Allie Wass

Hathor

a.k.a.: Hwt-Hr
Pantheon: Egyptian
Spouse/Lovers: Ra, Horus
Siblings: Ra, Apep, Serket, Sobek, Thoth
Parents: Ra; Neith and Khnum; Neith and Ra
Offspring: Duamutef, Hapi, Ihy, Imsety, Qebehsenuef, Horus
Deity of: love, motherhood, dance, fertility, beauty, music
Symbols: cow, lioness, falcon, cobra, hippopotamus, pregnancy, sistrum

These days comparing someone to a cow is unlikely to win you their favor. Long before "cow" was slang for a large or simple-minded person who would best contribute to humanity by being made into a jacket, it was a powerful image of nurturing motherhood. Cows, like mothers, are the source of milk. Cows, like mothers, can bear great burdens and hold strong. Cows, like mothers, provide food. Cows, like mothers, have sweet, kind eyes. Cows, like mothers, are often taken for granted. Cows, like mothers, are made of meat and leather.[1] For the Egyptians, no goddess was more closely associated with the divine bovine than Hathor.

As with most Egyptian deities, Hathor is depicted in a variety of ways. Sometimes she is a cow with a star-speckled hide, other times she is a woman with the head of a cow or simply a woman with the horns of a cow. Because of her close association with Ra and other sun gods, she regularly holds the sun disk aloft between her horns.

Her name means "The House of Horus" and she was variously viewed as the mother, lover, protector, or wet nurse of Horus. And since we are talking about Egyptian royalty, those roles were certainly not mutually exclusive. The living pharaoh was believed to be the embodiment of Horus and so the mother and/or wife of the pharaoh was connected to Hathor.

Her motherly duties didn't end with the birth of the king, though, as she was also the figure who helped the pharaoh with his post-death rebirth. This connects

---

[1] Take my word for it. Please do not eat and/or wear your, or anyone else's, mother. At least not human mothers, I'll let you make your own moral determination re: the eating and wearing of mothers of other species.

her to both the night sky and the daily rejuvenation of the sun. At times, she is even shown defending Ra in the solar barque on its nightly passage.

Often viewed as the mother of the sun god, and as the Eye of Ra, Hathor was her own grandmother. And just to make things even more uncomfortable, she also played the role of the Hand Goddess who helped the sun god unload his obelisk (as it were). And then, spurned by the same sun god, Hathor hoofed it out of town and became the Distant Goddess. Feline goddesses Bastet and Sekhmet got wrapped up into Hathor worship (or she into theirs) and they were taken as different aspects of the same goddess. Later, when Isis became the most favored goddess of Egypt, much of the Hathor tradition bled into Isis' tale.

It is telling how frequently cultures blend their goddesses together. In Hinduism, female deities are viewed as aspects or avatars of the template Devi. In Norse myth, numerous goddesses are named but most of them are taken to be nothing more than additional names for Freyja. In Egypt, even individually popular figures like Hathor, Sekhmet, Bastet, Isis, and Maat are virtually interchangeable in many of the mythic narratives. Why is it that culture after culture views their goddesses as simple variations on the theme of womanhood, while male gods are distinct figures?[1] Perhaps the easy though uncomfortable answer is patriarchy. Women, even goddesses, are only afforded a few distinct roles to fill (the mother, the virgin, the 'slut', or the vicious man-killer) whereas manhood comes in innumerable forms (the father, the savior, the craftsman, the scholar, the trickster, the warrior, the leader, the destroyer, the creator, the judge, etc.). It is an inevitable truth of male dominated cultures that men have more freedom to express themselves in a greater variety of ways than women do. Even goddesses fall victim to the limitations imposed by patriarchy.

Thoth

a.k.a.: Toth, Dhwty
Pantheon: Egyptian
Spouse/Lovers: Maat, Nehemtaway, Seshat
Parents: None; Neith; Ra; Seth; Hathor and Horus
Offspring: Seshat
Deity of: knowledge, moon, measurements, writing, records, reading
Symbols: ibis, baboon, moon disk, scrolls, pens, scales

---

[1] There are exceptions, of course. Male Egyptian sun gods blend quite a bit, for example.

"Thoth" by Caitlin Rausch

Thoth is most recognizable as the bird-headed scribe of the Egyptian gods. Unlike the numerous falcon-headed gods in Egypt, Thoth stands apart from the group with the long, thin neck and beak of the ibis. He is most commonly found in funerary texts observing the Weighing of the Heart ceremony and recording the results with his long, thin pen. He can also be found in the form of a baboon— bright red ass and all. In either form you may see Thoth balancing a moon disk[1] on top of his head.

There are multiple and conflicting accounts of the birth of Thoth. One holds that he was born from the head of Seth—possibly because of the semen of Horus that Seth accidentally swallowed. An origin more befitting of the wise god of words is the tradition which says that Thoth was a self-created god who spoke himself into existence. Lots of gods can beget things simply by naming them, but it takes a special kind of deity to beget themselves with the power of thought and word.

One of Thoth's greatest contributions to the world was giving us a 365-day calendar. He did this by gambling with the moon and gaining an extra five days to add on to the then 360-day calendar. More important than the five days themselves was that in winning them he made it possible for some of the most important gods of Egypt to be born. The story goes that after the brother-sister/husband-wife team of Geb and Nut (earth and sky, respectively) were forced to part their coital embrace, Nut was forbidden from giving birth to her womb fruit on any day of the year. By winning an extra five days Thoth created a loophole and the gods Osiris, Isis, Seth, Nephthys, and possibly Horus the Elder, could be born. Without their escape from the sky-womb, the world would not have had all the things (for better and for worse) brought to us by the first family of Egyptian myth. Ultimately, in this way, Thoth made the single most important contribution of any being to the course of history.

This text may be a bit biased toward Thoth, his endless wisdom, and talents because, quite simply, he wrote it. And not just this page, or this book, but every word ever written was inspired by Thoth himself. The Bible, the Koran, the Book of Mormon (the book), *The Book of Mormon* (the musical), *Catch 22*, *Tess of the D'Urbervilles*, *The Epic of Gilgamesh*, *Lemonade*, *Stairway to Heaven*, every tweet, and every issue of TV Guide were all written by an extension of the divine pen of Thoth. Or so we're told in documents written by Thoth.

---

[1] A moon disk is similar to a sun disk—the main difference being that the moon disk is usually gold instead of red and instead of being positioned between bull-like horns it is held up by a crescent moon shape.

"Bastet" by Christian Jackson

Bastet

a.k.a.: Bast, Pasht
Pantheon: Egyptian
Spouse/Lovers: Anubis, Ptah
Siblings: Ammit, Hathor, Horus, Sekhmet, Serket, Shu, Tefnut, Thoth
Parents: Ra; Isis and Ra
Offspring: Maahes, Khonsu, Nefertem
Deity of: cats, protection, family, dance, love
Symbols: cats, sistrum

Like the domestic cat, Bastet started from much more fearsome roots. Originally depicted with the head of a lioness, Bastet only became the more docile housecat after years of evolution. Bastet was an Eye of Ra and was used to deliver swift, brutal justice on behalf of the sun god. She was virtually interchangeable with Sekhmet until roughly the second millennium BCE when her depictions shifted from lioness to cat. Her capacity to mete out justice did not diminish, but her kinder, gentler aspect became more common.

During the Ptolemaic era, her darker, scarier side mostly fell away and Bastet was left largely as a goddess of motherhood, love, and music. The Greeks also took the decidedly solar goddess and, drawing connections between her and their huntress Artemis, made her a lunar lady. The Greeks often liked to pigeonhole other cultures' deities and syncretize them with their own pantheon, ignoring or changing the parts that didn't quite fit their model.[1] A cat head was fine because, well, it looked cool, but her sun disks became moon disks and Horus, who had only the loosest connection to Bastet in Egyptian sources, was taken to be her brother so that Artemis' brother Apollo could have an Egyptian analogue.

As well as being one of the goddesses associated with the Eye of Ra, Bastet also fills the role of the Distant Goddess. The Distant Goddess is a figure who abandons Egypt after having been rebuked for one reason or another[2] and only returns after a god, typically Thoth or Shu, convinces her to come back. Because of her time away, the Distant Goddess was often thought of as the goddess of

---

[1] Famous mythographer Joseph Campbell in his much-lauded work *The Hero with a Thousand Faces* similarly cherry-picked aspects of characters that fit his Hero model and downplayed the rest. Which may help explain Campbell's commercial success and the fact that other mythographers are way less fond of him than the general public.
[2] Most often it was for doing her job as the Eye of Ra and taking vengeance on humanity.

foreign lands and because she returned from the south (Nubia or some such) she brought with her the inundation of the Nile.

For Egyptian women, Bastet was an important figure. As cat and woman, she represented the tender, loving mommy aspects as well as the fierce defender mama. Generally a calm, nonchalant, cat lady, when it came time for her annual festival Bastet and her female followers got to cut loose. The women would drink, dance, play the sistrum, and maybe mummify a cat or two for the hell of it. Like a domesticated kitty, Bastet could be all purrs and pets or she could go on a catnip-fueled bender and become a whirl of hisses and claws. Don't be taken in by her internet-friendly appearance; when this cat got grumpy, blood started to flow.

Bes

a.k.a.: Bisu
Pantheon: Egyptian
Spouse: Beset
Deity of: family, pregnant women, babies and children
Symbols: dwarf, ostrich feather, lion (?)

Even in a world of gods with green skin or animal heads, Bes stands out from the crowd. The stout, jolly, dwarf god looks like nothing else found in Egyptian art. He is so out of place that for a great while scholars believed that he really was out of place and had been imported to Egypt by way of Nubia or another neighbor. More recent study, however, indicates that Bes is almost certainly Egyptian, born and bred. The only reason he looks so different from the other gods is that he is a really, really old deity. Pre-dating the aesthetics of the more familiar Egyptian art style, Bes may be an artifact of the predynastic history that somehow remained popular throughout the course of history.

One explanation for his longevity may be the fact that he held a very important job. Bes was a protector of pregnant women, newborn babes, and the household in general. In a time when pregnancy and delivery were often a death sentence, the Egyptians could hardly be blamed for wanting as many gods as possible to help women through their most vulnerable times. There were other gods and goddesses of women, children, and birth, but none were quite as adorable as the diminutive Bes. Archeological evidence suggests that some women were so appreciative of Bes that they would tattoo his image on their upper thigh.

"Bes Protecting a Child from Nightmares" by Darian Papineau

This may be a case of projecting modern sensibilities inaccurately onto ancient people, but Bes' unique, even comical appearance seems to make him a particularly kid-friendly guardian. Bald and chubby, with big round ears, a highly stylized beard, and a goofy look on his face, it's easy to imagine Egyptian infants looking up from their cribs and giggling at their silly protector. Considering that Bes' primary means of warding off the dangers of the world was by sticking his tongue out at them and doing a dance, he seems like the Egyptian answer to Barney the dinosaur.

Just as cartoon characters evolve over the years to reflect more modern aesthetics and changing sensibilities, Bes may not have been such an adorable figure in his earliest form. His odd shape, big tongue, beard, and round ears have led some to hypothesize that he was originally intended to be a lion rearing up on his hind legs. Whether intentionally or not, the image metamorphosed over the ages to become the tongue-wagging, dancing dwarf.

Khepri

a.k.a.: Chepri, Khepera, Khepry, Khopri
Pantheon: Egyptian
Siblings: Atum, Ra
Deity of: sunrise, rebirth
Symbols: scarab beetle, sun disk, blue lotus

The scarab is a well-known Egyptian symbol. Often portrayed in vibrant colors in the most majestic of Egyptian artifacts, it is easy to overlook the fact that the scarab is nothing more than a dung beetle whose claim to fame is that it rolls balls of poo around with it. Rather than being a bizarre side note, the poo-rolling was the most important aspect of the scarab for the Egyptians. The shit ball represented the sun and the beetle rolling it over the horizon was the god Khepri.

Many Egyptian gods had animal heads. From the falcon of Ra and Horus, to the black dog of Anubis, the felines of Bastet and Sekhmet, and the unidentifiable "Seth animal" of Seth, these fantastical gods contributed to the rest of the world's fascination with Egypt. Khepri is unique, though. He doesn't have the head of a beetle as Sobek has the head of a crocodile, instead he has a beetle *for* a head. A whole scarab—head, thorax, legs, and all—sits atop the neck of this most unusual looking god.

"Khepri" by Christian Sitterlet

More than just a buggy face, Khepri embodied rebirth or coming into being. In fact, his name is a verb meaning "to come into being." This stems from another important fact of dung beetle behavior: they lay their eggs within the dung ball. The Egyptians didn't witness the laying of the eggs, but what they did see was balls of poo splitting open and hordes of baby beetles scuttling out. To the ancient observers, they simply came into being.

The Egyptians believed the sun was reborn each morning. At night, as it passed over the western horizon the sky goddess would eat the sun. Then, it would travel by way of the solar barque through the innards of Nut (sometimes this is also seen as the afterlife realm called Duat) only to be reborn again the next morning. Of course, biologically speaking, if one eats something and then it comes out the other end the next morning, that's not really giving birth, is it? Perhaps the dung beetle image is even more appropriate than first imagined.

Since there was a plethora of Egyptian sun gods, Khepri never really achieved a starring role in any myths but he did get a daily cameo as the god who rolled the newborn sun over the crest of the horizon.

"Strength of the Gods" by Mandy Cantarella

Mesopotamian Mythology

Mesopotamia is the name the Greeks used for the land between the Tigris and Euphrates rivers. This area is primarily the modern country of Iraq, but in broader terms includes places like Syria, Iran (née Persia), Lebanon (née Byblos), Jordan, Israel (née Palestine), and so forth. The Iraqi capital of Baghdad is just to the north of the on-again, off-again capital of Mesopotamia: Babylon. The ancient city of Nineveh, which would eventually offer up many of the most significant mythological texts thanks to a long-forgotten library, was seated in the same area as modern Mosul.

Situated, as it is, in the middle of the east, and filled with important natural resources, Mesopotamia was a hub of activity and the birthplace of civilization. Called "The Cradle of Life," the land between the two rivers was not the birthplace of humanity, but it was the location of the oldest identifiable state-organized society. We know them as the Sumerians and they learned how to farm, how to make use of the life-giving rivers and eventually formed cities and the first known writing system. The unthinkably long history of invasions into this region began when the Akkadians took over and, rather than wiping out the Sumerians, merged their two cultures together to give us a Sumer-Akkadian culture. Next came the Amorites, who, under the famous Hammurabi, created the first known law code. After that the Assyrians, the Chaldeans, and the Persians came, each of whom brought their own innovations and, of course, their gods. And then there was Alexander[1], who came, saw, conquered, left, came back, and died in Babylon.

Because of the frequent influx of new cultures and influences, Mesopotamian mythology can be a bit of a quagmire. Add in the fact that each city had its own traditions and hometown deities, and it becomes very hard to say anything definitive about the whole of Mesopotamian beliefs. Then there's the fact that until the 18th century there was little to no attempt made to study and understand the culture and beliefs of the Fertile Crescent. This is in no small part thanks to the fact that various Mesopotamian groups such as the Babylonians and Canaanites act as the antagonists in the single most important religious text of the western world: The Bible. The Mesopotamians were not only the neighbors to the ancient Hebrews, but also their adversaries. Because of that, it was considered

---

[1] One of the great men of history, if we gauge greatness by influence and accomplishments. If, however, greatness is determined by goodness then the jury is still out on Alex.

something between unnecessary and evil to look too closely at their beliefs. Serious study in the field of Assyriology[1] didn't begin until the 1700s and only really took off in the 1800s.

Though they developed cuneiform, the earliest known form of written language, at a time when most people on Earth hadn't even given a thought to the written word, their chosen medium has proven to be both a blessing and a curse. Rather than writing on paper[2] that tends to fade or fall apart over the years, they pressed their wedge-shaped symbols into clay tablets, many examples of which have survived to the present. Clay is a sturdy format to work in, right until it isn't. Drop a clay tablet and you're left with fragments and dust. As a result, we have a decent number of Mesopotamian texts to study, but many of them are missing sizeable and sometimes crucial chunks. Among the longest and most complete texts are the creation tale called *Enuma Elish*[3], which chronicles the rise of Babylon's top god Marduk, and the thrilling poem known as *The Epic of Gilgamesh*. There are also extant samplings from a number of other creation myths and tales of the gods and goddesses. Because of the historic opposition and the difficulty of archeological efforts in the Middle East at present, we have an uphill climb toward a full look at the rich and complex tapestry of myth in ancient Mesopotamia.

---

[1] A term which encompasses not only the study of the Assyrians, but the other surrounding groups.

[2] Not their fault, really, what with paper having not been invented yet. Even papyrus wouldn't catch on in the area until around 1000 BCE.

[3] *Enuma Elish* gets its title from the opening words of the poem, which translates roughly as "When from above."

"The Tigris and Euphrates Rivers flowing from Ea's shoulders" by Darian Papineau

Ea

a.k.a.: Enki (Sumerian)
Pantheon: Mesopotamian
Spouse/Lovers: Damkina, Ninhursag, Ninsar, Ninkurra, Uttu
Parents: Kisar and Ansar
Offspring: Ninsar, Ninkurra, Uttu
Deity of: fresh water, wisdom, medicine
Symbols: water, fish, plants, goat

Ea is a difficult god to pin down. Like the water he represents, his form changes to fit whatever container you put him in. Sometimes he is the god of creation, other times he is the son or father of the creator gods. Sometimes he is the master of *me*[1], other times he is the father of the master of *me*, or the god who got drunk and foolishly gave away the power of *me*. Sometimes he is the god of fresh water, though his name literally identifies him as an earth god. Sometimes he is the king of the gods, other times he is the adviser to the king. The one common thread is that Ea is a powerful and more or less benevolent figure.

In the creation tale known as *Enuma Elish*, Ea was the penultimate hero god. Upon learning that the primeval fresh water god Apsu was planning to kill the younger generations of gods, Ea was the lone figure brave enough to do something about it. He assassinated Apsu and took over as the new fresh water god before impregnating his sister/wife Damkina with the god to beat all other gods: Marduk. Ea was the savior of the gods who then begat the next savior of the gods.

In *The Epic of Gilgamesh*, Ea saved humanity from the gods. Upon learning that the gods planned to kill humanity with a massive flood, Ea was the lone figure who cared enough about humanity to help us. He warned a man named Utnapishtim that a worldwide flood was coming and so he had better build a boat. While everyone else drowned, Utnapishtim survived to repopulate the world. This story connects Ea to both water and fertility but not in the manner that he is typically associated with them.

While the Mesopotamians made the important distinction between fresh water (often called 'sweet water') and salt water, there was no linguistic distinction

---

[1] *Me* (pronounced like "may") is the complex set of laws that govern the universe. Like the Ten Commandments or the Code of Hammurabi, the *mes* are inscribed on a series of tablets. The possessor of the "Tablets of Destiny" (or "Tablets of *Me*") has varying levels of mastery over destiny and the whole of the universe.

between water and semen. Ejaculate was merely a man's "water." Given that water causes plants to grow and semen makes babies grow, the connection is understandable, if not a little uncomfortable to think about. So, Ea was both god of water and semen. In one tale, Ea impregnated multiple generations of earth goddesses[1] by spreading his waters around a bit too carelessly. He got his comeuppance by being tricked into eating the fruit of his seed and becoming pregnant in eight parts of his body. Beyond the important message that incestuous rape is bad, this myth was meant to teach balance and warn against excess. Just as too much water kills a plant, so must a man be careful about overusing his water. Though Ea doesn't end up looking too favorably, this myth did not detract from the high degree of respect his worshippers had for him.

Another story where Ea fell victim to his own poor choices had much higher stakes. One tradition held that Ea was, if not the creator of the "Tablets of Destiny," at least their keeper for a time. Enter Ishtar, the sex goddess. Ishtar, sometimes identified as Ea's daughter[2], got good ol' Ea drunk and, in his inebriated state, convinced him to give her the "Tablets of Destiny." Apparently, Ea had a real weakness for both excess and incest. Luckily for us all, Ishtar ended up being the type of goddess who could be trusted with wielding the power of fate. Ea, however, never lived down the embarrassment of having drunkenly handed over the most powerful objects in existence.

Marduk

a.k.a.: Bel, Baal, Lugalbanda (Sumerian)
Pantheon: Mesopotamian
Spouse/Lovers: Zarpanitu
Parents: Damkina and Ea
Deity of: thunderstorms, destiny
Symbols: thunderbolt, scepter, bow, forked tongue dragon, dogs, horses

---

[1] His wife Ninhursag, then their daughter Ninsar, then their daughter/his granddaughter Ninkurra, and then their daughter/his great-granddaughter Uttu.
[2] Clearly, he has a type.

"Marduk" by Matt Renneker

Described as being too awesome for humans to look at, much less begin to comprehend, Marduk was a god amongst gods. He is a sterling example of the henotheism found in many cultures, and especially prevalent in Middle Eastern ones. Henotheism is a form of polytheism wherein the existence of many gods is accepted, but each city/tribe/household has its own primary deity. It is akin to being a fan of a particular sports team—just because the Washington Racist Mascots are your favorite team, it doesn't mean that other teams don't exist or that they aren't occasionally capable of winning. While Judaism and Christianity are modernly monotheistic, it's clear that the god of Abraham was henotheistic in his earliest conception. As the chief god of Babylon, Marduk is the occasional Biblical adversary of Yahweh known as Bel. "Bel" means "Lord" so it's a title rather than a proper name and one that is often affixed to Marduk or his regional variants.[1] Since the Hebrew Bible (or Old Testament, if you prefer) was written while the Israelites were in exile in Babylon, one of the primary functions of writing it was to distinguish themselves from their oppressors. It is not at all surprising, then, to find the Babylonian top god as the sparring partner of Yahweh. To complicate things further, Bel is derived from the word "Baal" which is both a generic word for "lord" as well as being the name of a separate Ugaritic (Canaanite) god. Since the Canaanites were also adversaries of the Israelites, Baal made some notable Biblical appearances, too. It's not abundantly clear that the authors of the Bible cared to distinguish between Baal, Bel, and the various gods using either title.

Like his Greek counterpart Zeus, Marduk was not the first born of the gods, but rather his birth represented the apex of creation. Also like Zeus, Marduk was a god of thunderstorms and the dealer of destinies. Marduk's "star" was Jupiter, which was the name of the Roman equivalent of Zeus. Similarities like these cannot help but point anthropologists toward a Proto-Indo-European culture that seeded many of the later religions found in Europe and the Asian Subcontinent. As an earlier god, we may think of Marduk as a cultural ancestor to Zeus.

One of the best known and most important Mesopotamian documents is a creation story called *Enuma Elish*. Like many other less-developed or less well-preserved Mesopotamian creation tales, *Enuma Elish* focuses on the rise of a primary deity rather than on the details of creation. The theogony and world-building are minor details in the tale of the ascension of Marduk. Tiamat, the salt water goddess, and Apsu, the fresh water god, along with their vizier Mummu,

---

[1] Such as Nabu, Adad, and others who are sometimes distinct characters from Marduk and sometimes not.

made a bunch of new gods who begat newer gods who begat again and again. Each generation of gods surpassed the previous in both stature and power, leading up to the crescendo that was Marduk. His father, Ea was the one god strong enough to defeat Apsu when Apsu and Mummu decided to kill all the younger gods for being too noisy.[1] Ea then assumed the role of fresh water god and within the realm of Apsu, Ea and his wife Damkina produced Marduk, the paragon of gods.

In retaliation for the slaying of her husband, Granny Tiamat forged an army of monsters to kill the younger gods. Each of the more senior gods, including their reigning champ Ea, chickened out when faced with the prospect of taking on Tiamat and her menagerie. Marduk alone was brave enough to lead the charge. Even in the form of a giant dragon-like creature, Tiamat was no match for Marduk. He ensnared her in a net made of winds and then shot an arrow from his lightning-strung bow down her throat, splitting her in half. Marduk then used half of her body to create the earth and the other half to craft the sky.

Having taken the "Tablets of Destiny" as the spoils of war, Marduk used his mastery over destiny to assign each of the gods their jobs. Apparently destined to rule destiny, *Enuma Elish* is not the only tale about Marduk obtaining the "Tablets of Destiny." In another, the birdlike underworld god, Zu, steals the tablets and Marduk is again the only god brave enough to do anything about it. It seems that whoever possessed the "Tablets of Destiny" was invulnerable to all attackers except Marduk. Perhaps, then, Marduk should be seen as being even more powerful than *me* itself.[2]

Marduk built the earth and sky, delegated the various positions to the gods, and was also responsible for creating humanity. When the gods complained about the prospect of having to build and maintain their own temples, Marduk used a handful of mud mixed with the blood of Tiamat's consort Kingu and made the first humans. Humans were then tasked with doing the menial labor, building of temples, shaping of statues, and making of sacrifices so that the gods could focus on more important things.

Enuma Elish ends with Marduk being given a series of additional titles and the powers associated with them. Some fifty new names make up the last one and

---

[1] As a parent, I get where they're coming from.
[2] Zeus, too, has a complicated relationship with the Greek keepers of destiny: The Fates. In some stories, he is just as subject to the Fates as anyone and in some tales, he is their father and rules over them. The relationship between Odin and the Norse goddesses of fate (the Norns) is also a tricky one.

a half tablets of the seven-tablet poem. Also featuring numerous instances of lengthy passages of repetition, *Enuma Elish* can be a bit tedious to read. One can only imagine how difficult it may have been for Babylonian youngsters to stay awake as they listened to the annual recitation of the poem as part of their New Year's celebration.[1]

Ishtar

a.k.a.: Inanna (Sumerian), Astarte, Anath

Pantheon: Mesopotamian

Spouse/Lovers: Tammuz (Dumuzi)

Siblings: Ereshkigal, Anu (An), Sin (Nanna)

Parents: ? and Anu; ? and Sin; ? and Ellil

Deity of: love, sex, fertility, war, language

Symbols: eight-pointed star

Ishtar is one of the most important goddesses of Mesopotamia and, in fact, may have been all the most important goddesses in Mesopotamia. It is only with great difficulty and little certainty that we can separate out the traditions of the Akkadian Ishtar, Sumerian Inanna, the Semitic Astarte, the Ugaritic Anath, the Aramaic Atargatis, and to a much lesser extent, the Egyptian Isis and Hathor, the Greek Aphrodite and Artemis, and the Roman Juno and Venus. Clearly, the goddess of love and war was an archetype that resonated far and wide.

Because of the effects of synthesized and/or fractured traditions, it is all but impossible to offer many definitive answers about her parentage. What is clear is that as the goddess of the planet Venus, she joined the moon god Sin[2] and the sun god Anu[3] in forming the triumvirate of the most important celestial bodies. Anu may be her father, her husband, or both, and Sin may be her brother or father—whichever way it shakes out, the three are definitely connected.

It was her role as goddess of love that was the basis for most of the significant myths surrounding her tradition. Though there are echoes of motherly love here and there, Ishtar was primarily a goddess of the physical act of love making. Sex. Lust. These were the true domains of Ishtar. Annual fertility rites

---

[1] The New Year was celebrated during the spring equinox rather than around the winter solstice as with the Julian calendar.

[2] Or Nanna to the Sumerians.

[3] Or An to the Sumerians.

"Ishtar" by Christian Sitterlet

would feature the king having public sex with the high priestess of Ishtar. Her priestesses also engaged in prostitution. Before sex became a shameful thing done only for the sake of procreation, and sex workers came to be viewed as somehow immoral simply for making money from sex, prostitution was far from frowned upon, so set your Puritanical preconceptions aside. Sex was good and, in fact, sex was necessary. To illustrate just how necessary, the Mesopotamians had a myth about what happened when the sex goddess died.

For no clear reason, Ishtar decided to travel down to the underworld realm to visit her sister Ereshkigal. On her way, she had to pass through seven gates and at each one she was instructed to remove a piece of her jewelry or clothing. Stripped of her clothes and, with them, her status, Ishtar entered the Land of No Return no better off than anyone else. And she was angry. She marched into Ereshkigal's palace, leaned in close with all the menace a naked goddess could muster, and Ereshkigal was so terrified that she sent out sixty diseases to kill Ishtar -- as perfect an example of overkill as one could imagine. Ereshkigal then had her dead sister's body hung from a hook like a trophy or a warning sign. With Ishtar dead, there was no sex anywhere. Not only were people not getting laid, but animals weren't mating, and plants weren't reproducing. The gods needed to correct the situation quickly or it would spell disaster. Luckily, Ishtar had a faithful servant who went to the heavenly gods for help when his mistress failed to return. The gods sent a messenger to retrieve Ishtar, but Ereshkigal told them that the only way Ishtar could leave would be if she chose someone to take her place. All around the world and the heavens, everyone was mourning for Ishtar and she couldn't bring herself to force a miserable fate on any of them. Until, that is, Ishtar caught a glimpse of the one man who seemed completely unfazed by her death: her husband Tammuz[1]. He was busy getting busy with his sister (or her sister, the translation is dicey) and so Ishtar happily sent the denizens of the land of the dead to grab him. From that time on, Tammuz hung like dead meat from a hook in the land of the dead for half of the year and for the other half of the year the sister (his or hers) took his place. That Tammuz was a god of crop fertility hardly needs to be said because this myth (like the better-known Greek story of Persephone) was used to explain the cycle of the seasons. When Tammuz rose from the depths each year, flowers would begin to blossom, rabbits would make baby rabbits, chickens would make eggs, and fertility rituals aplenty would be performed.

---

[1] Or Dumuzi to the Sumerians.

Ishtar also played an important role in *The Epic of Gilgamesh*. When Gilgamesh rejected her advances, citing various previous lovers of hers who had come to bad ends, Ishtar was so angry that she asked the gods to kill Gilgamesh. They sent the Bull of Heaven to do the job but Gilgamesh, along with his comrade Enkidu, successfully defeated the Bull. And then, Enkidu offered further insult to Ishtar by tossing raw, bloody Bull of Heaven meat in her face. Enkidu did not live long after that one.

Possibly the most vexing story about Ishtar involved the events leading up to her marriage to Tammuz. In a largely complete and completely bizarre poem, both the shepherd god Tammuz and a farming god named Enkimdu wanted to marry Ishtar. She preferred Enkimdu but Tammuz was her brother Shamash's choice for her. Enkimdu offered Tammuz everything he had to get the shepherd to back off and let him have Ishtar. He offered jewels, land, and then finally, he offered to give Tammuz Ishtar herself. And on that puzzling note, the poem ends. Or at least that is where the text that has survived to the present ends. Such are the myriad joys and frustrations that come from studying texts written on sturdy yet fragile clay tablets.

Ereshkigal

a.k.a.: Erkalla, Irkalla
Pantheon: Mesopotamian
Spouse/Lovers: Nergal, Ninazu
Siblings: Ishtar (Inanna), Ishkur, Utu
Parents: Ningal and Sin
Offspring: Namtar, Nungal, Ninazu
Deity of: death

Hades is the god of the realm of Hades. Hel reigns in Helheim ("Hel Home"). And so, it isn't too surprising that Ereshkigal is the goddess of Ereshkigal. Or Erkalla is the goddess of Erkalla. Or Ereshkigal is the goddess of Erkalla. Or Erkalla is the goddess of Ereshkigal. Or, just to break form, Ereshkigal is the goddess of Kurnugi. For the sake of clarity, we'll use the name "Ereshkigal" for the goddess and "Erkalla" for the place. An afterlife realm by any other name would still be as bleak. And Erkalla is one of the bleakest.

"Ereshkigal" by Amanda Zylstra

Though not a place of torture, it is hard to imagine anyone choosing Erkalla as a final destination. Repressively dark, Erkalla is surrounded by a series of walls, each with a single gate. If Ishtar's journey there is any indication of the treatment we all receive, at each gate an article of clothing is taken away. By the time you've made it through all seven gates, you are totally naked. The dead don't stay naked, though. Not completely, at least. Rather, the dead wear feathers and mimic birds. And they eat dirt. As birds do, apparently.

Ereshkigal's sister Ishtar made an infamous trip down to Erkalla, resulting in Ishtar's temporary death and, eventually, the cyclical nature of the seasons. It is in that myth that we learn the road to Erkalla is a one-way street. The other gods could not even travel there to save Ishtar for fear that they wouldn't be able to leave either. Instead, the benevolent Ea sent either faceless beings made from the dirt under his nails or a figure known as Good-Looks. The faceless creatures were not really alive and thus were not subject to the "No Exit" rule of Erkalla, and in the other version, Good-Looks was a sexless being[1] and because of that he could come and go from Erkalla as he pleased. While the challenge of getting Ishtar out of Erkalla was the main conflict of this myth, in other narratives the rules weren't quite so hard and fast.

The god Nergal was ordered by the gods to go to Erkalla to help Ereshkigal oversee the judging of the dead (or the judging of the gods in the land of the dead). Before going, the gods warned him that he ought not to eat or drink anything offered to him there. He also must not sit on anything, wash his feet, or have sex with Ereshkigal lest he be unable to ever rejoin the gods above. In preparation, he crafted a chair for himself and took it along so that when his feet got tired he would be able to take a load off. Of course, as it turned out, the food and drink of Erkalla were pretty easy to turn down, so Nergal did very well in following the advice of the gods. Until, of course, he caught a glimpse of Ereshkigal as she was bathing. Just as another Middle Eastern king found himself in trouble after spying on a woman bathing, Nergal could not help but give in to desire and he had sex with Ereshkigal. For not the only time in Mesopotamian mythology, the two had a seven-day marathon of sex. And when it was all over, Nergal snuck out.[2] He lied to the gatekeepers on his way out and made his way back to Heaven. So, despite breaking one of the rules, Nergal was still able to leave. When Ereshkigal woke up to find her bed short one lover, she was enraged. She sent the disease god, Namtar, with a message to the gods. The message told the gods that, in no uncertain terms,

---

[1] Sexless, but apparently not genderless as he is given male pronouns and called a "playboy."
[2] Typical man, amiright ladies?

if they didn't send Nergal back to her, she would raise up an army of the dead who would eat the living. Picture *The Walking Dead* but all the walkers are wearing only feathers. Much to Nergal's disapproval, he was sent right back to Erkalla. Raging, he killed the gatekeepers on his way back in. When he saw Ereshkigal he pulled her from her throne by the hair and then they made sweet, sweet underworld love for another week. Unfortunately, the end of that poem is non-extant so we don't actually know what came to be of Ereshkigal and Nergal but he is mentioned elsewhere as an underworld god, so presumably the two remained together.

There was a variety of other Mesopotamian underworld gods. Some, like Namtar, were seen as the offspring of Ereshkigal and were typically connected to either disease or subterranean rivers and the like. And there was the Ugaritic Mot who was a cannibalistic death god who may or may not have been connected to the same afterlife as Ereshkigal.

Gilgamesh

a.k.a.: Bilgamesh
Pantheon: Mesopotamian
Parents: Ninsun and Lugalbanda
Symbols: bull, lion

The Epic of Gilgamesh is one of the most significant works of literature in the history of the world. Despite having been forgotten or ignored for centuries, it may be one of the most influential texts ever written.

The titular character, Gilgamesh, is a demi-god, and king of the city of Uruk. Gilgamesh was a terrible king. He was arrogant, refusing to listen to counsel from even the wisest and most experienced of his advisors. He was immoral, grabbing women, and even raping them, believing that because he was famous he could do whatever he wanted and get away with it. Obviously, no modern society would ever willingly put a narcissistic, rapacious, destructive asshole like that in power, but try to imagine what it would be like if such a thing were to happen. The people of Uruk were helpless to stop Gilgamesh and so they cried out to their gods for help.[1]

---

[1] Back then there were no representatives you could contact to get a horrible leader kicked out of office and you had to wait and hope that the gods would do it for you. Nowadays removing a corrupt leader from office is much easier and requires appeals to democracy rather than deity.

"Gilgamesh" by David Manderville

63

The gods created a rival for Gilgamesh in the form of a beast-man named Enkidu. After a brief wrestling match, Gilgamesh and Enkidu became the best of friends, even calling each other "brother." The two went on to have rousing adventures defeating monsters and defying the gods. But, after Gilgamesh and Enkidu insulted the goddess Ishtar and killed the Bull of Heaven, the gods agreed to kill Enkidu in retaliation. Enkidu did not get a glorious battlefield death befitting a hero, but instead died slowly and painfully from illness. After witnessing his dear comrade's unromantic demise, Gilgamesh decided that he would do whatever it took to keep himself from a similar fate and so he sought out the key to immortality.

At the end of a very long journey, Gilgamesh encountered an immortal named Utnapishtim. He begged Utnapishtim to give him the secret of eternal life. Unfortunately for Gilgamesh, Utnapishtim gained his immortality by being the sole survivor of a worldwide flood. It is Utnapishtim's flood story that may be the most historically significant part of *The Epic of Gilgamesh*.

When George Smith found and translated *Gilgamesh* back in the 1870s he caused a stir by (accurately) dating its writing earlier than the written form of the very similar Biblical tale of Noah. Because the ancient Hebrews were neighbors to the Assyrians who wrote *Gilgamesh*, it is not surprising to find similarities in their mythologies. Beginning with Smith and continuing to the present, scholars have suggested that Utnapishtim's tale was the inspiration[1] for the story of Noah. While few modern people would argue that Utnapishtim's story should be taught as history and/or science, all too many believe that the Hebrew homage to it is both history and science. In that way, the influence of *Gilgamesh* looms large in the daily lives of many.

As significant as the flood narrative is, it did little good for Gilgamesh. That was not exactly an experience he could replicate to become immortal. Utnapishtim told Gilgamesh of a couple of additional routes to immortality but the king of Uruk failed them both. Defeated and depressed, Gilgamesh returned home to his people. And then he had an epiphany.[2] Gilgamesh realized that immortality isn't gained by not dying, but by being remembered for your deeds in life. He became a just and fair leader to his people, gave up his old, abusive, and corrupt ways. As a result, when he died after many years of service to his people, he was de   eply

---

[1] "Inspiration" being a gentle word that means "the story they totally ripped off to use for their own purposes."

[2] Maybe that's not quite the right word. After all, several people whom he encountered on his journey told him as much, but it didn't really sink in until journey's end.

mourned, and they passed his story on for generations. The historical Gilgamesh, whose biography likely bears little to no resemblance to the events of *The Epic of Gilgamesh,* was a Sumerian king. Over a thousand years and several major cultural shifts later, the legacy of Gilgamesh still so strongly resonated in the region that *The Epic of Gilgamesh* was composed to sing of his character and deeds. Several thousand years after that, we are still talking about Gilgamesh—what greater form of immortality is there?

The tale of Gilgamesh offers some truly valuable lessons. Perhaps the most important is that while a human may die, humanity lives on and it is the job of each of us to try to leave humanity better off than how we found it. We may not all be remembered by name for centuries but we do all have the capacity to leave our mark in shaping the future. And that's a lesson worth passing on.

"It's Dangerous To Go Alone" by Malena Salinas

Chinese Mythology

Since roughly 7000 BCE to the present, humans have lived in the area now known as the People's Republic of China. What began with farming villages in the Yangtze River Valley grew to the first recorded Chinese dynasty by around 2070 BCE. Dynasty followed dynasty followed dynasty and with each new group rising to power, the territory shifted and expanded. New ethnic groups were incorporated, rose or fell in power, and, of course, all along the way the myths and traditions changed and evolved. Despite the incredible expanse of time and space and diversity of perspectives, Chinese mythology has historically not been given the credit it deserves.

There are several reasons why Chinese myth has not received the attention that the myths of other cultures have enjoyed. Anne Birrell describes in her seminal book *Chinese Mythology: An Introduction* some of the obstacles that have held back the study of Chinese myth. As is the case with many others, the myths of China were passed down orally for most of their history. Even when the earliest Chinese systems of writing were developed, they lacked the subtlety and nuance required for the poetic and abstract language contained in myth. Eventually the written language evolved but rather than writing expansive mythic texts, the Chinese tended more often to sprinkle fragmentary pieces of myth within other texts. Rather than writing the Chinese equivalent of the Greek's *Theogony* or *The Iliad*, we get small bits of myth strewn throughout the whole of Chinese texts. It can obviously be a bit tricky to find and provide context to these fragments, but on the other hand, when we do find them, they have been largely unchanged, hidden away as they are like a Triassic mosquito in a piece of amber. Another hurdle to deciphering ancient Chinese myth, Birrell points out, is historic opposition. As new ethnic groups, new philosophies, and new perspectives took hold, the older gods and narratives were altered. Confucianism, in particular, brought with it a more puritanical morality and so much of the sexual material may have been suppressed or changed. This is one hypothesis for the prevalence of what are called *gansheng* myths. These are stories that very deliberately go out of the way to give absurd or elaborate origins for gods and heroes so as to avoid talk of sex. Since the Confucianists were quite successful in their cultural usurpation, we don't know if the received myths are as they were originally told or if the prudish Confucianists made them that way. Trying to figure out the original versus the received version is difficult, if not impossible.

Despite the difficulties, there are some notable Chinese mythic texts. One of the most significant is the *Shanhaijing* ("Classic of Mountains and Seas") which is a composite of mythic tales dealing with geographical features of China and it dates back to as early as the 4th century BCE.

Dated slightly later than *Shanhaijing* is the nonetheless important text called *Huainanzi* ("Writings of the Master of Huainan"). This twenty-one-chapter book contains stories of Nu Gua, Yi, Gun and Yu, Gonggong, and others. Written by Liu An, the ruler of the Huainan, he saw it as his most important legacy and a guidebook for future rulers to follow.

The most enigmatic source of Chinese myth is called *Tianwen* ("Questions of Heaven") and is written as a series of questions. Part of the larger text known as *Chuci* ("Songs of Chu"), legend holds that *Tianwen* was written on the walls of the temple by Qu Yuan after he had been unfairly exiled from the palace. It is a fascinating piece made even more so by its awkward format and the fact that the author exhibits not only anger but also skepticism about the ways of the gods and the universe itself.

Along with the (more or less) official mythology, China also has a great deal of folk traditions. Informed by the traditional religion, as well as Buddhism, Taoism, and Confucianism, there is an abundance of locally beloved characters, many of whom are still popular in modern Chinese culture.

"Panku" by Adrianna Allen

Panku

a.k.a.: P'an Ku, Pangu, Pan Gu
Pantheon: Chinese

Creation myths come in many shapes and sizes, but there are some recurring themes. For example, there is the cosmic egg that releases all the elements of life, or the primordial watery chaos containing everything in an undifferentiated state of nothingness, or the gigantic being whose disassembled body is used to create the world as we know it. While many cultures have etiological myths that contain one of these elements, the very ancient Chinese tale of Panku uses all three.

It begins with an egg. The egg broke open, and out from it came Yin, Yang, and a humanoid creature. This is essentially what it would be like if you went to make yourself a plate of eggs, cracked one open and found not only the yolk and white, but a hairy baby as well. The yolk is Yin, the egg white is Yang, and the hairy baby is Panku. Yin and Yang, like the undifferentiated chaos, are not deities or beings of any kind. They are elements and it is the interplay between the two of them that underlies all of creation. Yolk-y Yin is "congealed," the "heavy turbidness" that makes up the earth as well as the cold, dark, and feminine[1] aspects of the universe. The "limpid light" of Yang gives us the sky, warmth, light, and the masculine side of reality.

Freshly hatched from the cosmic egg, Yin and Yang were piled on top of each other, offering no room for anything else to exist. So, newborn Panku lifted up the lighter Yang and pushed down the heavier Yin. Every day for thousands of years, Panku grew ten feet taller, forcing the earth and sky ten feet further apart. After 18,000 years of this, the two were far enough apart that Panku no longer feared them crashing back into each other and he could take a break. Like a weary cop being taken out by a stray bullet on the day of his retirement, Panku relaxed for the first time in his life and immediately (though peacefully) died. And that's when Panku really became useful.

---

[1] Western sensibilities tend to lend negative connotations to words like cold, dark, and heavy and they are not ideas that are generally associated with femininity. The Taoist view does not take these concepts as either inherently malignant or benevolent but rather they are simply one part of the great equation of life. So, if you're offended by femininity being likened to these things then it's probably more about your weird hang-ups than anything else.

Panku's final breath[1] became the wind and clouds; his booming voice became peals of thunder. His left eye became the sun and his right eye the moon[2]. Panku's limbs formed mountains found in each of the cardinal directions. Both his blood and his semen created the waters, possibly as a nod to both fresh and salt water. His flesh became the earth and the hair that sprang from it became plants. While creation myths routinely undersell the stars, Panku's story gets closer to accounting for the number of stars than many others—the stars were formed from the hairs of his head and scruffy beard. But what of us? What of humans? Humans (or specifically, the "black haired people") were born of the dead, hairy giant's fleas. Which, sounds kind of insulting. I mean, how dare they compare humanity to a group of parasites that feed off the earth and offer nothing in return? Not only is the comparison quite apt, but it's meant to be kind of flattering in that fleas feed on blood and we, as the fleas of this proto-god, are nourished by god juice. The divine, the primordial, and the eternal give us life. We are not simply parasitic, we are uniquely parasitic and our host is the being responsible for creation.

Nu Gua

a.k.a.: NuWa, Nu Kua
Pantheon: Chinese
Spouse/Lovers: Fu Xi
Siblings: Fu Xi
Offspring: humanity
Deity of: creation, fertility
Symbols: knotted cord, carpenter's square, moon with a frog inside

Given the expanse of time and space encompassed within Chinese history, it isn't surprising to find that there are multiple versions of many of their myths and mythic figures. Nu Gua is an important figure in a variety of Chinese creation and flood myths.

In one tale, the primordial fertility goddess Nu Gua was lonely—which is a natural reaction to being alone. So, she took it upon herself to create humans that

---

[1] Probably a sigh of relief.
[2] This is another familiar mythic trope: the sun and moon coming from or representing the eyes of a single being.

71

"Nu Gua" by Ashley Campos

would both keep her entertained and worshipped. She began by scooping up some of the rich clay along the banks of the sacred Yellow River. She molded the clay carefully, and meticulously crafted a collection of perfectly proportional and physically flawless human beings. All this care and meticulousness was incredibly time consuming, however, and she realized that if she was going to populate the whole earth (or even just China) it would take a very long time indeed. So, she found a shortcut. Taking a length of rope, she dragged it through some moist mud. The mud that fell from the rope formed humans quickly and efficiently even if it was with a disturbingly low level of quality control. The first people, the ones crafted from the goddess' own hands, became Chinese nobility. Her lazier sophomore effort gave rise to the rest of us. Clearly this was a myth written for, if not by, Chinese nobility. They, those perfect people, are like sandcastles built by an artisan and us poor folk are like drip castles made by a child who enjoys the feel of slimy sand slipping through their fingers.

Nu Gua was attached to multiple flood narratives. In one, we may take her to be the same character as the one who made humans from mud, or it might be an entirely separate variation. When one or all four of the pillars that held up the sky were knocked down, a flood ensued. To make matters worse, as often happens with mythic weather disaster tales, monsters came out and attacked the soggy humanity. Nu Gua used her skills in metallurgy to mend the sky with five melted, multi-colored stones to stop the flooding. Then she reinforced the work by cutting off the legs of a giant turtle and using them as the new pillars to hold up the sky. Then she killed off the monsters. This Nu Gua was seriously badass.

The name Nu Gua appears in another story about a great flood and the origin of humans, though the character herself is a bit different. In this tale, Nu Gua was a young girl whose father managed to cage a thunder god. When he went into town to get supplies with which to pickle the thunder god[1], Nu Gua and her brother Fu Xi were told to keep an eye on the imprisoned god. When the god begged the children for a tiny sip of water to slake his thirst, the kind-hearted children complied. And that innocent gift of water brought about a flood that killed 99.99% of all people on Earth.

A sip was all it took for the thunder god to regain his strength and break out of his cage. Thankful for the assist, the god offered the children one of his teeth as a gesture of his appreciation before returning to the heavens. Possibly because he told them to, and possibly because a tooth is just a really gross gift to hold on

---

[1] Presumably a large jar and some brine.

73

to, Nu Gua and Fu Xi buried the tooth. From the tooth grew a tree and from the tree grew an enormous gourd. When their father returned home with a craving for some pickled thunder god, he was upset to see that (1) the god was gone; (2) there was a new tree with a giant gourd on it in his yard; and (3) it was raining cats and dogs.

Still a bit peeved from his imprisonment, the thunder god had set the sky to deluge mode and dry land was becoming increasingly difficult to find. Nu Gua and Fu Xi's father took to his iron boat to weather the storm while his children climbed into the tooth-tree gourd. Apparently, no one else on Earth thought to climb into a boat or other buoyant object and thus everyone else drowned. The water continued to rise until the boat and gourd literally bumped into the heavenly home of the Jade Emperor. Father implored the ruler of the gods to stop the rain. The Jade Emperor, still groggy from having been woken up from his afternoon nap, quickly turned off the waterworks. Whereas in flood narratives like that of Noah, Utnapishtim, and others the water recedes slowly, in this Chinese tale, the water was immediately whisked away and the boat and the gourd plummeted from Heaven all the way to the earth below. Dad, in his mighty iron boat, was crushed by the fall but Nu Gua and Fu Xi, in their tooth-tree gourd, survived.

The problem faced by lone survivors of worldwide floods is the same no matter if they're Mesopotamian, Greek, Nordic, or Chinese: How to repopulate? Some have magical means of doing so, and some must resort to old-fashioned acts of incest—the Chinese found an interesting middle ground. While it's true that there are far fewer of the tawdry sexcapades in Chinese myth than there are in almost any other culture, sometimes even they are forced to admit to an indiscretion. Lacking any other option, Nu Gua and Fu Xi, the only humans left, decided that they must procreate with each other. They checked with the gods first to make absolutely certain that what they were about to do was what must be done, and once the gods had offered their sign, Nu Gua and Fu Xi committed a taboo act out of necessity rather than desire. But, to avoid repeated incestuous relations, Nu Gua gave birth, not to a child, but to a lump of flesh[1]. Fu Xi sliced and diced the pile into little pieces which were then carried away by the wind. Wherever the pieces landed around the globe (or at least China), they became new humans. Thus, people again peopled the world and all it took was a few icky moments, rather than generations of gene pool-stagnating interactions.

---

[1] In some translations, it is a gourd rather than flesh, but the ultimate effect is the same.

Even though the stories we have of Nu Gua are less than cohesive, she is widely regarded as a fertility goddess and protector of humanity. She seems to be a very ancient deity, possibly pre-dating even the primordial giant Panku by up to six centuries. What we see over the course of the evolving use of the name Nu Gua is a gradual de-powering of the goddess. Initially, she was viewed as an Empress of heaven, then a hands-on creator goddess, and then as the sister/wife of Fu Xi who needed both a male counterpart and special dispensation from the gods before she could create humanity. Her visual representation morphed through the ages as well, most often some variation on the theme of a woman combined a snake.

Fu Xi

a.k.a.: Fuxi, Fu Hsi, Paoxi, Baoxi
Pantheon: Chinese
Spouse/Lovers: Nu Gua
Siblings: Nu Gua
Offspring: humanity
Deity of: creation and invention, divination, cattle, spring, measurements, music
Symbols: compass, sun with a three-footed crow inside, net, *Bagua*, fire

Fu Xi is credited with giving humanity a wide array of gifts, not the least of which is life itself. He and his sister Nu Gua, after establishing the institution of marriage, gave birth to humanity. Technically, Nu Gua gave birth to a blob of flesh that Fu Xi then chopped up with his ax and, once the wind scattered the pieces, Earth was repopulated. This tale, though one of the best known, only entered into the traditions of Fu Xi and Nu Gua after both had had long and successful careers of their own.

One of Fu Xi's most lauded gifts to the ancient world was the Eight Trigrams. Also called the *Bagua*, these symbols are hugely important in Taoism because they describe the intricate and interwoven laws of nature and, specifically, the interactions between the building blocks of reality: Yin and Yang. If you could master the symbols you could use them to decode the universe, be able to understand the present, and predict the future. Fu Xi figured them out by studying

"Fu Xi" by Christian Sitterlet

the heavens and the earth and he gifted them to humanity. Divination plays a significant role in Taoism and Chinese culture in general and Fu Xi gets the credit for much of it.

Some of Fu Xi's gifts to humanity were less abstract and more practical for daily life. He was credited with inventing musical instruments, various tools of measurement ranging from the compass to the calendar, writing systems, and mathematical principles. Not only was he regarded as the father of humanity, but he was also their savior.

Early humans were poor hunters and so they often suffered from a lack of food. Fu Xi helped his people by showing them how to catch fish by hand. And amazingly, that worked pretty well. Well enough, at least, to upset the Dragon King. The fish were the subjects of the Dragon King and he grew very angry at Fu Xi for teaching humans how to catch them. And so, he commanded that neither Fu Xi nor any human would be allowed to catch fish by hand. Fu Xi was vexed as humanity once again went hungry. Just as Buddha created Buddhism while sitting under the bodhi tree and Isaac Newton was struck by the inspiration to invent gravity when he was struck by an apple, so too did Fu Xi find his answer at the foot of a tree. Lying down under the shade of its branches, Fu Xi looked up and saw a spider knitting its web. He then completely ripped off the spider's intellectual property and created a net. He tossed the net into the river and when he pulled it out again it was filled with flipping, flopping fish. He passed this invention on to humans who were then able to catch way more fish than they ever had with their bare hands. Joke's on you, Dragon King.

Fu Xi's appearance morphed through the ages to reflect the changing ideas of his role. The earliest depictions of Fu Xi showed him as a serpent or dragon with a human head. Later, he appeared with a human upper body and a snake-y bottom half. It was around the Han Dynasty when his story was linked with Nu Gua that the two were portrayed with interlaced serpentine lower bodies. In a bit of reverse euhemerism[1], Fu Xi is now often regarded as a legendary human king and, accordingly, is portrayed without any snakelike attributes.

---

[1] Euhemerism is the idea that myths are based on historical events or people. Identifiable instances of Euhemerism (named for the Greek proponent of this idea, Euhemerus) are quite rare. More commonly we have evidence of mythic figures who were retroactively regarded as real humans to reflect changing philosophical and religious trends.

"Yu the Great" by David Manderville

Yu

a.k.a.: Da Yu, Yu the Great
Pantheon: Chinese
Spouse/Lovers: Tushanshi
Parents: Gun
Offspring: Qi
Symbols: yellow bear, yellow dragon, *xirang*

Yu is[1] one of the great culture heroes of China and is known for saving humanity from one of the many great floods in Chinese myth. Yu's achievements, however, begin with the failings of his father Gun.

In the Mesopotamian flood narrative found within *The Epic of Gilgamesh*, the entire world floods in the span of seven days and six nights. When the ancient Hebrews adapted it and put Noah in the lead role, the flood took forty days. The Gun/Yu-centered flood narrative in China works on a very different timetable. There is still the hyperbolic language with the waters rising so high that they lap against the sky itself, but rather than a wiping of the slate, killing off all of humanity and starting afresh with a ton of incest, the Gun/Yu tale seems both more grounded and more frightening. The flood was devastating and rather than having one family climb into a boat, Gun took action to try to stop the flood itself. In doing so, he defied and even stole from them, bringing down to the earth *xirang*. *Xirang* is a self-renewing soil whose cultural counterpart shows up in some Indigenous American and African creation myths. Gun used the ever-growing soil to stem the tide of the overflowing rivers, like using sandbags to shore up a failing levee. The gods did not appreciate Gun's efforts and so the heavenly executioner, Zhurong[2], struck him dead.

Though dead, the body of Gun did not rot and decompose. Rather, it lay unchanged and undisturbed for three years until someone shoved a sword into its belly. The body of Gun then broke open and from his abdomen emerged Yu the Great riding a yellow dragon. While a miraculous, sexless birth is practically a given for most Chinese divinities, Yu's creation is unique in that there is no female element involved at all.

---

[1] Apologies to the grammar police.
[2] Different names of the heavenly executioner appear in different sources. Typically, it is a variation on the fire god and the implication is that swift justice is delivered in the form of a thunderbolt (ie. fire from the heavens).

Picking up where his father left off three years earlier, Yu combatted the flood waters with *xirang*. For some reason, this time the gods were totally cool with it. Again underscoring just how different this flood narrative is from so many of the others, three years in and the flood was still happening. Yu's efforts to repair the damage and control the waters took another thirteen years. One gets the impression that whoever first told this myth was well aware of the devastating and prolonged consequences of massive flooding.

We must not oversell the 'realism' of this flood, however. As with many other mythic natural disasters, the flooding brought out opportunistic monsters whom Yu had to defeat. One was Xiangliu who had nine human heads on a snake body. But Yu, with the help of friends ranging from river gods to turtles, defeated all the troublemakers.

Yu is an important figure not just because he saved humanity, but also for the selfless and tireless way he did it. We are told that Yu made great personal sacrifices in devoting himself to his cause. He wouldn't take a break to go home, he forsook all romantic entanglements, and married at the ripe old age of thirty, only to head out again five days later to continue his work. In some accounts, his ceaseless efforts had a deleterious effect on his health and resulted in him having a pained, shuffling walk.

Yu remains one of the most significant and single-minded heroes of Chinese myth. Gun's attempt and failure to save humanity led to the birth of Yu and through his son, Gun's legacy was secured. The theme of the son carrying on the work of the father as well as that of the unrelenting zeal with which Yu pursued his altruistic goal resonate deeply with the Chinese and ought to set an example for us all.

Jade Emperor

a.k.a.: Yu Di, Yu Huang, Yuanshi Tianzun, Heavenly Grandfather, "Peace Absolving, Central August Spirit, Exalted, Ancient Buddha, Most Pious and Honorable, His Highness the Jade Emperor"
Pantheon: Chinese
Spouse/Lovers: Xiwangmu, Mazu, Wang Ma etc.
Offspring: Zhi Nu, Shi Quning, Yen Kuang etc.
Deity of: governance, emperors
Symbols: jade, imperial vestments

"Jade Emperor" by Mallory Heiges

Sometimes it really is about who you know rather than who you are. Yu Di, the Jade Emperor, was an extremely obscure figure in the Chinese pantheon until the actual earthly emperor Zhen Cong was visited by Yu Di in a dream and he was named as the patron of the ruling family and, therefore, the most powerful of all deities. Why did Zhen Cong pick this particular, little-known deity? Hard to say, but it is arguably not because the god truly visited him in a dream.

The Jade Emperor's star quickly rose and he became the most powerful god of the most powerful of the three domains: Heaven. Beneath him was the earthly domain and last of all, the underworld realm. As other cultures reflect their social structure in the way they view their gods, so too did the Chinese. Perhaps because of the late date (the Jade Emperor became part of the official religion around 1000 CE) and the comparatively complex governmental system in place at that time, the Chinese viewed the court of the Jade Emperor as a bureaucracy. Just as the commoner had no direct contact with the earthly emperor, humans had no direct contact with the Jade Emperor. Prayers couldn't even be offered up to the man on the throne but had to be written down, and could passed on to the local deities by being consigned them to the flames. Considering that many commoners were not literate, this meant that they would have yet another degree of separation and would have to find a scribe to copy down their prayers for them.

No other pantheon generated quite as much paperwork as the gods of China did under the Jade Emperor. Beneath Yu Di were gods who oversaw each city, beneath the city gods were gods of the household, and beneath the household gods were gods who lived within and kept tabs on each person. Each deity would write regular reports that were given to the gods above them, who would write reports to the gods above them, and so on and so forth until the Jade Emperor got a stack of communiques from the earthly domain.

The Jade Emperor is a pragmatic figure who refrains from direct contact or direct action. He is a great delegator and is primarily known for practicing a management style called *wu wei* (literally "non-doing"). The less action or effort exerted to solve a problem, the better. The level of bureaucratic red tape resultant from the multi-layered hierarchy meant that the gods worked slowly and deliberately or not at all. However, as with any bureaucracy, the middle-managers range from relatively inoffensive to outright corrupt. Many of them could be bribed to offer more favorable reports up the chain of command. This was mutually beneficial for both the human bribers and the bribed gods because positive reports meant they must have been good at their jobs and so would be considered for promotions up the heavenly ladder. Thank goodness, some thousand years later that kind of corruption has been weeded out and now the only way to gain political influence is by being experienced, competent, honest, and deserving of merit[1].

Xiwangmu

a.k.a.: Wangmu Niangniang, Queen Mother of the West
Pantheon: Chinese
Spouse/Lovers: Yu Di
Siblings: Fu Xi, Nu Gua
Offspring: Zhi Nu, Sun, Moon
Deity of: immortality, western Heaven
Symbols: peaches, predatory cats

Xiwangmu is a relatively late addition to the Chinese pantheon but she is one of the more popular figures in the modern religion. In her earliest form, Xiwangmu was a fearsome goddess[2] of punishment, disease, and disaster with the tail of a panther, the teeth of a tiger, and dressed in skins. Comparable to the Greek goddess Artemis, Xiwangmu was more comfortable among the animals than the courts of Heaven. But her Artemisian version was only the first in the evolution of the Queen Mother of the West. She stands as a concrete example of how changing religious and social ideals often neuter the more violent and frightening gods (and especially goddesses). Over time, Xiwangmu's tail fell off, her teeth were capped, and she adopted the royal robes befitting a respectable deity.

The Queen Mother of the West, appropriately enough, was linked romantically to the King Father of the East for a time. Known as Dongwanggong[3], he too had bestial aspects, including the tail of a tiger and the face of a bird. It was during the time of this romance that Xiwangmu became connected with the gift of immortality as well as health, wealth, and fertility. Though her tradition is light on narrative pieces, her specialities made her a popular goddess to pray to.

Distancing herself from Dongwanggong, Xiwangmu continued to grow in respectability. Her originally vicious characteristics disappeared and she became a

---

[1] . . .
[2] The gender of Xiwangmu is not clear in the earliest sources but since the character is later considered a female we will use those pronouns to avoid additional complications.
[3] To those of you who are still in middle-school or have the sense of humor of a middle-schooler: you are welcome.

"Xiwangmu" by Naomi K Illustrations

beautiful, demure queen surrounded by beautiful, demure maidens. It is this kinder, gentler version of the Queen Mother of the West that shows up in the story of Yi the Archer, giving him the well-meaning but ultimately unfortunate gift of the Elixir of Immortality. In a similar vein, she is referenced in the much beloved folk novel *Journey to the West*. The protagonist, Sun WuKong the handsome Monkey King, was put in charge of the garden of the peaches of immortality only to eat them all and then destroy the banquet Xiwangmu had organized for the gods.

More often than not, for the past 1500 years or so, Xiwangmu has been viewed as the consort of Yu Di, the Jade Emperor, supremest of all supreme Chinese divinities. In one tale Xiwangmu and Yu Di were the parents of the sun and the moon. The two were said originally to occupy the sky together but when the sun made unwanted and untenable sexual advances toward his sister they were separated. Yu Di had wanted to kill their son, but Xiwangmu being all motherly and not-so homicidal begged her husband to spare his life. From that day forward, sun and moon had to take turns in the sky which, as a side benefit, differentiated night from day.

In at least one tradition, Xiwangmu was linked to the much earlier deities of Nu Gua and Fu Xi. Xiwangmu was said to be the younger sister of the two and worked side by side with Nu Gua[1] in her efforts to patch the sky after it had been ripped open, causing a devastating flood. Despite being the Robin to Nu Gua's Batman, Xiwangmu is currently much more popular than her elder sometimes siblings. More commonly called Wangmu Niangniang now, she has shrines throughout China where she offers her supplicants success in their endeavours, be they financial or procreational.

Yi

a.k.a.: Houyi, Zongbu
Pantheon: Chinese
Spouse/Lovers: Chang'e (Heng'e, Zhang E)
Symbols: archery, sun, peach wood

---

[1] Called Lishan Laomu in the northwestern Chinese variation.

"Yi" by Sarah Lindstrom

Way back in antiquity there were ten suns. Each day of the week[1] one of the suns would leave the great tree Fusang[2] and travel across the sky only to return to the tree in the evening. The suns, grandsons of the Supreme Deity, took turns in an orderly manner until one day when they didn't. For some reason, all ten suns took to the sky one morning. The tenfold amount of heat and light made the earth uninhabitable. Rivers and seas dried up, plants died, and humanity suffered. And, of course, monsters came out to play. Earth was doomed.

Enter Yi.

Yi was the greatest archer on Earth or in Heaven. He loosed nine arrows and one by one the superfluous suns dropped from the sky. He would have killed the tenth and final sun, too, but it was smart enough to hide[3]. Yi also dispatched the monsters, including a giant bird, snake, and boar, and a creature with nine heads, one with teeth like chisels, and a dragon-headed leopard beast.

Then the sources begin to diverge in their accounts of the exploits of Yi. Some of the divergences are minor, such as: did Yi kill the river god He Bo and the wind god Feng Bo or did he merely maim them? Other differences are more significant, especially concerning the fate of Yi and his wife Chang'e.

One tradition holds that, despite Yi having saved the world, the Supreme Deity was quite cross at the archer for having killed off nine-tenths of his grandsons. Yi, who had been divine, was then cast out of Heaven, and his wife Chang'e was forced to go with him. She was less than thrilled about losing her divinity. Yi visited the palace of the Queen Mother of the West who, among other things, was quite generous in doling out immortality. She gave Yi an Elixir of Immortality. Planning to share it with his wife, Yi brought the elixir home and put it away until he had purified himself adequately to deserve becoming immortal once again. Chang'e had no patience and so she stole the elixir and drank it all herself. She then floated up to the moon where she became either a frog or just a lonely moon goddess.

Another tradition keeps many of the same events, but assigns different motives to the characters. The Queen Mother of the West offered the Elixir of Immortality to the mortal Yi as thanks for his sun killing. Yi, a human leader, stowed the elixir away until he was ready to leave his people. Meanwhile, his apprentice, Fengmeng learned of the elixir and went to steal it while Yi was away. Chang'e caught Fengmeng mid-burglary and, to prevent him from getting it, found

---

[1] The traditional Chinese calendar had a ten-day week.
[2] "Leaning Mulberry;" also called Fu Mu or "Leaning Tree"
[3] The sun only returned to the sky after being called to by a rooster.

no other option but to drink it all herself. She immediately began to float away. Yi returned home just in time to see his wife whisked away from him forever. So Chang'e is taken either as a greedy woman or a sympathetic figure but the result is the same: she is left to occupy the moon all by her lonesome. Other than the white jade rabbit that lives there with her, of course. And possibly a frog. Unless she is the frog.

Though Yi is most famous for his world-saving archery skills, he is not exempt from less flattering characterizations either. In some traditions, Yi became a mortal king but was a terrible leader because he was more interested in target shooting than he was in leading. He was so hated by his subjects, in fact, that they killed him and tried to feed him to his sons *Titus Andronicus* style. His sons refused and then they too were killed. Or, Yi may have been killed by his Padawan, Fengmeng when the student realized that he would never surpass his master in archery. Fengmeng beat Yi to death with a peachwood club. Because of that, and because the Chinese word for peach is similar to the verb meaning "to cast out," peachwood was said to scare ghosts and is still used in ritual exorcisms. Yes, the popular religion of China allows for exorcisms.

Zao Jun

a.k.a.: Zao Chun, Tsao Shen, Zhang Lang, Kitchen God, "Stove Lord,"
Pantheon: Chinese
Spouse/Lovers: Unnamed Wife and Unnamed Lover
Deity of: kitchen/stove, household
Symbols: stove

Better known as "The Kitchen God," Zao Jun has surprisingly little to do with cooking. In fact, the only thing he ever put on the stove was himself.

The story goes that Zao Jun was a mortal man who abandoned his wife for a younger one. It wasn't long before he and his new lady friend fell on hard times and she, in turn, abandoned Zao Jun. Loveless and alone, Zao Jun went blind from overwhelming poverty and became a beggar[1]. For years he traveled from town to

---

[1] This story perpetuates the idea found in many ancient (and some modern) cultures that both disability and/or poverty are proof of wrongdoing on the part of the differently abled or impoverished. To be clear: neither blindness nor homelessness is the result of divine punishment.

"The Kitchen God" by Rayne Karfonta

town asking for help and (on a good day) he managed to receive a subsistence level of food.

One day, as Zao Jun went house to house and held out his bowl for meager bites of food, he knocked on a familiar door. Being blind, he had no idea where he was but the woman behind the door immediately recognized him. Even in his disheveled state the woman knew that this was the man who had left her all those years before. Rather than laughing or slamming the door or slapping the blind man, the woman invited her ex into her home[1]. She sat him down at the kitchen table and spread out before him a feast of all his favorite foods. When he took his first bite of the scrumptious delights, his vision returned. He saw before him more food, more lovingly prepared and presented than any he'd had in years. When he turned to see who had been so sweet and generous to him, he was amazed to see his former wife smiling gently. Despite all he had done to her, she showed him kindness. Zao Jun's amazement gave way to deep shame. Racked with guilt, and with the taste of his wife's cooking was still on his lips, Zao Jun threw himself onto her stove. Apparently, a long bout with poverty and blindness had rendered him especially flammable because he was consumed by the flames almost instantly. His wife tried to pull her prodigal husband off the stove but only came away with a partially charred leg.

Another account of the life of Zao Jun gives him a slightly more sympathetic trajectory. Rather than leaving his wife by choice, she and he were forced to split by a richer, more powerful man who wanted her as his own. From there, the trajectory is the same and Zao Jun ends up tossing himself on the stovetop like so much stuffing mix. Either way, it was the final beat of his life that is echoed in his post-life position working with the Jade Emperor's Administration.

As the Stove Lord, it was Zao Jun's duty to keep tabs on every household, while seated at the true center of the home: the kitchen. At the end of the year, Zao Jun would make a report based on his surveillance of you and yours and bring it to the Jade Emperor. To send him on his way, an image of Zao Jun would be burned on the stove. If you wanted to ensure that the Zao Jun would report only good things about your household you could put some honey or sweet paste on the lips of the image before burning it, thus making it so he could only speak sweet words. It's a bit like sticking $20 in your letter to Santa so he forgets about a year's worth of naughty behavior.

---

1 She blew a perfectly good opportunity for some schadenfreude that few of us would pass up so willingly.

"Lei Gong & Dien Mu" by Malena Salinas

Lei Gong & Dien Mu

a.k.a.: Lei Kong, Lei Shen, Dian Mu, Tian Mu, Tien-Mu
Pantheon: Chinese (Taoist)
Deity of: thunder (Lei Gong), lightning (Dien Mu)
Symbols: hammer, drums, mirrors

It is entirely understandable that thunder and lightning have often been viewed as the tools of divine retribution. The ominous thunder portends disaster and lightning strikes with such power and accuracy that it must be anything but random. We may not know what that person was guilty of or what wrongs that specific tree or metal rod committed, but surely it was the intent of the gods to make them pay. Though ostensibly one phenomenon, lightning and the commensurate sound it produces have been viewed as two separate but clearly related events by many. In Chinese Taoism, they are the products of the husband and wife team of Lei Gong and Dien Mu.

As is often the case in Chinese myth, Lei Gong was the result of a miraculous, sexless birth. Possibly because of the prudish sensibilities of the Confucianists or maybe because of the prudish sensibilities of those who came before the Confucianists, there is a trend in Chinese myth called *gansheng* myths. Sex is icky and thus should never be talked about in public[1] and so many gods and heroes were given bizarre but totally pure and innocent origins. A hero may have been born because his mother stepped in a giant footprint[2], or because mom swallowed magic pearls[3]. In the case of Lei Gong, it was an elaborately-eared hunting dog who found an egg in the wilderness.

In reality, thunder is the much less dangerous of the two elements, but in myth it is the thunder god Lei Gong who has the much fiercer appearance. With wings, clawed feet and hands, a beak where his mouth should be, and lush bluish-green skin, Lei Gong would hopefully inspire so much fear with his looks alone that he would stop most evildoers before they did evil. For those too corrupt or too foolish to stop themselves from committing crimes against humanity or

---

[1] Which is still the approach to Sex Education in much of the United States and the kind of thinking that leads to rampant teen pregnancy, the spread of STIs and worst of all, kids getting married super young so they can have officially sanctioned sex.
[2] Fu Xi's origin, in some sources.
[3] Insert your own crude joke here.

against the gods, Lei Gong would offer a final warning shot by striking his hammer; if that didn't do it, he would deliver swift justice with a chisel.

Lei Gong's wife Dien Mu has a striking image herself. Looking much less monstrous and more like an average, well-dressed Chinese woman, Dien Mu carries a couple of accessories that really light up the sky: she produces lightning by bouncing light back and forth between two mirrors. While Dien Mu is often depicted alongside her husband, there is not exactly what you'd call a rich tradition of Dien Mu myths. One story holds that Dien Mu became a goddess after Lei Gong wrongfully killed her. Lei Gong thought he saw her wasting food and for that he struck her dead. Apparently, Lei Gong is a bit of a hard-ass. But the Jade Emperor shed some light on the subject and explained that Lei Gong hadn't seen what he thought he saw and that Dien Mu was innocent. To make up for the wrongful killing, Dien Mu became a goddess, the wife of Lei Gong, and his assistant in meting out justice. To make sure Lei Gong didn't make the same mistake again, it was Dien Mu's job to light up the sky so he could see clearly who was innocent and who was truly guilty. This, of course, is why lightning comes before the thunder[1]. Dien Mu is also the goddess of the North Star and fortune tellers.

Thunder God and Lightning Goddess were only two of the members of the Legion of Shitty Weather. Cloud Boy (Yun Tong) pulled the chariot of the storm gods, explaining why clouds preceded storms. Rain Man (Yuzi) was definitely responsible for the rains by dipping his sword into a pot of water. And a bag full of wind was wielded by either Wind Lad or Wind Lass (Feng Bo or Feng Popo).

Xingtian

a.k.a.: Xing Tian
Pantheon: Chinese
Deity of: perseverance

Never give up, never surrender. No matter how many setbacks you encounter or how severe the opposition, you can, will, and must persist. So says the tenacious Chinese warrior giant Xingtian.

---

[1] Actually, it's because light travels faster than sound. Science takes the fun out of everything. And by "fun," I mean inaccurate, baseless beliefs.

"Xingtian" by Cynthia Lynn Cooper

Xingtian did not like the Supreme God. He thought him unfair and unfit and so he decided to take him out. It didn't go great for Xingtian. The Supreme God, in fact, lopped off Xingtian's head. A normal person, even most extraordinary people, would have the sense to give up after decapitation. A normal person would have the sense to accept martyrdom. Xingtian was not a normal person. Not even by giant standards. When the Supreme God separated Xingtian's head from his shoulders, headless Xingtian groped around in the hopes of finding the head and recapitating himself. When the Supreme God moved to split the severed head with his mighty sword, a nearby mountain split open, the head rolled in and the mountain closed up again. Unable to recover his head, Xingtian did the next best thing and used his nipples for eyes and his navel for a mouth. And then he kept fighting.

Though his appearance is comically absurd, Xingtian's story is deeply inspiring. Like the Celtic hero Cu Chulainn who strapped himself to a rock as he died so that he could go down swinging, Xingtian represents an inexhaustible spirit of determination. Long regarded as the embodiment of perseverance, Xingtian offers strength and encouragement to those who continue to fight the good fight even when all hope seems lost. By any reasonable standard, Xingtian lost the battle; nevertheless, he persisted. While we may not be able to sprout eyes from our nipples (yet), we can follow his example by refusing to give up or give in.

Gonggong

a.k.a.: Kung Kung, Kanghui
Pantheon: Chinese
Deity of: water
Symbols: dragon/serpent

Gonggong is a heavenly troublemaker whose temper tantrum nearly wiped out humanity. Most often depicted as a dragon or a dragon with the head of a ginger haired person, Gonggong was not content with his menial tasks as an underling in the heavenly court. He wanted to be the top god and so he challenged the baddest badass of them all, Zhurong, to a fight.

Zhurong was the god of fire and the official executioner of the gods. When someone in Heaven, Hell or on Earth was causing trouble, Zhurong was the one who brought swift, fiery justice. As such, he was not the type of guy most would

"Gonggong" by Taryn Marcinowski

choose to step into the Octagon with, but Gonggong did it anyway. Perhaps the highest praise we can offer to Gonggong is to acknowledge that he survived the bout. He didn't win, of course, but Zhurong didn't murder him, so it still went better than expected. Gonggong was too close to the situation to fully appreciate that fact, so rather than being happy that he avoided getting his ginger head lopped off, Gonggong threw a fit.

Like a toddler whose favorite toy has been taken away, or like my wife playing a video game, Gonggong raged and tossed himself about. In the throes of his epic tantrum, Gonggong slammed against Mount Buzhou, one of the pillars that held up the sky, which also caused the cords connecting Heaven and Earth to break. The firmament tipped, spilling the waters above down to the earth below. This flood caused by Gonggong was corrected by Nu Gua patching the hole in the sky and bolstering it with the severed legs of a giant turtle. Or maybe it was Nu Gua working with her sister Xiwangmu. Or maybe neither of them was involved and the long road to fixing the damage done by Gonggong became the undertaking of Gun and his son Yu. Or maybe Nu Gua (or Nu Gua and Xiwangmu) repaired the sky, and then Gun, followed by Yu, did the groundwork, rerouting rivers, and renewing the damaged soil. There are so many flood narratives in Chinese myth, which either account only for the beginning of the flood or deal strictly with the reconstruction post-flood, that attempts have been made throughout the years to marry the various traditions together. The earliest recorded versions of Gonggong's story appear alongside Nu Gua myths but fall short of drawing direct correlations between them.

Not surprisingly, there is a lack of agreement over what happened to Gonggong after all the trouble he caused. Some say he was killed by Zhurong or another heavenly avenger, some say he was banished by Yu or someone else. There is also a tradition that gives Gonggong's deeds great etiological importance, suggesting that celestial objects move across the sky as they do because the sky is still tipped slightly and that the rivers in China flow east because the earth is off balance.

"Kuan Yin" by Matthew Olack

Kuan Yin

a.k.a.: Kuan Shi Yin, Guanyin, Quan Yin, Kwan Yin, Avalokiteshvara (Sanskrit), Kannon/Kwannon/Kanzeon-Bosatsu (Japanese), "The One Who Hears the Cries of the World"

Pantheon: Chinese and most forms of Buddhism

Bodhisattva of: compassion, mercy

Symbols: dragon, lotus, white robes, child, willow branch, dove, prayer scroll, prayer beads, many arms, seated Buddha on her headdress

One of the most important figures in any branch of Buddhism, Kuan Yin goes by many names and takes many forms but is always there to help when needed. Back in India in the early days of Buddhism, he was known as Avalokiteshvara, but Buddhism and Avalokiteshvara really came into full flower when they made their way to China. Somewhere along the Silk Road, the Sanskrit male Avalokiteshvara became the Chinese sometimes male, but most often female, Kuan Yin. Kuan Yin made their mark in Japan as Kannon, in Hong Kong as Kwun Yum, as Gwanse-eum in Korea, Prah Mae Kuan Eim in Thailand, and Quan Am in Vietnam. While their name and gender may change, they are always regarded as a figure of great mercy and compassion, called "The One Who Hears the Cries of the World."

In Buddhism, there are enlightened ones (buddhas) and those who dedicate themselves to helping others achieve enlightenment, known as bodhisattvas. Kuan Yin is a bodhisattva and, as such, has earned all the karmic merit required to attain Buddhahood but instead hangs around to help the rest of us reach enlightenment.

Avalokiteshvara was first born from the Amitabha Buddha but when Avalokiteshvara observed all the suffering in the world, his head shattered to pieces[1]. Amitabha pieced his head back together, but apparently the buddha of infinite light was not great at puzzles and somehow ended up making nine heads from the pieces. This made it so Avalokiteshvara could take in all the suffering. Rather than simply observing the misery of others, he wanted to do something to help. And so, Avalokiteshvara grew a thousand arms to offer aid to those in need. Before making his way east, Avalokiteshvara took the time to convert the people of Tibet and a clan of female ogres to Buddhism.

In China, Avalokiteshvara became Kuan Yin and more and more tales showed him taking on a female form. To this day, you can find representations of

---

[1] Mind you, this was *before* the election of Trump.

Kuan Yin as male or female. Many times, different versions stand side by side, the idea being that mercy has no gender. Which, consequently, suggests that we all have the capacity and, more importantly, the responsibility to offer great compassion, regardless of the parts between our legs or the identity between our ears.

One of the reasons Kuan Yin is often depicted as a young woman is her connection to the tale of Princess Miao Shan. The third daughter of a king, Miao Shan did not want to be married off as her sisters had been. Her sights were set not on romance, but on a life dedicated to helping others. More than anything, Miao Shan wanted to be a nun[1] and administer to the sick and suffering. However, when you are the daughter of a king, the most valuable thing you can do is marry well to help increase the wealth and/or power of the king, so her dad was less than thrilled by her religious aspirations. Eventually he relented and allowed her to go to a monastery, but he instructed the other nuns, under punishment of death, to treat his daughter as badly as possible, believing that she would quickly relent and agree to marry whomever he chose for her. Afraid to incur the wrath of the king, the nuns gave Miao Shan all the worst jobs and generally treated her like shit. Miao Shan, however, gladly took on everything they threw at her and at night, when the other nuns were sleeping, she went out and did even more work. His plans having failed, the king became angry. So angry that he had the monastery set on fire. But, wouldn't you know it, Miao Shan put out the flames with her bare hands. Then the king sent someone to chop off her head but Miao Shan was so pure that his sword shattered against her neck. So, he had to strangle her by hand.

After dying, Miao Shan was brought down to Hell on the back of a magical tiger. She was so full of compassion that, even in Hell, Miao Shan continued to help the suffering. In short order, she had transformed Hell into a paradise which did not make Lord Yama, the ruler of the underworld, very happy. Yama could not tolerate her killing the whole hellacious vibe he had been cultivating over the years and so he tossed her back to the land of the living.

Meanwhile, Miao Shan's father had been punished for his cruelty by being stricken with a horrible illness. The only medicine that could cure him had to be made from the flesh of a person completely without anger. He asked the daughters whom he hadn't killed and, like Regan and Goneril, they refused to help their suffering father[2]. Miao Shan heard about her father's troubles and without even being asked she gave of herself to save him. She sacrificed her arms and eyes to

---

[1] A Buddhist nun, of course, not a Catholic one.
[2] Go see *King Lear* if that reference is lost on you.

cure the man who had her killed. When the king learned who had saved him, he ran to his resurrected daughter and embraced her—which kind of feels like him showing off that he still has arms, but it probably wasn't meant that way. Because of her boundless compassion, Miao Shan was reborn and rearmed (many times over) as the bodhisattva Kuan Yin.

Kuan Yin hears the cries of the world and lends as many helping hands as she can to correct injustices. She offers food to the hungry, care to the sick, she breaks the chains of those wrongly imprisoned, and always has an extra couple of arms for those who just need a hug. She's not just a teddy bear, though; she's also a fierce mama bear protecting those who need protection with a ferocious zeal. Kuan Yin is the original social justice warrior[1].

Kuan Yin has a lot of work to do and she's very hands-on about it. A full-time job in and of itself, Kuan Yin is said to fill each grain of rice with her own nourishing milk, thereby having a direct influence on the daily lives of a large chunk of the population of Earth. Much beloved for her constant compassion and aid, she is also a popular figure in literature. The unparalleled folk novel *Journey to the West* features Kuan Yin as the bodhisattva who not only selects the pilgrims for the journey but helps them along the way.

Monkey

a.k.a.: Sun WuKong, Handsome Monkey King, Great Sage Equal of Heaven, Stone Monkey, Fiery Eyes, Buddha Victorious in Strife

Pantheon: Chinese (folk tradition)

Strictly speaking, Monkey is not a figure from mythology. Strictly speaking, he is a literary figure from a folk novel that is filled with mythic themes and characters but cannot properly be regarded as 'mythology.' But because his story is arguably the most culturally-significant Chinese tale of Buddhism and badassery, and because Monkey is inarguably the greatest character in all of world literature, he's worth including here.

The folk novel *Journey to the West* by Wu Cheng 'en is one of the so-called "Four Classic Novels of China." The story has been retold hundreds of times in the form of operas, plays, puppet shows, movies, television shows, cartoons, comics, video games, board games, and basically any other storytelling format you

---

[1] A term that should never be taken as a pejorative.

101

"The Handsome Monkey King" by Malena Salinas

can imagine. Though the Chinese have delighted in this tale for nearly 500 years, it was almost completely unknown in the western world until the 20th century.

In the 1940s Arthur Waley translated about a third of the original hundred-chapter epic into English. Rather than keeping the original title, he wanted to highlight the most dynamic character, and so his translation was titled *Monkey: A Journey to the West*. Since then, various other translators have offered up more or less complete versions in English but the story of Monkey and his pilgrimage has yet to enjoy the kind of cultural penetration in the West that it has in the East[1].

The story begins with Monkey being born from a magic stone egg that came out of a larger stone that sat on top of a mountain. So, typical birth story stuff. Called "Stone Monkey" (for obvious reasons) he found a group of regular monkeys playing by a waterfall. The monkeys dared each other to jump through the waterfall to see what was on the other side, but none of the monkeys were willing to take the leap. Except, of course, Stone Monkey, who was the kind of monkey to act first and worry about consequences later, if ever. He told them that he would jump through the waterfall if they promised to make him king afterward. Assuming that he was going to end up as a smooshed monkey, the others readily agreed. But rather than painting the rocks with stone monkey blood, he leapt through the waterfall and found a beautiful kingdom on the other side. He convinced the others to check it out and soon they moved into the "Water Curtain Cave" and made Stone Monkey their king. His first order of business was to drop the word "stone" and change his name to the Handsome Monkey King.

The Handsome Monkey King ruled his monkey people happily for some time, until he became consumed with thoughts of his own mortality. Sure, he was a king now, but someday he was going to die, and then what? After death, he would become subject to King Yama in the dark and dreary afterlife. That simply would not do for our Handsome Monkey King. And so, he left his people and embarked on a Gilgamesh-like quest for immorality.

After a decade of searching, Monkey learned of an immortal teacher named Patriarch Subodhi. The Patriarch was reluctant to take Monkey on as his student, until Monkey's enthusiasm for the teachings (and their potential to unlock great power) won him over. Monkey was given the religious name "Sun WuKong"[2] and he proved to be a quick study, learning many impressive skills. Most notably,

---

[1] Fans of the *Dragon Ball* manga/ anime may recognize many aspects of the character Goku that are drawn from the figure of Monkey.

[2] Translated as something along the lines of "Aware of Vacuity" or "Awakened to Emptiness."

Monkey learned seventy-two transformations, and cloud soaring[1]. Eventually Monkey's prowess became something of a distraction for the Patriarch's other students and so he was asked to leave.

Returning to his people, Monkey taught them how to defend themselves. He armed and trained an entire army of monkeys, but, alas, he could find no weapon that could withstand his own great strength. Only by menacing a dragon-king was Monkey able to obtain a magical staff (or cudgel) that could grow and shrink to any size he desired. After bothering more dragon-kings in order to expand his wardrobe, Monkey took a nap and woke to find himself in Hell. Undeterred, Monkey used this as an opportunity to cross his name out of the book of death, thus ensuring that he would never die. Even the lords of Hell were unable to stop the unruly primate.

All of Monkey's monkeyshines eventually caught the attention of Heaven. Called before the Jade Emperor, Monkey was given a job rather than being made subject to disciplinary action. The lofty-sounding position of "pi ma wen" made Monkey very pleased. Until, that is, he learned that it wasn't a title so much as it was an appointment to the position of heavenly stable boy. Outraged, Monkey left Heaven and gave himself a new title: The Great Sage Equal of Heaven. Of course, many in Heaven took it as the insult Monkey intended it to be, and they demanded punishment. The Jade Emperor astutely pointed out that Monkey could call himself whatever he wanted, because just saying it didn't mean anything. Nevertheless, The Great Sage was called back up to Heaven and given an even more important job: that of the Keeper of the Peaches of Immortality. Lacking any impulse control, Monkey glutted himself on all the Peaches of Immortality[2] before they could be harvested for the heavenly banquet. This became a problem and war broke out between Monkey and all the heavenly armies. And Monkey won. Because he's just that cool. With the Jade Emperor helpless to stop Monkey from causing havoc in Heaven, they were forced to call in the big gun: Buddha.

Yes, Monkey took on Buddha. The Buddha. Founder of Buddhism. Siddhartha Gautama. That guy.

Buddha made a simple deal with Monkey: if Monkey could jump out of Buddha's hand, the throne of Heaven would be yielded up to him. "No problem," said Monkey, since he could jump 180,000 miles in one leap and Buddha's hand was, well, the size of a hand. He bounded from Buddha's palm, jumping so far that he traveled beyond the created world, and all the way to the very edge of

---

[1] Which is the ability to travel great distances by surfing on a cloud.
[2] At this point, Monkey has become immortal several times over.

existence. There he saw the five pillars that held up the sky. To prove that he had been there, he scrawled his name on one of the columns and then, just because he's that kind of guy, Monkey took a big ol' whizz on the pillar. Then he jumped all the way back and landed in Buddha's palm. "Hand it over, Buddha buddy," Monkey demanded. But Buddha laughed. Monkey had failed, Buddha explained, and as evidence, he showed Monkey his hand. There, on one of Buddha's fingers were the words, written in Monkey's own hand: "The Great Sage Equal of Heaven Was Here." And then he took a sniff and was nearly knocked back by the stink of simian urine. No matter how powerful Monkey believed himself to be, there was no one bigger or more powerful than the enlightened Buddha. This was a lesson which Buddha drove home by changing his hand into a mountain and imprisoning Monkey beneath it.

For 500 years, Monkey was trapped under the mountain. You would think that after 500 years of humiliation, Monkey might emerge a little bit more introspective and respectful, but you'd be wrong. It took more than that to tame his primate proclivities and he only truly changed after being recruited/forced into helping a monk.

Hsuan Tsang (also called Tripitaka), a Buddhist monk, freed Monkey as he began his pilgrimage to India to retrieve some of the original writings of Buddha. This pilgrimage is the titular *Journey to the West* and makes up the next eighty-seven[1] chapters of the novel. Along the way, their merry band of pilgrims grew to include a dragon who ate Tripitaka's horse and then became its identical replacement; Pigsy, another exile from Heaven whose soul got lost on the way to reincarnation and he ended up as an insatiable, muckrake-wielding pig-man; and the Sandy Monk who needed to atone for his own past sins including eating previous pilgrims and wearing their skulls as a necklace. Tripitaka and his disciples faced all manner of dangers, from cruel kings to cannibal monks, to Princess Iron Fan[2], a flaming mountain, and more before they finally managed to obtain, and return with the sutras. It is a ripping good yarn with more high adventure than *The Odyssey*, more giant monsters than a season of *Power Rangers*, and more badass bodhisattvas than *Game of Thrones*.[3] It is easy to see why both Monkey and *Monkey* have sparked the imagination of so many for so many years.

---

[1] Monkey's origin fills chapters 1-7, Hsuan Tsang's origin (which is even more convoluted than Monkey's) is told in chapter's 8-12 and 13-100 are the journey proper.

[2] The very first full-length, animated film from China is *Princess Iron Fan* (1941) and it is an adaptation of part of *Journey to the West.*

[3] To my knowledge, *Game of Thrones* features exactly zero bodhisattvas of any degree of badassness.

"Essence of Japanese Mythology" by Kyle Smith

Japanese Mythology

Japan is a unique place, though not quite as original as their cultural mythos would have us believe. The idea of Japanese Exceptionalism has been and remains a prominent part of how the Japanese see themselves. Aspects of this exceptionalism include the belief that their language, culture, and people all had their own, special creation, free of outside influences. There is even a tradition that says that people of Japanese origin have slightly longer intestines than other people. Where this belief came from, why it persists, or even why extra gut length is believed to be advantageous is perplexing to say the least. While it is true that Japan is unlike any other place in the world, it is disingenuous to say that it became that way with no outside influences. To paraphrase John Donne, no nation is an archipelago entire of itself.

When we talk of Japanese mythology, it is important to distinguish between the official, state-sanctioned myths and the local folk traditions. Known as the Great Tradition, the official form of Japanese myth comes primarily from two sources: the *Kojiki* and the *Nihon Shoki* (or *Nihongi*). Written in Chinese characters[1] in 711 CE, the *Kojiki* tells the tale of creation, the birth of the gods, and the early mythic history of Japan all the way to an accounting of recent (to the time) events. The *Nihon Shoki* is much the same, with a few variations, and because it was written later, includes even more recent history.[2] Clearly, the *Kojiki* was the main source for the authors of the *Nihon Shoki* and so, without the former we likely would not have the latter.

The *Kojiki*[3] and the *Nihon Shoki* are repositories of Shinto mythology. Because Buddhism and other outside influences were becoming more and more prevalent in Japan, the imperial court made a concerted effort to record, and to thereby retain, the older native Shinto beliefs. Of course, over time, other religions and mythologies (particularly Buddhism and Taoism) did get a foothold in

---

[1] The written Japanese language wasn't advanced enough by that time.

[2] It was written down only about ten years later, but was composed nearly forty years after the *Kojiki*.

[3] Unlike the family-friendly received Chinese mythology, Japanese traditions aren't quite so shy about the tawdry details. Sexual and even incestuous relationships are present in the *Kojiki* but, unless you speak Latin, you may not know that from reading an English translation. The first and still the most readily available translation of the *Kojiki* into English was done by the right-prudish Basil Hall Chamberlain in 1882. Being the good Victorian gent that he was, rather than translating the so-called naughty bits into English, he thought it more tasteful to render them into Latin. Because it's not dirty if it's in Latin.

107

Japanese culture and were often mashed up with Shintoism to create a uniquely Japanese fusion. The bonding together of these traditions is known as syncretism and it is rampant in Japan. Syncretic figures who are worshipped both in Shinto and Buddhism are plentiful.

The Great Tradition carries with it a distinct political objective and changes to it are as deliberate as they are rare. The Little Traditions are incredibly dynamic and represent the local myths of individual communities. Because many of these tales have been passed down orally for generations, they are mutable and it is all but impossible to identify any definitive form—which is exactly what makes them so important and beloved to the common people. There is strength in adaptability and, no doubt, a special pleasure in having myths that are specific to one village or family.

Born from Little Traditions, local superstitions, and individual nightmares comes the uniquely Japanese menagerie known as yokai. Also called *ayakashi* or *mononoke*, the yokai are a variety of spirits, magical creatures, and terrifying monsters who are blamed for all manner of worldly ills from the mundane to the massive. Along with some of the better known yokai, which are featured in this text (Tsukumogami, Kappa, Tengu, Kitsune, and Tanuki), there are limitless others. Some can be helpful, like the Akaname, who licks your bathtub clean overnight. Some just want to harass you, like the faceless Shirime who drops his clothes, bends over, and reveals that he has an eye in his butt. Some want to kill or maim, like the Kushisake Onna or "Slit Mouth Woman" who stalks the streets of Japan looking for someone to disfigure. Of course, the most notorious legacy of the yokai is as the inspiration for the devious little creatures hiding all around us known as *Pokémon* (and the myriad other *Pokémon*-like games and cartoons).

"Izanami & Izanagi" by Ella Newman

Izanami & Izanagi

a.k.a.: Izanami-no-Mikoto, Izanagi-no-Mikoto, "The Female Who Invites," "The Man Who Invites"

Pantheon: Japanese (Shinto)

Offspring: Amaterasu, Susanoo, Tsukiyomi, Hiruko, Kagutsuchi-no-kami, Takemikazuchi, Futsunushi etc. (also the islands of Awaji, Honshu, Kyushu, Oki, Shikoku, and Tsushima)

Deities of: creation, life and death

Izanagi and Izanami are the most important couple in Japanese myth and are directly responsible for creating the islands of Japan, the sun, the moon, the subjugation of women, human mortality, and more.

They are not the first gods (or kami) to exist, but, as with many other cultures, the early generations of gods do little more than set the stage for the more important characters. The world, and assorted other things less important to the Japanese than the islands of Japan, already existed when Izanagi and Izanami appeared. Izanagi was entrusted with a bejeweled spear which he thrust into the water and stirred around. While this method is a time-tested and ineffective form of birth control, Izanagi pulling out his spear proved to be a terrific way to create the first island of Japan. He and Izanami left the heavens to live on that island.

While they were there, Izanagi and Izanami noticed differences in each other's anatomy. Izanagi had an outie and Izanami had an innie, genitally speaking. But before they brought their compatible parts together, they united in marriage. It was a simple ceremony wherein they each walked around a pillar in opposite directions, met, and greeted one another. Then they had sex.

The first sign of trouble was when Izanami gave birth to Hiruko. While describing most children as parasites is as accurate as it is unpopular to say, Hiruko was literally a leech. Horrified by this armless, legless bloodsucker, Izanagi and Izanami placed their child in a boat and pushed it out to sea. Retracing their steps, they concluded that the reason their first child had been so horrifying was because they had performed their wedding ritual incorrectly. Or rather, Izanami had, in that she broke the most sacred of all rules of the patriarchy: she had spoken before her husband. So, they redid the ceremony, this time Izanami behaved herself and only spoke after Izanagi had his turn. Much like how the Abrahamic religions blame Eve for, well, everything bad, the story of Izanami has long been used in Japan to justify male supremacy.

After their re-marriage, things went much better for everyone. Everyone but Izanami's birth canal, that is, because she then gave birth to the other islands of Japan. Giving birth to a squishy, armless, legless leech sounds way less painful than squeezing out Honshu and the rest of the archipelago. After that, Izanami birthed an array of other kami of things like trees, mountains, rivers, and so forth. Everything was moving along great, the world was filling up with kami, Izanagi was happy, and Izanami wasn't allowed to say that she wasn't. And then a second disaster struck: Izanami gave birth to Homusubi, the kami of fire.

If giving birth to an island sounds unpleasant, imagine how much worse off you'd be giving birth to a ball of fire. Homusubi torched Izanami from the inside out. As she delivered the little spitfire, her body was so destroyed that she also gave birth to kami of vomit, urine, and excrement. And not one of each, but a pair of each because sometimes you need a female piss god and sometimes you need a male one. Izanami died the first death in all the world. Izanagi was so upset that he decapitated Homusubi—an act which led to the creation of even more kami.[1]

In deep mourning[2], Izanagi traveled to the afterlife realm of Yomi. In the total darkness of Yomi, Izanagi somehow managed to track down his deceased wife. He told her to come back to the land of the living with him—but Izanami was beholden to new masters: The Lords of Yomi. She would, she told her husband, ask the rulers of the dead if she might be allowed to leave with him. In the meantime, she instructed Izanagi, he was not allowed to see her. In mythology, one is usually safe in assuming that when an order of this nature is given, it will almost immediately be ignored. As Pandora opened the jar she was entrusted with, as Orpheus couldn't help but look back for Eurydice, so too was Izanagi compelled to sneak a peek at his wife. He waited until she was asleep and, lighting a comb as a torch, he crept close and saw what Izanami had become. It's a sad fact that death does many things to the body, none of them good. Izanami was no longer the beautiful woman she had been, but was a rotten, decaying corpse. Maggots poured from the holes where her eyeballs had once been. Worms crawled in, the worms crawled out, the worms played pinochle in her snout. Izanagi let out a horrified scream which woke Izanami, who was more than a little upset to find that her husband had broken the one rule she'd given him.

---

[1] The *Kojiki* says that in total they birthed fourteen islands, thirty-five kami (not counting Hiruko) as well as the eight born in the death throes of Izanami, eight from Izanagi's sword after the decapitation and eight from the corpse of Hamusubi.
[2] Possibly just because he was now stuck raising two poo gods all by himself.

Izanagi ran. Izanami sent dozens of demons, ghosts, and other scary sounding beasties after him. With some quick thinking and a handful of peaches[1], Izanagi managed to escape the deadly denizens of Yomi and he blocked off the exit just before Izanami could catch him. Infuriated, Izanami swore to kill one thousand people every day as retaliation for Izanagi's actions. Izanagi simply replied that he would create one thousand five hundred people every day and thus we have the genesis of human mortality and of planetary overpopulation.

As one might expect, this whole experience left Izanagi feeling a bit yucky. It is important to understand that Japanese mythology is less about a struggle between good and evil and much more about clean vs. defiled. The dead are not evil, but they are dirty. Creatures who feed on carrion are not bad; they are just unclean. Traveling to the land of the dead was one of the least clean things a person could do and so upon making his escape Izanagi desperately needed to wash himself. Washing, both literally and philosophically, are important aspects of many Shinto rituals and, mythologically speaking, the inception of that idea was the bathing of Izanagi after he escaped Yomi. As he washed himself, he accidentally created fourteen more kami. They came from his discarded dirty clothes, the washing of particular parts of his body, washing in a particular part of the river, and so forth. The final three were Amaterasu (the supreme sun goddess who was born from his right eye), Tsukiyomi (the dark moon god born from his left eye), and the tempestuous Susanoo (who was born from Izanagi's nose).

As with many other creator gods, Izanagi does not play much of a role in stories beyond this. Izanami rears her head now and again as a queen of the dead, but the roles of Izanami and Izanagi reach their climax early on and then recede into the background of Japanese mythology.

---

[1] Like the Chinese peaches of immortality, in Japanese myth peaches are associated with divinity and can be effective deterrents against demons. It has been suggested that this is because the Chinese word for "peach" sounds similar to the word meaning "exit" or "cast out." Peachwood is used in Chinese exorcisms, apparently for this reason. Sidenote: there is such a thing as Chinese exorcisms.

"Amaterasu" by Madeleine Graumlich

Amaterasu

a.k.a.: Amaterasu-O-Mikami, Ohirume-no-much-no-kami, "Heaven-Shining-Great-August Deity"
Pantheon: Japanese (Shinto)
Siblings: Susanoo, Tsukiyomi
Parents: Izanami and Izanagi
Offspring: the emperors of Japan
Deity of: sun
Symbols: sun, mirror, sword, beads

Ancient Japan was, by no means, a feminist paradise.[1] Which makes it even more surprising to find a woman seated at the top of the Shinto pantheon: Amaterasu, the sun goddess.

Amaterasu was born when the creator god Izanagi took a bath after escaping the afterlife realm of Yomi. In purifying himself, Amaterasu was born from his left eye, her brother/celestial counterpoint Tsukiyomi was born from the right, and a third sibling, the tempestuous Susanoo, was born from Izanagi's nose. Izanagi then assigned them their domains: Amaterasu would take the throne of Heaven as the goddess of the sun, Tsukiyomi would rule the night, and Susanoo would be the lord of the sea. Even though she was neither male nor the first born[2], and that power in Japan was primarily based on male primogenitor, Amaterasu was given the highest honor. This may be a holdover from Japan prior to the influx of Chinese influence where it may have been a little bit more open to women holding power.

When Amaterasu assumed her position, her brothers were something less than helpful. She asked one of them (the *Kojiki* says it was Susanoo, the *Nihon Shoki* says it was Tsukiyomi) to attend a party thrown by Ukemochi, the food goddess, in her stead. Rather than bringing Amaterasu home a doggy bag, they killed the food goddess. This was either the impetus for Amaterasu avoiding Tsukiyomi and therefore creating the cycle of day and night, or it was just another shitty thing that Susanoo did. Of course, the most notable bout with a sibling that

---

[1] To be fair, neither were any of the other cultures touched on in this book. Sadly, (and I'm sure *shockingly* to most women) the "fairer sex" has not historically enjoyed the same power and prestige as men have in many places and times in world history.
[2] All told, Izanagi fathered over sixty children before this trio.

Amaterasu endured was her nigh-apocalyptic struggle with Susanoo for dominion over the sky.

Amaterasu and Tsukiyomi took to their jobs right away, but Susanoo was a bit less obedient. He was too busy whining about (A) missing his mother; or (B) not getting to be the sun god. As a result, he was banished to go live with Izanami in the afterlife realm of Yomi, but before he did so, he went to see Amaterasu. The sun goddess believed that Susanoo was trying to make trouble and so she made ready to deal with trouble. She armored up and even pinned up her hair as a male warrior would. At his coming, Amaterasu stomped the ground in the traditional pre-battle *shiki* ritual[1] with such force that her legs sank into the earth up to her knees. Technically, this was probably the first use of the *shiki* ritual so Amaterasu was a ground breaker in two ways. Susanoo either didn't have the intention or guts to face his sister in battle and so they decided to hold a kami-making competition. Amaterasu either won or lost depending on how you do the math, but the result was the same: Susanoo went on a defilement bender. He caused destruction, pooped in her temple, and tossed a flayed horse through a window. When the skinless horse tumbled into her weaving hall, Amaterasu and all her handmaidens, understandably, freaked the Hell out. One of them reportedly got so scared that she tried to run away, hit her genitals on part of a loom, and died. For her part, Amaterasu had had enough of that nonsense and went to hide out in a cave.

When the sun hides itself away for a few hours, it's no big deal; in fact, it's what we call "night." However, when the sun goes away with no intention of returning, it presents a real problem. While Amaterasu hid out in her cave, Earth grew dark and cold and (as is often the case when natural disasters strike) monsters came out. The assembled kami did everything they could think of to draw her out of the cave and back to her rightful place in the heavens. They tried to compel her back to the sky by asking cocks to crow for her, the thinking being that it worked every other morning. The rooster ruse did not cause her to rise. So instead, they tried something a bit more complicated: just outside the entrance to the cave was a tree and from that tree they hung some beautiful jewels and a mirror. Then, they called on the goddess of the dawn, Ama-no-uzume. Ama-no-uzume started to dance while the other kami looked on. As the dance overcame her and she began

---

[1] *Shiki* is the stomping ritual most often seen before sumo wrestling bouts and may get its inspiration from beetles battling. Watching and betting on beetle battles is also a popular pastime in Japan.

to expose herself, the assembled kami all laughed[1] riotously. Hearing the shouts of joy, Amaterasu couldn't help but be curious and so she peeked out of the cave. There, before her, was a radiant figure and so she stepped out for a closer look. The moment she did, the muscular doorman kami grabbed her so she couldn't go back in, while another god hung up a sign at the entrance to the cave saying no one was allowed inside. Amaterasu was thus drawn out of hiding because she couldn't help but admire her own reflection, which just goes to prove that, despite her position as top deity, she was not immune to sexist storytelling.

Though she provides the earth with the light and warmth it needs to survive and remain relatively monster-free, that is arguably not her most important contribution, at least not in the eyes of the Japanese. As mother of the first emperors, Amaterasu is the ancestor of the imperial family of Japan. When a new emperor is crowned, they are given three gifts: a mirror (Yata-no-Kagami), a string of jewels (Yasakani-no-Magatama), and a sword (Kusanagi-no-Tsurugi). The mirror and jewels are held to be the very same mirror and jewels that helped draw Amaterasu out of her cave, and the sword was given to Amaterasu as a peace offering by Susanoo after he had redeemed himself for his earlier dirty deeds. By passing down these objects as the Imperial Regalia, they are making a direct connection from each successive emperor all the way back to Amaterasu herself.

Amaterasu's temple in Ise is the holiest of all Shinto sites and, as a testament to just how important it is, it is rebuilt every twenty years. Made from wood from the adjoining sacred grove, every two decades the existing shrine is taken down and a new one is created. And this has been the tradition since some time in the 5th century. Amaterasu is not some long forgotten deity from ages past. Her worship remains very active and important to the Shinto religion.

Tsukiyomi

a.k.a.: Tsukiyomi-no-Mikoto, "His Augustness Moon-Night-Possessor"
Pantheon: Japanese (Shinto)
Siblings: Amaterasu, Susanoo
Parents: Izanami and Izanagi
Deity of: moon, night
Symbols: moon

---

[1] Generally speaking, if you are stripping and everyone starts to laugh, it is not what you'd call a good sign, but in this case, it was meant as a positive thing.

"Tsukiyomi" by Qing Zhu

In many cultures, the moon is ruled by a female deity. Whether it is the fact that women, like the moon, experience a predictable monthly cycle[1], or it is because the moon and women are both taken to be less powerful than the sun and masculinity in many patriarchal cultures, or for both reasons, the feminine moon is quite widespread in the mythologies of the world. In Japan, the script is flipped and they have a female sun and a male moon.

Tsukiyomi, the Shinto moon god, was the middle child of Izanagi's post-underworld cleansing. Creator god Izanagi narrowly escaped Yomi, the dark and dirty realm of the dead, and then bathed himself to take all the ickinesss of death off him. After Amaterasu was born from his left eye, Tsukiyomi was born from his right eye, which was then followed by Susanoo being born from Izanagi's nose.[2] In some traditions, Tsukiyomi was born from Izanagi's hand in which he held a mirror. Though possibly accidental, the idea that the moon is connected to a mirror is surprisingly appropriate, given that the moon is not a light itself but merely acts as a reflector for the rays of the sun.

Tsukiyomi cannot compete with his siblings in many ways, but he does help account for some very important aspects of the natural world. In the *Nihon Shoki*, we are told of a party thrown by Ukemochi, the goddess of food, which Amaterasu was too busy to attend. In her stead, she asked her brother Tsukiyomi to go for her. An invite to a feast with the food goddess is nothing to sneeze at so Tsukiyomi gladly agreed to go. He arrived a bit too early, however, and witnessed Ukemochi creating the food. As with sausage, you're better off not knowing how it gets made, because Ukemochi spat out fish, coughed up rice, and pooed meat out of her body and onto a plate. Since, in Shinto, cleanliness is next to kami-ness and filth is tantamount to evil, Tsukiyomi was so horrified that he struck the food goddess dead. Though dead, Ukemochi continued to provide food to humanity with cattle and various grains coming from her head, eyes, stomach, and genitals. When Amaterasu learned of what her brother had done, she was so upset that she would no longer allow him to occupy the sky the same time she did. Thus, Tsukiyomi inadvertently led to the abundance of food the earth has to offer and he caused the rotation of the sun and moon. In the *Kojiki*, the same story is told except it features Susanoo rather than Tsukiyomi. Though understandable due to Susanoo's famously adversarial relationship with Amaterasu, the *Kojiki* version lacks the

---

[1] That is a huge over-simplification of menstrual cycles, by the way.
[2] The *Kojiki* tells us that there were fourteen total kami born from Izanagi's ablutions, including Chimata-no-kami, a phallic god of crossroads born from Izanagi's discarded pants. The last three are far and away the most important.

additional dimension of the solar/lunar cycle and robs Tsukiyomi of the only significant narrative in which he is featured.

Oftentimes, "Tsukiyomi" has been translated as a combination of the words for moon (*tsuki*) and darkness (*yomi*). As seemingly apropos as that may be, it apparently isn't correct. Scholarship now suggests that the "yomi" part is not the same as, say, the name of the dark afterlife world Yomi, but is actually a form of the word meaning something like "reckoning." So rather than simply being "Moon Dark," Tsukiyomi is the "Moon Reckoner" and is therefore linked to time measurement, an important and self-evident function of the moon. This puts him in league with other moon gods like Egypt's Thoth who is less a god of darkness and more a god of time, calendars, and measurements. Tsukiyomi's job isn't all that sexy, but it is nonetheless important.

Susanoo

a.k.a.: Susano-wo, Susa-no-O, Takehaya, Susanoo-no-Mikami, Kumano, Ketsumiko-no-kami, "His-Swift-Impetuous-Male-Augustness"
Pantheon: Japanese (Shinto)
Spouse/Lover: Kushinadahime (Kamu-o-ichi-hime)
Siblings: Amaterasu, Tsukiyomi
Parents: Izanami and Izanagi
Offspring: Isukeyorihime, Suserihime
Deity of: storms, sea, death
Symbols: sword

Susanoo has something that very few mythic figures have: a character arc. He goes from being a nasty, defiling antagonist, to being the heroic protagonist, to taking on the role of the elder statesman.

Born from Izanagi's schnoz during his post-Yomi cleansing, Susanoo turned out to be a real mama's boy. Even though Izanami had very little to do with his creation and nothing to do with his upbringing, Susanoo mourned deeply for her. Izanagi had assigned Susanoo the position of god of the sea, but Susanoo wanted nothing of it. Despite the huge importance of being the ruler of the sea, especially coming from Japan where the sea is literally all around, Susanoo chose rather to sit and cry over his separation from his father's dead sister-wife Izanami. The *Kojiki* tells us that he sat and cried long enough that his beard grew down to his stomach.

119

"Susanoo" by Aaron Kroodsma

Izanagi, in his last act before fading into mythic obscurity, told Susanoo that if he missed his 'mother' so much he could just go to Hell.

Before departing for the afterlife realm, Susanoo decided to pay his sister, Amaterasu, the ruler of Heaven, a visit. Assuming that Susanoo was spoiling for a fight, Amaterasu geared up. She put on full armor, grabbed her weapons, and then stomped[1] so hard that her legs ended up buried to her knees in the ground. When Susanoo arrived and saw Amaterasu ready to deliver an epic smack-down, he was caught off guard. "I come in peace," he told her and explained that he only stopped by Heaven to say good-bye before departing to go stay with mom in the afterlife. Amaterasu was skeptical of his claim and Susanoo offered to prove it by engaging with her in some kami making. Depending on how you look at it, or how it is translated, this may be either a peace offering of sorts or it may be a challenge to prove who should rightly occupy the throne of Heaven. Amaterasu went first, she took Susanoo's sword, broke it into three pieces and then, as translator Basil Hall Chamberlain charmingly puts it "crunchingly crunche[d]" the bits and spat out three female kami. Then, Susanoo took some of Amaterasu's beads, "crunchingly crunche[d]" them up and spat out five male kami. Amaterasu claimed that since the five men were made from her beads they were technically her offspring and, therefore, she was the winner the competition (if, indeed, it was a competition) because not only did she make more, but she made males, which are, of course, more important than females[2]. Susanoo countered by arguing that since the three dainty ladies were birthed from his sword, they provided proof of his sincerity and gentle intentions. The *Kojiki* and the *Nihon Shoki* disagree over which is the actual winner, but it doesn't really matter because Susanoo then proceeded to defile as much as he could. This was either a victory lap or the tantrum of someone who had been cheated out of his victory. He ran about destroying rice fields, filling in irrigation ditches, and tossing literal shit around in the temple of Amaterasu. And, finally, when Amaterasu and her maidens were in their weaving hall doing some weaving, Susanoo tossed a flayed horse in through the window. This sent Amaterasu into hiding and with the sun goddess away there was nothing but bad news in Heaven and on Earth.

The assembled kami eventually managed to coax Amaterasu out of hiding and peace was restored, but Susanoo needed to pay for all the trouble he caused. If you've ever seen a samurai movie, you know that one of the greatest indignities

---

[1] Modern Sumo wrestlers still do this traditional wide-stance stomping before a bout.
[2] An especially bizarre argument given that she is female and the most supreme of the gods. This is what internalized sexism does to women, I suppose.

a Japanese warrior can suffer is having their hair cut off. Susanoo got both his hair and beard cut off, and his fingernails and toenails ripped out, which is less of an indignity and more just horrid to think about. Susanoo was then sent to walk the earth like Caine in *Kung Fu*.

Disgraced and displaced, Susanoo became something of a Ronin. Ronin is actually a much later term used for masterless samurai and even currently for drifters and people who are 'between jobs' but it's a similar type of idea. Ronin Susanoo came upon a couple and their daughter weeping in the wilderness one day. In his translation of the *Kojiki*, Chamberlain calls the father and mother "Foot-Stroking-Elder" and "Hand-Stroking-Elder" respectively. Since it is literally impossible to refer to them by those names without eliciting childish giggles from reader and writer alike, we will simply call them the parents of Kushinadahime (Princess Kushinada). Susanoo asked them why they were crying and the parents of Kushinadahime explained that Koshi, an eight-headed and eight-tailed dragon, had eaten their other seven daughters and it was nearly time for it to return to eat their eighth and final daughter. Susanoo offered to help defeat Koshi the dragon for them. Kushinadahime's parents said that if he could keep their daughter safe then she would be his bride. So, they wouldn't be losing a daughter so much as they'd be gaining an august, swift, impetuous, dragon-slaying son-in-law.

To keep Princess Kushinada safe, Susanoo turned her into a comb. He then stuck the comb in his hair which, apparently, had grown back by this time. He then commissioned the construction of eight giant vats. Placing the vats outside the dragon's cave, he filled them with sake. When the dragon came out, it saw the sake and greedily lapped it up with each of his heads. As will happen, when one drinks too much, the dragon passed out. And apparently the dragon was a very heavy sleeper because not a single head awoke while Susanoo walked around and chopped off each of them. A river of blood wasn't the only thing Susanoo found inside Koshi; contained in one tail was the "Sword of the Gathering Clouds of Heaven."[1] This sword was the Japanese equivalent of Excalibur, and, to show how much Susanoo had amended his previous ways, he gave it to Amaterasu as a peace offering. The two reconciled, Susanoo was restored to his previous glory and then became the lord of storms.

---

[1] *Ame-no-Murakumo-no-Tsurugi* in the *Nihon Shoki* or *Kusanagi-no-Tsurugi* (trans. "Grasscutter Sword") in the *Kojiki*. But since "Sword of the Gathering Clouds" sounds less like a manual lawnmower, we'll use that name.

Susanoo next appears in the story of the hero Okuninushi. The would-be hero Okuninushi was killed[1] by his eighty brothers and found himself in the land of the dead. There he met Princess Suseri, the daughter of Susanoo. Susanoo, despite being reconciled with Heaven, had nevertheless taken up a position alongside his 'mother' Izanami as ruler of the dead. Okuninushi wanted to marry Suserihime but over-protective pop Susanoo made him complete several potentially deadly tasks first. Not potentially, if we're being honest. They were *intentionally* deadly tasks that Okuninushi managed to survive only with some divine intervention from Suseri and a helpful field mouse. After surviving the unsurvivable and then stealing both Susanoo's weapons and his daughter, Okuninushi gained the acceptance of Susanoo, married Suseri, and became the ruler of Izumo (modern Shimane region of Japan), the earthly region where Susanoo's most important temples were located.

Though he never attained the throne of the Heavenly Plains, Susanoo is a more active and more significant player in Shinto tradition than either of his immediate siblings or any of his extended pool of myriad other siblings. He plays the villain, the hero, and the over-protective father, and he still finds the time to rule both storms and the afterlife.

Hachiman

a.k.a.: Hachiman-jin, Hachiman Daibosatsu, Yahata-no-kami, "Eight Banners"

Pantheon: Japanese (Shinto, Buddhist)

Spouse/Lovers: Hime-gami

Parents: Jingo and Chuai (parents of Ojin)

Deity of: warriors, war, archery, writing, culture, agriculture, fishing

Symbols: *tomeo*, samurai, kamikaze, doves

Over a third of all Shinto shrines are dedicated to the syncretic Shinto/Buddhist kami/bosatsu[2] Hachiman. The patron god of Japanese warriors from the samurai to the kamikaze, Hachiman's story begins with the legendary 15th emperor of Japan.

---

[1] Twice.

[2] *Bosatsu* is the Japanese term for bodhisattva, which is a term that means someone who has reached enlightenment but has chosen not to move on to Nirvana.

"Hachiman" by Lindsay N. Poulos

As all good heroes of dubious or non-existent historicity, Ojin had a miraculous birth. His father, Emperor Chuai, died before Ojin was born and thus, Empress Jingu became the de facto ruler. And Jingu was a badass. She decided to take the opportunity to conquer Korea but, knowing that giving birth might slow her down on the battlefield, she chose not to give birth. Empresses can do that, apparently. She wrapped her pregnant belly up tightly and tied a rock over it so that the fruit of her womb would be forced to ripen for as long as she wanted it to. And so, with bound belly Jingu conquered Korea. It took three years, but she did it without bloodshed, so more power to her. After all was said and done, she returned home to Japan and her son Ojin was born. At his birth, eight banners fell from the heavens and, one assumes, a sigh of relief fell out of Jingu. If Ojin and Jingu are based on real historical figures, Jingu's prolonged pregnancy may be an exaggeration (maybe it just felt like three years for her) or it could be a way to lend legitimacy to the Ojin whose father reportedly died some three years before his birth. Clearly, since there's no way at all that Jingu might have had sex with anyone else ever, it must be that she stubbornly held the babe in until she decided she was ready to give birth.[1]

Ojin, who is regarded to have been born around 200 CE and ruled from 270-310 CE, had a remarkable career in his own right. Arguably his most important contribution was engaging in cultural exchange with the likes of China and Korea. It was through these porous cultural borders that the Japanese learned things like Korean weaving methods and the Chinese system of written language.

By the year 725 CE, Ojin had been deified and his first Shinto shrine was dedicated. As a god, he was known as Hachiman, who was part of a trinity along with his mother Jingu, and his wife Hime-gami. Popular in both Shinto and Buddhism, he is a bosatsu and is often depicted in the garb of a Buddhist monk. As a nod to the possible historical successes of Ojin, Hachiman is the god of writing and culture. His earliest popularity as a god came from the samurai who worshipped him as their personal guardian. Many samurai even adopted Hachiman's *tomeo*[2] symbol as their insignia. Eventually his popularity with the samurai spilled over into the population at large and, to this day, Hachiman has more Shinto shrines dedicated to him than any other figure except for the all-important Inari, god of rice, agriculture, business, success, and sake.

---

[1] Refusing to let a baby come out when it's ready to do so is not an advisable practice.
[2] Translated roughly as whirlpool or "vortex," and it looks something like three commas chasing each other around. Like the familiar Taoist "Yin/ Yang" symbol but with one more.

DAVID FLETCHER

The eternal protector of Japan, Hachiman's legacy inspired both bravery and fear. Back in 1274 CE Japan was facing invading Mongol-Korean forces and, frankly, their chances didn't look good. The invaders had dramatically superior numbers and all the Japanese could do was pray for a miracle. And they got one. A massive typhoon struck the Mongol fleet, destroying about a third of their ships and killing roughly 13,000 of Kublai Khan's men. The storm was so devastating that the Mongols abandoned their plans to attack Japan. Some seven years later, a significantly larger Chinese-Korean-Mongol fleet decided to give it another shot. And, in 1281, the Japanese were once again saved by the divine wind sent by Hachiman. More than half of the enemy forces drowned in the typhoon and only a handful of ships survived. It was one of the most decisive defeats of Kublai Khan's career and is the stuff legends are made of. The most shocking thing about it all is that this story seems to be true. Sure, numbers (especially in texts this old) can be sketchy but it appears to be a fact of history that in both 1274 and 1281 Japan was saved from Mongol invasions by typhoons. While we can debate which, if any, deity might have been responsible for the devastation of the Mongol fleets, the effect on the Japanese consciousness was very real. The Japanese believed, and it was hard to argue with them given the circumstances, that when they were facing insurmountable odds, Hachiman would be there to save them. Fast-forward to the 20th century. The closing days of World War II were not the best for Japan. They were facing a much larger military force and it was starting to look like they may lose. And so, the only option they were left with was to once again call forth heavenly justice to save them. With no Hachiman-sent typhoons appearing, approximately 4,000 Japanese pilots became the divine wind themselves, or as they called it: *kamikaze*. This time, the kamikaze did not successfully turn the tides of battle but they nonetheless had a lasting impact on the way the world perceived Shintoism and the Japanese.

Not long after the official end of WWII, Emperor Hirohito did something no other Japanese ruler had done: he denied his divinity, proclaiming himself not a demi-god, but simply a man. Soon after that, Shinto ceased to be the official religion of the land. These changes were motivated more by politics than by religion—it was Japan's way of healing relations with the outside world who were suspicious and fearful of them. Considering that the U.S. interred innocent men, women, and children of Japanese descent and used the most devastating weapon ever forged by human hands on Japan *twice*, it seems like Japan may not be the only ones who need to make reparations. Perhaps someday.

"Raiden" by Tessa Brown

Raiden

a.k.a.: Raijin
Pantheon: Japanese (Shinto)
Spouse/Lover: O-Chiyo
Deity of: thunder
Symbols: lightning, drums

The Japanese thunder god Raiden will be familiar to many of a certain age for his appearance in the *Mortal Kombat* video game series. Or for his portrayal by the very not-Japanese actor Christopher Lambert in the movies based on the *Mortal Kombat* video game series. Other than the lightning that issues from his eyes, video game Raiden looks like a guy wearing a traditional Asian conical hat and a white ninja outfit. It's basically the outfit that your racist uncle would throw together to dress up for his office Halloween party as 'an Oriental.' This may be the one example in history of video games making a character look less visually interesting than the original version.

Authentic depictions of Raiden look more demonic than human. He is typically red, mostly naked, with clawed hands and feet, pointed ears, sharp teeth, black eyes, and sticky-uppy hair like an anime character. He creates thunder by striking a series of drums that hover behind him in a circle. He is a fearsome-looking individual, made all the scarier by his insatiable hunger. For belly buttons.

Navels are delicious, apparently. Raiden is so hungry for navels that some Japanese people still wear a special piece of clothing to protect their belly buttons from him. Given that the umbilicus is the source from which we receive our earliest sustenance, it is perhaps less surprising that Raiden is on the hunt for them than it is surprising that many other cultures don't have much to say on the subject.[1]

As tough as Raiden is, he doesn't work alone. He is frequently accompanied by Fujin, the wind god, who has a similar demonic appearance and carries with him a sack full of wind. And if Fujin is the Robin to Raiden's Batman, then Raiju is his Ace the Bat-Hound. Part canine, part feline, part weasel, Raiju is a four-legged beastie made of lightning who also has a penchant for belly buttons, only he likes to take naps in them, rather than eat them. So, maybe it's not so weird to protect your navel after all.

---

[1] The most notable exception being Hinduism which is rife with navel imagery.

Raiden is far from the only Japanese thunder god. There is also Takemikazuchi, a thunder deity who was born from the blood of Kagutsuchi (a.k.a. Homusubi) when Izanagi lopped off his head. Perhaps Takemikazuchi's most important contribution to the world is subduing Namazu, the catfish responsible for earthquakes.[1] There are also the Ni-o (or Kongo-rikishi) known as the "Thunderbolt Strongmen" who guard temples, and a veritable shit ton of unnamed[2] thunder kami throughout the land.

Shichi Fukujin

Pantheon: Japanese (Shinto, Buddhist, Hindu, Taoist)
Members: Ebisu, Daikoku, Bishamon, Benzaiten, Jurojin, Fukurokuju, Hotei

The Shichi Fukujin are the Japanese super team of good luck. Made up of seven deities of various origins, they travel together in the ship *Takarabune* offering up wealth and prosperity to those who deserve it. While they are frequently pictured together in their dragon-headed boat with a bedazzled sail, each of the Shichi Fukujin is an important figure in their own right.

The only purely Japanese member of the group, Ebisu, is a god of prosperity in business, crop fertility, and most importantly, fishing. Dressed in traditional fisherman's garb, he holds a fishing rod and a big ol' fish. The *tai* fish is a popular one in Japan and is often eaten at celebrations because its name is a homonym for the word for "celebration." A wandering deity who shows up when and where he wants to, Ebisu's presence can be a good thing, indicating incoming bounty, but if you don't treat him right, he can cause the opposite. Possibly the most bizarre and delightful aspect of Ebisu is that he is either deaf or pretends to be. The other gods aren't entirely buying his hard-of-hearing act and so they regularly test him to see if, in fact, he can really hear. Because of his lack of hearing or because he wants to perpetuate that rumor, Ebisu often ignores his petitioners.

The father of Ebisu, Daikoku (or Daikokuten) is an import from Indian Buddhism and is a fat, jolly god of prosperity. Round-bellied and smiling, Daikoku sits on large bales of rice. The bales are so full that they overflow and are picked

---

[1] Yes, you read that right.
[2] Or with names that vary from region to region.

"The Treasure Ship and the Luck Gods" by Whitney Ruhlman

at by rats—but Daikoku has such abundant wealth that he is happy to share it with the little rodents. The way he doles out his wealth to us is by striking his mallet a*nd raining down a golden shower of coins. As happy as Daikoku is, his background is surprisingly dark. His name is the Japanese variant of the Indian death lord Mahakala and can be literally translated as "Great Blackness." Despite the allusions to death, Daikoku remains an infectiously happy, short-legged man who generously shares his overflowing wealth.*

Far from the rotund Ebisu and Daikoku, the next of the Shichi Fukujin is armored and armed. Though Bishamon (or Bishamon-ten) is a member of a Japanese team of gods and is dressed like a Chinese warrior, he is Hindu in origin. In Hinduism, he's known as Kubera and he began as a thief whose attempted pilfering of a temple of Shiva was so ridiculous that Shiva made him a god. The sillier aspects of his predecessor notwithstanding, Bishamon is the most serious and serious-looking of the Shichi Fukujin. He is a patron of warriors and god of battles, but also of happiness. Yes, he looks scary but that's only because he's scary good at defending Buddhist law. Or so we're told.

Benzaiten (or Benten) is the lone female of the group. Like Bishamon, she is passed down from Hinduism. There she is associated with the goddess Sarasvati. Benzaiten carries a Japanese lute (*biwa*) and represents music, the arts in general, love, and feminine power. Since she is skilled in music, dance, art, conversation, and more, Benzaiten is the patron of geishas. She is often accompanied by Ugajin, a snake with the head of a woman (or a man). The two figures are sometimes collectively called Uga Benten.

Jurojin came to the Shichi Fukujin by way of Taoist China. While Bishamon is the warrior, Jurojin is the scholar. As a tall, thin, generously-bearded, elderly man, Jurojin represents longevity. He is accompanied by one or more of his animal friends, including a deer, a tortoise, or a crane. Each of the animals is symbolic of longevity, as well: the antlers of the deer reflect its age, tortoises live exceptionally long lives, and the crane, I guess, has a long neck/beak/legs/wings?

Fukurokuju is also of Chinese origin and is also an old man. He too represents longevity, but with Fukurokuju it is expressly a long, happy life that he has to offer. He is a short old man with an enormously long head. Let's be honest: it is a phallically-long head, a fact which did not escape the Japanese, as is evidenced by the fact that the figure of Fukurokuju was used for *harigata*, a type of ancient Japanese dildo. That may account for why Fukurokuju always has a broad grin. The actual reason for his long head is that it reflects his great wisdom, but since in Taoism wisdom and sex are often intertwining ideas, it is not inappropriate that he enjoyed a role as a 'marital aid.'

Rounding out the Shichi Fukujin is the delightfully rotund Hotei. Hotei (or Budai or Pu-Tai) is the most frequently misidentified figure in Buddhism, if not in the whole of world religions. You've seen him, with his bald head, bulbous earlobes[1], joyous grin, and great big belly and have probably heard him referred to, or even referred to him yourself, as Buddha. He is not Buddha, at least not *The* Buddha, Siddhartha Gautama (or Shakyamuni to the Japanese), the founder of Buddhism. He is *an* enlightened one, but not The One. Perhaps placating westerners who can't be bothered to differentiate, Hotei is sometimes called "Laughing Buddha" or "Fat Buddha" but he is, in no uncertain terms, a distinct character from Buddha. It's essentially like a non-Catholic pointing to any Saint and calling it Jesus. All that aside, it is easy to understand why Hotei enjoys such popularity within Buddhism. He is the bald, beardless Santa Claus of the east who carries with him a large sack of gifts and brings joy to children.

Though the Shichi Fukujin come from many places and come in different shapes, they share a very Japanese message: good things come to those who work for it. Yes, they dispense riches and other gifts, but they don't do so willy-nilly. They give to the deserving, which is why they are so popular amongst the working class and not-so-much with the upper class. Of course, that leads to the unavoidable conclusion that those who do not experience good fortune are simply not working hard enough for it, which is a fairly toxic way to view the impoverished.

Fudo Myo-o

a.k.a.: Acala (Sanskrit), Budong Mingwant (Chinese), Miyowa (Tibetan), "Immovable"
Pantheon: Japanese (Vajrayana Buddhist)
Deity of: protection, steadfastness
Symbols: flames, weapons

Not all Buddhist figures are gentle or jolly; some are downright scary. In fact, the Myo-o (or "Bright Kings") have been known to convert people to Buddhism simply by scaring the dukkha[2] out of them. There is more than a dozen of these

---

[1] A sign of wisdom. Ebisu, Daikoku, and Fukurojuku also have the enlarged lobes, as do numerous other Buddhist figures, including The Buddha.
[2] *Dukkha* is the first of the Four Noble Truths in Buddhism. The idea is, essentially, that suffering is the result of desire. Also, it is a word that makes children (and this author) giggle.

"Fudo Myo-o" by Tyler Space

Bright Kings in Japanese Buddhism. Of those, five are the most important and of those five, the one at the center of it all is Fudo Myo-o.

Depicted as an angry-looking blue demon, Fudo Myo-o is the immovable barrier against evil. He is typically seen sitting on a rock to indicate his stability and his lack of interest in comfy seating. Perhaps it is the gluteal discomfort that causes the sour expression on his face, with furrowed brow and pointy fangs protruding from his grimacing mouth. Then again, his grumpy puss may be due to his obnoxious-sounding servants: "What Is It About?" Boy and Gangly Kid. No matter what the cause of his foul mood, you would do well to keep your hostility toward the *dharma* (the teachings of the Buddha) at bay when Fudo Myo-o is around, because he keeps a rope and a sword handy and does not hesitate to use them.

Fudo Myo-o has toughness and tenacity to spare. He's not just about dharma-chopping baddies, but he also grants steadfastness and stability to those who ask for it. Hardcore Buddhist monks draw on power from Fudo Myo-o before meditating under a waterfall. If cold showers aren't your cup of tea, Fudo Myo-o also likes to play with fire. Basically, if you want to endure something unpleasant from walking on hot coals to going to an elementary school holiday pageant, Fudo Myo-o will keep you keeping on. It is not hard to see why Fudo Myo-o, the personification of resolution and persistence, is one of the most active and popular figures in Vajrayana Buddhism[1]. More infamously, Fudo Myo-o is popular amongst the Yakuza who frequently have his visage tattooed on their bodies.

Seated in the center of the Myo-o conclave, you will very often find Fudo Myo-o surrounded by four other Bright Kings. Each of the others represents one of the cardinal directions and has their only specialty.

Representing the North is Kongoyasha Myo-o—the Devourer of Demons—who, you guessed it, eats demons. And, by demons, I mean desire, which is the great cause of suffering in Buddhism. And also, actual demons. Kongoyasha (or Vajrayaksa in the original Sanskrit) might be even more fearsome in appearance than Fudo. Like Fudo, he is blue or black in color, and he has one or three heads, and four or six arms. His central head has five eyes and the others have three. In each hand, he holds weapons and occasionally less-menacing Buddhist symbols like a bell or wheel. He is typically seen posed in a rather

---

[1] Vajrayana Buddhism (also called Tantric or Esoteric Buddhism) is the strain of Buddhism most popular in India and Tibet.

aggressive posture, juxtaposed with the beautiful, peaceful lotus on which he stands.

From the South comes Gundariyasha Myo-o. He has one to three heads, approximately eight weapon-wielding arms and, as an extra fun little flourish, he wears snakes around his ankles. Gundariyasha Myo-o's day job is doling out the heavenly nectar.

Gozanze Myo-o, from the East, is the Conqueror of the Three Planes. He has roughly three heads, eight or so arms holding weapons, including the "Arrow of Mercy," which he uses to keep folks on the straight and narrow (or, in Buddhist terms: The Middle Way). Perhaps the easiest way to identify Gozanze Myo-o from the rest of the group is that he's the one standing on the heads of two other deities who just happen to be the Buddhist form of the Hindu god Shiva and his wife. Anyone with the guts to stand on Shiva[1] is someone whom you should not upset.

The last of the Five Bright Kings is the western Daiitoku Myo-o. Daiitoku holds the record amongst the Myo-o with an astonishing six heads. Like many deities he has six arms, but unlike most Buddhist or even Hindu figures, he also has six legs. While it seems that someone with six legs has no need of assistance in getting around, Daiitoku rides a bull (which is a symbol of perseverance and enlightenment).

There are yet more Bright Kings including the red-skinned Aizen Myo-o who is worshipped by sex workers and other performers. The green-skinned Rojuki Myo-o is the manifestation of the Buddhist mantra "om mani padme hum[2]." Ususuma Myo-o is available to help menstruating women and the sick. Kojaku Myo-o, the lone gentle Bright King, rides a peacock and protects against poison. There's also Bato, Buteki, Daisho, Dairin, Eshaku, Munosho, and more.

Of all the Myo-o, though, Fudo remains the central Bright King, both figuratively and literally. He is the stalwart, immovable protector of Buddhism, his flames can burn away your impurities and, for some reason, if you wash your money, Fudo has been known to cause it to multiply.[3]

---

[1] Including the Hindu Dark Goddess Kali.

[2] I could try to explain this powerful six syllable Buddhist phrase, but truly understanding it is a one-way ticket to enlightenment and since I am neither a bodhisattva nor a Buddha, I would be woefully underqualified for the task. Suffice it to say, the whole of Buddhist teaching, the nature of suffering and how to remove it, is said to be contained within this deceptively simple sounding mantra. So, you've got that going for you, which is nice.

[3] Does that make him the god of money laundering?

"Kishimojin" by Chloe Stewart

Kishimojin

a.k.a.: Kariei, Kishibojin, Kangimo, Koyasu Kishibojin, Hariti (Sanskrit), Guizi mu shen (Chinese), Gwija mo sin (Korean)

Pantheon: Japanese (Buddhist née Hindu)

Offspring: Ten Demon Daughters or somewhere from three to 10,000 demon children

Deity of: children, childbirth, motherhood

Symbols: nursing infant, pomegranate

Kishimojin is proof that redemption is possible. She began her career as a baby-eating demoness and she had three, five, seven, ten, a hundred, five hundred, seven thousand and forty-two, or ten thousand children and they too lived off human flesh. It wasn't until the Buddha stepped in that she amended her ways.

To teach her a lesson, the Buddha captured her most beloved child. She was understandably distraught when her favorite little baby-eating baby was nowhere to be found. His adorable little demon face went on the ancient Indian equivalent of milk cartons, while his mother hung up missing persons posters, and organized search parties—the full Johnny Gosch treatment. When Kishimojin deeply and truly understood the pain and suffering a parent experiences at the loss of a child, Buddha let the boy out from under his begging bowl where he had hidden him. Granted, kidnapping seems like a shitty thing for the Enlightened One to do, but apparently, he's a little bit more Machiavellian than we give him credit for, because the ends justified the means. From that time on, Kishimojin swore to protect all the little children. As a full-on reversal of her initial modus operandi, Kishimojin took to nursing infants herself rather than nibbling on them.

The reformed Kishimojin was associated with taking care of infants and helping both mother and child through childbirth. She became the go-to lady for not just successful births, but *easy* births. As the Epidural Queen (not an actual name) she made it easy to bring children into the world and then, unlike some modern religious/political groups we could name, she also cared about what happened to them after they exited the womb.

Because of her efforts to protect wee ones, Kishimojin is sometimes linked to Jizo, the bosatsu who watches over children and takes special care of lost children. She also has echoes of Kwannon (Japanese for Kuan Yin) the bosatsu of compassion who is also frequently shown holding or nursing a baby. With so many mythic protectors of women and children, it's no wonder that so many in society don't feel the need to extend additional protections to them. I mean, heck, if a former baby-eater is keeping an eye out for them what more could we real, mortal humans do?

Other than the nursing babe, the image most closely associated with Kishimojin is a pomegranate. While the pomegranate is the food that condemns Persephone to a winter home in Hades, and is sometimes taken to be the real fruit from the Garden of Eden, here it carries an even more complex meaning. The numerous seeds inside the pomegranate are a symbol of fertility and serve as a horn of plenty for her vast quantities of children. The blood-red color harkens back to the cannibalistic origin of Kishimojin as well, and some Japanese people will not eat pomegranates because, apparently, they taste like human flesh.

Tsukumogami

a.k.a.: Tsukumo-gami, "Object Spirits"
Pantheon: Japanese (folk tradition, yokai)

It can be hard to get rid of family heirlooms, even those that have long outlived their usefulness. Grandma's old gramophone? Your daughter's first pair of baby shoes? Dad's favorite umbrella? Sure, no one is using them anymore, but it's hard to let go, nonetheless. In Japanese folk tradition, it's not just hard for the people but for the objects as well.

Household objects that have been used (or at least kept around) for a long time aren't ready to be dropped off at Goodwill or sold for pennies on the dollar at a yard sale. When they do get discarded, they hold a grudge and may just come back to bite you. Or sometimes just to lick you.

In Japanese folk tradition everything, not just everyone, has a kami. After a time, usually thought to be about a hundred years, the kami causes the thing to come to life and take on a monstrous, if not terribly threatening form. These are called the Tsukumogami or "Object Spirits" and everything from an old broken jar (Kameosa) to mosquito netting (Shironeri) to a mirror (Ungaikyo) will come back to taunt, frighten, and pester humanity. Like spurned lovers, they are filled with resentment for having been cast away, but are typically more annoying than they are dangerous[1].

---

[1] Spurned lovers can prove to be very dangerous indeed, especially to women. So, when you get dumped, get over it and move on. Let her go and you worry about working on yourself.

"Attack of the Thing Wraiths" by Christian Sitterlet

Two of the best-known types of Tsukumogami are the haunted umbrella (Kara-Kasa or Kasa-Obake) and the lantern (Bura-bura or Chochin-Obake). The handle of the old umbrella becomes a gnarled leg for the Kara-kasa to hop around on and one great big eye and a disturbingly long tongue seemingly burst from the folded umbrella. Though highly prevalent, the Kara-kasa usually won't do any real harm, it will just hop up behind you and lick you when you aren't looking. Bura-bura is about on par with Kara-kasa except that, as a paper lantern, it floats and has a little flame in its mouth.

Within the broad category of Tsukumogami, we can find subcategories. For example, there are the haunted instruments such as Biwa-bokuboku (*biwa* is a Japanese lute-type instrument), Koto-furunushi (a floor harp), and Shamisen-choro (a three-stringed guitar-type instrument). They won't hurt you, but they will play their music loudly when you're trying to sleep. Some Tsukumogami are revitalized articles of clothing like the popular one-eyed living sandals called Bakezori or Kosode-no-Te, the animate kimono. Kitchen objects like Yamaaoroshi, an animate grater, could be just as dangerous as a regular grater— only this one will laugh when you scrape your knuckles. Morinji-no-okama is the mean-spirited Japanese version of Mrs. Potts from *Beauty and the Beast*. Clocks, prayer beads, paper, the blankets on your bed, the stirrups on your horse, and virtually anything else you can imagine might come to life and bug the crap out of you in one way or another.

But wait, there is some good news: Tsukumogami hate electricity. So, all your modern technologies from radios to televisions to computers and smartphones are unlikely to haunt you after you've discarded them. Part of the reason for that is because all these newfangled devices get replaced too quickly to build up any serious mojo, which is great because if every cell phone, laptop, or television that we've replaced for a newer, sexier version were to rise up, we'd all be in serious trouble. Grandpa's slippers coming to life is way less worrisome than devices with access to our private information and browser history going rogue. I'll take a bitter umbrella licking my elbow over an iPhone with malicious intent, any day.

Kappa

a.k.a.: Kawappa, Kogo, Mizushi, Dangame, Kawataro, Komahiki, "River Child"

Pantheon: Japanese (folk tradition, yokai)

"Kappa" by Mandy Cantarella

Kappa are one of the best-known types of Japanese yokai. They are water-dwelling, humanoid, reptilian creatures with a distinctive indent filled with water on the top of their heads. Though there are numerous, adorable, modern depictions of these creatures of the deep, they are not to be trifled with and have long been feared throughout Japan. They have been known to kidnap, rape, kill, and even eat humans who come too near the rivers and ponds they call home.

Prevalent throughout Japan, the modus operandi of the kappa is to grab people standing near or swimming in a body of water and pull them under. Some kappa are content to drink your blood as you drown, but sometimes they are a bit more invasive in their pursuit of a snack. Kappa love to eat human souls, which, incidentally, can be found in a gland located in your anus. Yes, that is where the soul resides and kappa are more than happy to rip your intestines out through your butt and suck the soul out. If you find yourself in the grip of a hungry kappa, all is not lost: you can save your soul and your butthole if you offer up a cucumber instead. Cucumbers[1] are the only food kappa prefer over anal souls. If you don't have a cucumber on you, the super-strong amphibious fiends will surely kill you. Not to get all victim blame-y, but it really is your own fault if you're going to walk around Japan without a cucumber. Just to be extra safe, toss a cucumber with your surname written on it into any potentially kappa-infested body of water; that way, you and the rest of your family will get a pass from the thankful kappa. Unless, of course, as a conflicting tradition holds, putting your name on a cucumber all but guarantees a kappa attack. Damned if you do. Damned if you don't.

Not every encounter with a kappa is a life or death struggle. Some kappa are content simply to harass women by looking up their skirts, or frighten and annoy unsuspecting people by farting a loud fishy fart in their direction. Kappa will also occasionally give you an opportunity to defend yourself by engaging you in a wrestling match before they kill you. If kappa should challenge you to wrestle, they will inadvertently leave themselves open to their greatest weakness: politeness. Before grappling with the wet and webbed hands of the kappa, you should bow deeply to your opponent. Being a courteous intestine-slurping turtle-monkey, the kappa will return the gesture and bow to you, causing the water to spill out of the dish on top of its head and you will have, quite literally, killed it with kindness.

Kappa have been known, from time to time, to be friendly. Especially if you offer them a cucumber, a kappa may offer you their help with fishing, farming, or administering medicinal care. There are even some shrines dedicated to specific

---

[1] Sushi aficionados will recognize "kappa maki" as the name of cucumber rolls, a nod to the cucumber's number one fans.

kappa who have been especially beneficial to society. For the most part, though, you would do well to bribe the kappa with a snack before putting too much faith in its willingness to do right by you.

Tales of kappa serve a very specific purpose in Japanese folklore. Like all good boogeymen, the specter of the murderous reptoid is used to scare the bejeezus out of children and, in this case, make sure they keep clear of drowning hazards. Even today, in modern Japan, you can find signs warning about the possible presence of kappa by lakes, ponds, and rivers. Admit it: a sign that says, "No Lifeguard on Duty - Swim at Your Own Risk" is much less compelling than a sign that implies that an angry sea-monster, who wants to eat your soul from your butt, is nearby.

Tengu

a.k.a.: Karasutengu, Kotengu, Daitengu, Konoha tengu, Yamabushi tengu, "Celestial Dog"

Pantheon: Japanese (folk tradition, yokai)

There are several different types of tengu living on the mountains and in the forests of Japan, but each is a variation on the human/bird hybrid. Some are more bird than human, others are more human than bird, but all of them are powerful and dangerous to those who cross them.

Karasutengu (also called kotengu), are the most avian type of tengu. They appear as human-sized crows, and are dressed as yamabushi[1]. Sometimes karasutengu are shown having a humanoid body with only the wings and beak of a crow. Though not as powerful as other strains of tengu, these bird-men are renowned for their skills with both weapons and magic and can be quite malicious. Unlike crows who feed largely on carrion, karasutengu will attack and feed off living humans. They like to torture humans who wander too close to their homes but they will also go out of their way to menace people just for the heck of it. For some reason, karasutengu especially enjoy torturing religious clergy. Apparently, they get their kicks by driving monks and nuns crazy before killing them. Perhaps the reason they hate clergy so much is because tengu are believed to be the spirits of arrogant people, particularly prideful monks, who need to be taught a lesson in humility. They aren't always bad news, though. If you have something shiny to

---

[1] Ascetic monks who often lived as hermits in the mountains.

"Tengu" by Lindsay N. Poulos

bribe them with (whether it has actual value doesn't matter much to these hoarders) they may impart some of their vast knowledge of weaponry, swordplay, and sorcery.

A second type of tengu, called konoha tengu (or daitengu, or yamabushi tengu) are generally more benevolent, but are also capable of much greater destruction. These tengu, also dressed like yamabushi, look mostly human most of the time, apart from their wings and bright red faces. And they have prodigious, phallic red noses. The bigger the nose, the more powerful the tengu.[1] Living quiet hermit-like lives, these konoha tengu mostly keep to themselves. When they are crossed, however, they have been known to cause large-scale destruction with earthquakes, tsunamis, and the like. If you approach one humbly and respectfully, though, they may just take you on as an apprentice. Many of the great samurai and heroes of legend were trained by these winged, red-faced monks. Unlike the lesser tengu, the konoha tengu often have individual names and/or regions where they are believed to reside. A tengu named Enkai of Mt. Haguro reportedly taught Tsukahara Bokuden a new form of fencing, making him one of the great swordsmen of the 16th century. Daitengu Sojobo lived on Mt. Kurama and acted as the Yoda to Minamoto no Yoshitsune's Luke Skywalker. Minamoto is regarded as one of the greatest heroes of Japanese history and some legends[2] hold that he eventually left Japan and made his way to Mongolia where he took the name Genghis Khan. If that were true[3], and if it were also true that Sojobo was his trainer[4], then that one tengu would be partly responsible for one of the most successful leaders in human history and the single most genetically successful human of all time.

The fact that the term "tengu" literally translates as "heavenly dog" is a bit perplexing. The most likely explanation for this is that the word is an import from Chinese and originally referred to an asteroid whose tail was evocative of a dog. It was the destructive force of the meteor that was connected to the angry bird-men and not the literal meaning of the word. The look of the tengu (especially the karasutengu, which go back the furthest historically) was likely inspired by the Hindu/Buddhist bird-man Garuda, who acted as the messenger of the gods. The konoha tengu may trace their roots back to the red-faced and big-nosed Shinto figure Sarutahiko. Confusingly enough, Sarutahiko translates to "monkey man"

---

[1] Really, it's less about size and more about how you use it. I'm told.
[2] "Legend" here is used as a term to mean: "outlandish lies that are nonetheless entertaining."
[3] It's not.
[4] That is also not true.

but it is, apart from the lack of wings, the spitting image of the later konoha tengu. Yet another tradition suggests that the tengu may have begun as the offspring of Susanoo, a Shinto god who, partly because of arrogance, was booted from Heaven and forced to make amends. Clearly, the family tree on which the tengu perch is a gnarled and confusing one.

Kitsune

a.k.a.: Oinari, Yako, Zenko, Tenko, "Red Fox"
Pantheon: Japanese (Shinto, folk tradition, yokai)

Around the world, foxes are regarded as being especially clever. Japanese folk tradition holds that foxes are not only smart (as smart as or smarter than humans, in fact) but that they are also exceptionally long-lived. Like the Tsukumogami, after about a hundred years or so the fox is endowed with magical powers and joins the ranks of the yokai. The older, wiser, and more powerful a fox becomes, the more tails it sprouts. A fox with nine tails is at the peak of its abilities[1].

Called kitsune (literally: "red fox"), they are revered and feared throughout Japan. Inari, the god of fertility and agriculture, has more shrines dedicated to him than any other Shinto deity and at those shrines, you will find kitsune statues by the dozens. The kitsune are, in those instances, taken as the messengers and guardians of Inari. These benevolent kitsune are called *zenko* ("good fox") and are only troublesome to those who would do harm to Inari or one of his shrines. Not all kitsune are quite so magnanimous, though.

Kitsune are shapeshifters and unlike the more mischievous tanuki, kitsune are often out for blood. One of their most frequent tricks is to disguise themselves as beautiful women, lure men back to their homes, and then drain them of their blood. This type of kitsune, called *yako* ("wild fox"), occupies a realm in Japanese folk tradition somewhere between a werewolf and a vampire. Sometimes it's a simple one-night stand and at other times it's a long con in which a kitsune impersonates a person for years and years, even bearing children. If you suspect a woman at the bar or even your wife of many years may be a kitsune, there are a few ways to test the theory. First, kitsune have a natural aversion to dogs so if she's scared of your Chihuahua, that's a red (fox) flag. Secondly, kitsune have a hard time maintaining their disguise, especially hiding their tail(s), when drunk. So, if

---

[1] When a fox earns all nine tails, its fur turns gold, and it is known as a *tenko* ("celestial fox").

"Kitsune" by Malena Salinas

she gets drunk and you see a red tail or two creeping out from under her skirt, you'd do well to make a run for it as soon as possible.

Not only can kitsune disguise themselves as people, but they can also possess humans. They enter your body through your nipple, or under a fingernail, and take control of your body. If you keep the fox happy, a kitsune possession may not be all that bad. But, if you do not keep the fox happy, you may grow physically or mentally ill. Worst of all, if you manage to survive a kitsune possession you will never again be able to enjoy tofu (which is apparently a favorite food of the foxes). Attempting to root out kitsune possession in Japan is the equivalent of a witch hunt wherein accusations are generally leveled at people for personal reasons, like envy, rather than actual proof of wrongdoing. Beautiful women are especially suspect because, of course, they bewitch men so well, so easily, and so often. And once again we have a culture wherein men demonize the object of their desire simply for it being desirable.

Kitsune have other, more subtle ways of manipulating their victims. Appearing as a fire-fox (something like a *will o' the wisp*), they will lead nighttime travelers off their course and to their doom. They can also shoot fire or lightning from their mouth, fly, turn invisible, and transform into virtually any shape. While there are plenty of good kitsune out there, unless it is on official business for Inari, you would do well not to cross the path of any fox.

Tanuki

a.k.a.: Tanooki, Bake-danuki, Japanese Raccoon Dog
Pantheon: Japanese (folk tradition, yokai)
Notable members: Danzaburou-danuki, Shibaemon-tanuki, Yashima no Hage-tanuki, Soko-tanuki, Tanuki-bayashi, Jubakobaba, Inugami Gyoubu

Most of the yokai are imaginary[1] creatures, but the tanuki are 100% real. Often translated into English as "raccoon" or even "badger," the tanuki is an animal native to Japan and is more closely related to foxes and domestic dogs than to either the raccoon or badger. "Raccoon dog" nicely describes its appearance, despite it being a taxonomically-misleading name. Westerners are probably most familiar with tanuki as the suit Mario wears so he can fly. And though flight is not a gift that real tanuki possess, there is little that the yokai variant is incapable of.

---

[1] Or are they?! Booga-booga.

"Tanuki" by Malena Salinas

Known as devious but not necessarily malicious tricksters, tanuki play an active role in Japanese folk traditions. They are shapeshifters who, like many trickster figures, are more interested in feeding their appetites, and sowing confusion than in causing any large-scale trouble. One of their favorite tricks is to pay for goods and services with gold that turns out to be nothing but leaves as soon as they walk away. Some will shave your head when you're not looking, or disguise themselves as a bottle of sake that refuses to be picked up. In the tales of violence inflicted by tanuki, it is often accidental and usually the tanuki pays dearly for it.

Some tanuki, however, are outright benevolent. There is Soko-tanuki who disguised himself as a monk for so long that even after his identity was revealed, he remained a respected figure thanks to his years of hard work and dedication. Yashima no Hage-tanuki is one of the "Three Famous Tanuki" and was the protector of the Taira clan and renowned as the greatest shapeshifter of all. Though Danzaburou-danuki didn't always have the purest motives, he is credited with keeping kitsune, the more malicious trickster foxes, away from Sado Island.

The most striking feature of the tanuki is not its adorable raccoon-like face, but its bulbous scrotum. Yes, tanuki have sizable sacks. Even real tanuki have disproportionately large cojones, but the yokai version of them is typically portrayed with absurdly large bollocks. Like so big that they can toss them over their shoulder and carry them around like that, or they can strap them up and play them as drums, or stretch them out and use them as a fishing net, or attack and even smother humans with them. There is a children's rhyme about the tanuki that you might hear on a Japanese playground even today. In English, the song goes something like "Tan-tan-tanuki's balls/ they swing-swing/ even without wind." All this talk of testes is enough to make a puritanical American blush, but tanuki statues, figurines, and stuffed toys (with ball sacks accounting for nearly half of their body mass) can be found throughout Japan, from shop to shrine. And they aren't there purely for ornamentation or shock value; rubbing a voluptuous set of tanuki gonads is a way to ensure fortune and prosperity. So, if you're looking to be successful, don't neglect the tanuki balls.

"Darkest Dreams" by Tessa Brown

Celtic Mythology

There was no Celtic Empire. The people that we now call the Celts did not call themselves that, nor did they think of themselves as belonging to the same group as the diversity of people we now lump together as being Celtic. They lived in places as disparate as Scotland and Turkey. They did not speak the same language and they did not worship the same gods. There is no singular "Celtic mythology."

The people whom we call Celts at one time covered not only the United Kingdom, but also most of mainland Europe. Unifying these groups under the label of "Celtic" is merely an over-simplified classification forced on them by much later scholars. Just as the indigenous peoples of North America have a vast array of lifestyles, languages, and beliefs with some recurring, similar thematic elements, so too did the Celts of Europe. To make matters even worse, the myths of most of the Celtic world were not recorded at all, or only in flimsy Roman accounts that were heavy on judgement and light on understanding. Julius Caesar himself wrote some of the earliest accountings of Celtic gods and goddesses, often imposing Greco-Roman archetypes onto them.

The only lengthy versions of any Celtic myths come to us from the Irish and their neighbors in Wales. Even those were set down by medieval Christians centuries after the old religion had died out. Therefore, the only received Celtic myths come to us from a tiny corner of the Celtic world and are glossed over with a thick coat of Christian shellac. At times, it is easy, and at other times impossible to chip away the Christian influence from the characters and tales to find their original forms underneath.

The four most significant written sources are the *Book of Invasions* (also called the *Lebor Gabala Erenn* or simply LGE), *Ulster Cycle* (or *Ulaid Cycle*), *Fenian Cycle* (or *Fionn Cycle* or *Ossianic Cycle*), and the Welsh *Mabinogion*. Here we will focus purely on the Irish sources. *The Book of Invasions* tells a foundation myth of Ireland and features the exploits of characters like Tuan Mac Starn and Lugh as well as the epic battles of the Fomorians, Tuatha de Danann, Fir Bolg, and Milesians. The Ulster Cycle deals with the Ulaid people, the ancestors of the modern northeastern Irish county of Ulster. The primary protagonist of the Ulster Cycle is the tenacious hero Cu Chulainn. The Fenian Cycle tells the tale of Finn McCool and his people, the Fianna. Finn's own son Oisin is held to be the poet who chronicled the tale, hence it sometimes being called the Ossianic Cycle.

"Tuan Mac Starn" by Annamarie Borowiak

Tuan Mac Starn

a.k.a.: Tuan mac Carell
Pantheon: Celtic (Irish)

One of the few sources of Celtic myth that has survived to the present is called the *Lebor Gabala Erenn* or *The Book of Invasions*. It tells, through a heavy medieval Christian filter, how Ireland was settled through a series of invading groups and the ensuing battles. Tuan Mac Starn provides the through line for the *LGE* as the only person to have witnessed first-hand the history of Ireland from its very inception.

In the received mythology, Tuan Mac Starn (Tuan, son of Starn) was the nephew of Parthalon who was a descendant of Noah. Given that ancient Celts living in Ireland had probably never heard of the Biblical character of Noah, we can conclude that this was likely not the original way the story was told. More than likely, Tuan Mac Starn was originally conceived of as a descendant of the God of the Dead[1], as the Celtic people in general were thought to be.

Whether descended from the God of the Dead or Noah, Parthalon and a group of his followers stumbled upon a tiny island that history would come to know as Ireland. When the Parthalonians got there, Ireland was far from the land it would later become. Much smaller, with only a handful of lakes and one field, the island would grow as its population boomed. Not long after their arrival, Parthalon and his followers were attacked by a terrifying tribe of monsters known as the Fomorians. Representative of the forces of darkness, or with the Christian filter applied, the descendants of Noah's cursed son Ham, the Fomorians weakened but didn't defeat the Parthalonians. Disease proved a more formidable foe, leaving Parthalon and all his people dead. Except one: Tuan Mac Starn.

Tuan Mac Starn was left all alone on the preemie Ireland for decades. He grew old and, possibly, a bit unstable. When nine survivors of a massive shipwreck washed up on the slightly larger Irish shore, Tuan was too scared to make contact. Instead, he transformed. Tuan became a stag, and because apparently deer will elect anyone, he became king of all the deer of Ireland. Meanwhile, the survivors,

---

[1] The Irish Celtic God of the Dead and, in fact, death itself were not objects of fear. To the contrary, Irish Celts believed in a lovely afterlife on an island somewhere west of Ireland, variously known as The Isle of the Blest, The Isle of the Young, Tir Na-nog, and so on. The God of the Dead was likely a benevolent figure more akin to a creator god than the type of dark and gloomy deadheads you'd find in many other cultures.

led by Nemed (yes, another descendant of Noah) flourished and then flopped. The thousands of Nemedians born from the original nine all either died off or left Ireland for less-green pastures. Tuan responded by transforming into a boar and becoming the reigning monarch of boar-dom.

Sometime later, a group of descendants of Nemed returned to Ireland. They had traveled to Greece or Spain (what's the difference, if you're an ancient Irish Celt?) where they had been enslaved. Eventually, they rose up and headed back to Ireland where they were known as the Fir Bolg. Decades of living as a boar did not make Tuan any more sociable, so he transformed yet again into a sea-eagle. Since Tuan was not one to do things half-assed, he campaigned hard and became the king of all birds of prey.

The Fir Bolg were not the only Nemedian tribe to find their way back to Ireland. A second group known as the Tuatha de Danann came in from the Faroe Islands, just north of Ireland. Through one of the more circuitous routes ever embarked upon in myth, Tuan would become a member of the Tuatha de Danann. The then-aging avian Tuan transformed yet again, this time into a salmon. He did not, however, have time to become the king of all spawning fish because he was eaten whole and uncooked by the very hungry unnamed wife of a man called Carell.

Of course, that is not the end of the tale of Tuan, only the end of Tuan Mac Starn. Having been swallowed whole, the soul of Tuan survived and became a gestating fetus in the womb of Carell's wife[1] and was then reborn as Tuan mac Carell. Tuan mac Carell became a well-known Celtic scholar and historian because, thanks to his shape-shifting, regeneration, and rebirth, he alone witnessed the history of Ireland first hand. Mac Carell retained the knowledge of mac Starn's long life and, in fact, was the person credited with relaying the story that would be set down into the text we call *The Book of Invasions*. Not only does Tuan's tale provide a nice through line, connecting all Irish history through one ever changing set of eyes, but it also makes clear the Celtic belief in reincarnation.

We cannot say for certain that all Celtic groups believed in reincarnation, but it is clear that at least the Irish Celts did. Their form of reincarnation was a bit different than the eastern versions more familiar to modern audiences. It wasn't part of the laborious process for each of us to accrue karma over numerous lifetimes to eventually reach enlightenment, but was something reserved largely for the best and brightest. Rebirth was by no means a given. Additionally,

---

[1] Mercury poisoning is not the only reason to be wary of too much sushi, as it turns out.

155

reincarnated souls did not always come back as living beings but could return as geographical features, objects, or locations. Frequently, people would come back as their own descendants, but were just as likely not to come back at all, or to come back as a pond or a tree.

Fomorians

a.k.a.: Fomoire, Fomhoraigh
Pantheon: Celtic (Irish)
Notable Members: Balor, Bres, Ethniu, Elatha

According to the *Book of Invasions*, the Fomorians were descended from Ham, the cursed son of Noah. Ham, for the record, was cursed for laughing at Noah when he was passed out drunk and naked[1] and not because of his very unkosher name. Biblically, the descendants of Ham were the Canaanites, a very real group of people who were enemies of the Hebrews who wrote the Bible, whereas in the received Celtic mythology they are the monstrous Fomorians. In the original form of these stories the Fomorians doubtlessly represented the forces of darkness who were eventually defeated by the forces of light.

It is no accident that the Fomorians held the ultimate adversarial position to the invading founders of Ireland. They fought with the early Irish settlers known as the Partholonians and then, most notably, nearly defeated the radiant gods (or godlike beings) of the Tuatha de Danann. Just as the people of Moses needed to defeat the Canaanites to claim their Promised Land and become Israelites, so too did the settlers have to defeat the Fomorians to claim their destiny and inhabit Ireland. While it is impossible to say how much of this story comes from the pre-Christian traditions of the Celts, it is clear that by the time Irish Christians were writing it down they viewed themselves as the new 'Chosen People' and echoed the trials and tribulations of the Israelites whenever possible. To be fair, both the Jews and the Irish have a solid history of mistreatment, persecution, and tragedy so it's not an unfair comparison to make.

The exact nature and appearance of the Fomorians is not abundantly clear from the surviving sources. Some sources seem to suggest that they are not only from the darkness, but from the deep blue sea and may be conceived of as some type of fish monsters like the Creature from the Black Lagoon or the even more

---

[1] Genesis 9:20-27

"The Fomorians are Coming" by Emily Luyk

terrifying angler fish[1]. Some translations suggest that they are beings with only one leg, one arm, or both. There is very little consistency in their depiction, though there is general agreement that many Fomorians are monstrous in appearance, size, or both. But then, of course, there are numerous exceptions because some half-blooded or full-blooded Fomorians live amongst the exceptionally beautiful Tuatha de Danann and fit in perfectly well. Bres, Lugh, and the Dagda all led the Tuatha de Danann for a time despite having one or more parents of Fomorian origin. Bres turned out to be a bad and cruel leader, but that can't be blamed on his Fomorian father because Lugh and the Dagda were two of the most successful and best-loved of all the Tuatha de Danann. The Fomorians, like the Norse Jotun, are probably more accurately thought of simply as the outsiders, separated more by attitude than by genes.

The Second Battle of Magh Tuirdeh pitted the fearsome Fomorians against the tenacious Tuatha de Danann. After the half-Fomorian Bres was satirized out of office by a cheeky Tuatha poet, he found his father, and convinced the Fomorians to take on the Tuatha. The kingship having been yielded to the newly

---

[1] Those things are the stuff of nightmares. And that's without even getting into how they reproduce.

enlisted Lugh by the slightly skittish Nuada of the Silver Hand meant that Lugh faced his own maternal grandfather, Balor, king of the Fomorians. Ultimately, of course, the forces of light were successful and in one grisly moment both Balor and most of his army were killed off.

Tuatha de Danann

a.k.a.: "The People of the Goddess Danu"
Pantheon: Celtic (Irish)
Notable Members: Nuada, Bres, Lugh, The Dagda, Brigid

A race responsible for Celtic belief in fairies, leprechauns, and the like, the Tuatha de Danann also provide an origin story for the distinctive appearance of many Irish people. When an earlier invading group known as the Nemedians left Ireland, some of them traveled south to mainland Europe, some headed north to the Faroe Islands. Years later, a group of Nemedians (then called the Fir Bolg) escaped enslavement in the south and re-settled in Ireland. Not long after that, the descendants of the Nemedians who had gone north came back to Ireland as well. They were called the Tuatha de Danann, or the Children of the Goddess Danu. These separate points of origin are said to explain the diversity of the Irish. Yes, some Irish people are pale, freckly, and ginger, but some are slightly less pale and have slightly darker hair color. The fairer Irish are born from the godlike race of Tuatha de Danann, whereas the swarthier Irish are born of those who came from closer to the Mediterranean.

The Goddess Danu is all but unknown. Despite being the matriarch of the Tuatha de Danann, no stories remain about the goddess herself. Clearly, she was a mother goddess, possibly also an earth goddess, a fertility goddess, or a sun goddess of some type but that is all we know of her. Likely, Danu is yet another very ancient matriarchal goddess whose tradition was almost entirely snuffed out by later patriarchal belief systems. At least Danu's name is retained—many other goddesses in her position are lost to history without even that much.

The people of Danu are radiant and powerful and are the purest representatives of the forces of light found in the *Book of Invasions*. It was the Tuatha de Danann who were responsible for the only outright victory against the evil Fomorians. This myth's function was clearly to establish that light beats dark. But that battle, known as the Second Battle of Magh Tuirdeh, had a prequel in which the Tuatha faced a decidedly less evil foe.

"Mother of the Tuatha" by Amanda Zylstra

159

When they first arrived in Ireland, the Tuatha de Danann found their distant cousins the Fir Bolg already there. The First Battle of Magh Tuirdeh was fought between the Tuatha de Danann and the Fir Bolg for supremacy in Ireland. While the Tuatha won the fight, their king Nuada lost his arm and, with that, his kingship. The Tuatha and the Fir Bolg divvied up the country, giving the Fir Bolg the county of Connacht and the other three-quarters of the isle went to Danu's kids.

Thanks to their new leader Lugh and a sex act that won over the favor of war goddess the Morrigan[1], the Tuatha de Danann defeated the Fomorians in *The Battle of Magh Tuirdeh 2: Electric Boogaloo*. Despite their ability to beat back evil itself, the Tuatha de Danann proved unable to defend themselves against the next group to invade.

In a lightly historically-based tale, the Milesians (or the Sons of Mil, a group from the Iberian Peninsula) invaded Ireland next. They fought with the Tuatha until the Tuatha called for a weekend truce. The fighting stopped for a day and the Milesians went back to their boats anchored off the coast. And then, Danu's Children played dirty and called up a magical storm to wreck the Milesian ships. But alas, the Milesians happened to have a poet on hand who, like all poets, had oratorical powers to calm the storm. Despite their underhanded tactics, the Tuatha de Danann lost the fight. The Milesian poet[2] was then asked to divide the land between the two groups. He generously split the land fifty-fifty—the Milesians got everything above ground and the Tuatha de Danann got everything below ground. The godly beings were then forced to live in caves and trees, hidden away from the eyes of the mortal world. In this way, the Tuatha de Danann gave way to belief in fairies, leprechauns, and the various other magical figures hiding at the periphery of the Celtic world.

---

[1] See the Dagda for more info.
[2] Clearly the poet who wrote this story placed a very high premium on the importance of poets.

"Lugh" by Christian Jackson

Lugh

a.k.a.: Lug, Lugus, Lu, Lamfada, Smaildanach
Pantheon: Celtic (Irish)
Spouse/Lovers: Deichtine, Bui, Nas
Parents: Ethniu & Cian, Manannan (foster-father)
Offspring: Cu Chulainn, Ebliu, Ibic
Deity of: light, crafting, the arts
Symbols: wheel, light, tools

Finding the original form of Lugh is something of a "needle in a haystack" scenario. Or more accurately, a "slightly different piece of hay in a haystack" scenario. Other gods, legends, fairy tales, folk tales, and other traditions make it nearly impossible to pick out the pre-Christian Celtic form of the character. Julius Caesar himself muddled things up when he wrote about a Celtic god whom he associated with the Roman Mercury.[1]

The surviving form of the story of Lugh's birth reads more like a fairy tale than anything else. Once upon a time, there was an evil king named Balor. A prophecy stated that King Balor would one day be killed by his own grandson. To prevent such a fate, Balor had his only child, a baby daughter, imprisoned in an impossibly tall tower. Further thumbing his nose at the gods, the tower was guarded by only women so that baby Ethniu would never even know men existed, let alone become pregnant by one.

And then Balor made a classic fairy tale villain mistake: he stole a cow.

There were three brothers, blacksmiths, who owned a cow that provided endless supplies of milk. Balor wanted that cow so he disguised himself as a little redheaded boy and tricked the brothers into fighting amongst themselves. While they were distracted, he nabbed the cow. When the brothers realized they had been duped, and furthermore, that Balor had done the duping, they teamed up with a powerful druidess. One of the brothers, named Cian, disguised himself as a woman, and he and the druidess snuck into Ethniu's tower. Cian impregnated Ethniu, but being as sheltered as she was, Ethniu did not even realize what had happened. The next morning, she told her guards that she had been visited by a woman who was also part snake and that the snake had done something very confusing to her. It dawned on the guards what exactly they had allowed to

---

[1] A bit of a stretch even by Caesarean standards.

happen. They told her she must have been dreaming and subsequently, as her belly grew larger and larger over the next nine months, they told her she was simply eating too much. One can only imagine how confused poor Ethniu must have been when three male babies tumbled out of her. The guards, hoping to avoid facing the wrath of Balor, gathered up the newborns in a carpet and went to toss them into the sea. On the way, a pin came out of the carpet and one of the babies fell out, unbeknownst to the guards. The baby, named Lugh, was raised by the sea god Manannan and grew up to learn many trades and skills including carpentry, poetry, music, battle, and accounting.

Lugh eventually made his way to Tara, the home of the Tuatha de Danann. He was told there that he could enter only if he was the very best at something. He said that he was a very accomplished warrior, but was told that they already had a great warrior. He said that he was a great poet, but was told that they already had a great poet. Each of his skills was met with the same response until Lugh asked the gatekeeper if they had amongst the ranks of the Tuatha de Danann someone who was accomplished in everything. They did not yet have a jack of all trades and so Lugh was not only allowed in, but was shortly thereafter proclaimed king. Turns out, the Tuatha de Danann had a real meritocracy.

Lugh went on to lead the Children of Danu to their greatest victory. *The Battle of Magh Tuirdeh 2: The Legend of Curley's Gold* ended with Lugh, as prophesied, killing his maternal grandfather Balor. No surprise that the prophecy came to pass, of course, but the way it did is one of the most gruesomely awesome scenes in all of mythology. When he wasn't disguising himself as a ginger child, Balor was an enormous hulk with one giant eye that shot out death rays. But Balor had grown old and he no longer had the strength to open his eye by himself. Instead, four men with a series of ropes and pulleys had to hoist up Balor's eyelid for him. When the lid-lifters let go for a moment, Lugh threw a rock at Balor's eye, sending it out the back of Balor's head where its death beams killed the assembled Fomorian forces.

Lugh was also recognized as the owner of some wonderful toys. He had an unbeatable spear, a magic sword from his foster father, a pigskin that cured all injuries, as well as a horse, a boat, and a hound (each of which had its own special powers). Many of these objects and others were obtained by Lugh forcing the three[1] sons of Tuireann to make up for killing Cian. He gave them a series of nigh-

---

[1] The Celts are really big on triplicates. Lugh's father is one of three brothers, Lugh is one of three brothers, there are three sons of Tuireann, the Morrigan, and Brigit are tri-part goddesses, etc. ad nauseum.

impossible tasks to gather the magical devices he was too lazy to go get himself. In the end, they succeeded but it cost all three son their lives and then Tuireann, their father, died of grief.

The great Celtic hero Cu Chulainn was the son (through a convoluted series of events) of Lugh as well as a reincarnation of Lugh.[1] In the story of Cu Chulainn, Lugh helped to guide his son through a magical minefield by becoming a spinning wheel of light to show him the path. The circle of light often associated with Lugh may have represented the sun, the cyclical nature of the seasons, or even just literal wheels. Because of Lugh's diverse studies, he may be viewed as the patron of arts, crafts, warriors, poets, and more.

The Morrigan

a.k.a.: Morrigan, Morrigu, Morrighan, Mor-rioghain, Anand, "Phantom Queen"
Pantheon: Celtic (Irish)
Spouse/Lovers: The Dagda
Siblings: Badb, Macha, Nemain
Parents: Ernmas
Deity of: fate, war, death
Symbols: crow

She is the Great Queen, or the Phantom Queen. She is three goddesses in one, or one goddess of a triumvirate. She is dark and menacing, but comes from a race of bright, beautiful gods. She is a goddess of death and a goddess of fertility. She is a washerwoman and a crow feasting on carrion. She is the inspiration for the enemy of King Arthur and a cousin of the Valkyries. She is enormously popular yet only vaguely understood. She is the Morrigan.

To get a clearer conception of the Morrigan, we must first consider the Celtic view of death. In the received mythology, it is clear that Irish Celts envisioned an ideal afterlife. Far from the torture or torturously boring afterlife realms like Hell, Hades, or Helheim, the Celts saw death as a ticket to paradise. Presumably even before Christianity made its mark on the Celtic world, they believed in a vaguely Heaven-like realm. Variously referred to as the Isle of the Blest, the Land of the Young, Hy-Brasil, or Tir na n-Og, their afterlife was not found above or below,

---

[1] Not unlike Jesus who is believed to be God and the Son of God.

"The Morrigan" by Madeleine Graumlich

but was envisioned as an actual island somewhere west of Ireland. There, your youth would be restored, you would remain healthy and happy, and you would get to enjoy the lush green surrounds while floating in a sparkling diamond sea. The God of the Dead was not the Spirit of Christmas Yet to Come, but was the father of humanity, if not also the gods. The Morrigan then, as a death goddess, is both fearsome and benevolent. Yes, her appearance portends death, but hey, at least it'll be a nice death. Perhaps the complex relationship the Celts had with death helps to explain the complexity of the Morrigan.

The Morrigan, as with other Celtic goddesses, was often conceived of as three distinct yet interwoven goddesses. "The Morrigan" may be the name of one of the three goddesses that makes up the group or may be the collective term for the three sisters. Not only are the sources not particularly clear on this point, but there's also no reason to assume that it was necessarily one or the other. Either way, the Morrigan held a great deal of importance in the Celtic world.

One of the Tuatha de Danann, the Morrigan helped ensure victory over the Fomorians in *The Battle of Magh Tuirdeh 2: Cruise Control*. She may have played a part simply as a great warrior who fought in the battle, or possibly she chose the victor herself because, as a goddess of fate she favored the Tuatha de Danann after the Dagda had shown her a good time. *The Battle of Magh Tuirdeh 2: Armed and Fabulous* was not the only battle over which the Morrigan held sway. In various traditions, the Morrigan could be found in the form of a washerwoman washing the bloodstained clothing of warriors before the battle, indicating who was doomed to die. She could foreshadow who would die or, like the Valkyries of the Norse, she could appear as a raven after the battle to choose amongst the dead.

The Morrigan had a complex relationship with the great hero Cu Chulainn. At first, she fell in love with him like Ishtar for Gilgamesh. Rather than simply rejecting the goddess, Cu Chulainn and the Morrigan fought, leaving the goddess injured. Cu Chulainn blessed her when she came to him in the form of an old woman, which both healed the wounds he had given her and earned him her blessing for the rest of his life. The Morrigan even tried to warn Cu Chulainn against engaging in his final, fatal battle, but he didn't listen so all she could do was alight on his shoulder in crow form to indicate the moment of his death.

It is not difficult to see why the Morrigan is so popular in the neo-pagan movement. Yes, she's dark and goth-y and has crow imagery and a cool name like "the Phantom Queen," but that's not all she has to offer her modern fans. Often viewed as a very ancient mother goddess of the earliest European matriarchal tribes (despite a dearth of evidence to support this), the Morrigan is used as a symbol of female empowerment. She is a woman who both gives life and takes it back whenever she wants. While a lot of neo-pagan traditions are based on speculation and "wouldn't it be cool if . . ." kinds of thinking, it is hard to begrudge an appreciation of such a mysterious, badass goddess.

The Dagda

a.k.a.: Daghdha, Eochu, Aed Abaid of Ess Ruad, Fer Benn, Daire
Pantheon: Celtic (Irish)
Spouse/Lovers: Boann, the Morrigan, Ethniu, Danu
Siblings: Allod, Delbaeth, Fiacha, Ogma
Parents: Danu and Elatha
Offspring: Angus, Brigid, Bodb Derg, Cermait, Midir
Deity of: fertility, agriculture, magic, manliness
Symbols: club, cauldron, massive phallus

The received Celtic mythology is chockablock with daring men, badass women, monsters, magic, and epic battles. It is therefore all the more charming to find a character like the Dagda seated at the head of the table. The Dagda is a father god but, unlike your average paterfamilias, he's goofy and approachable rather than stern and authoritarian. The Dagda isn't "the Father" so much as he is "the Dada" or "the Daddy."

Of enormous size and strength, the Dagda was no slouch on the battlefield, but his signature accessories betrayed a softer side. Where Odin had a spear, hungry wolves, and birds who fed on carrion, the Dagda came equipped with a cauldron of boundless food and a club that could restore life just as easily as it took it. Sure, if he wanted to kill you, he would do so without hesitation, but he could also flip his club over and bring the fallen back to life should he have a change of mind.

While you wouldn't want to run into the Dagda on the battlefield, you could be beaten just as handily by him in an eating contest. In a tale that shows that even the denizens of the dark known as the Fomorians have a lighter side when the Dagda is around, they invited the father of the Tuatha de Danann to a party. Knowing that he had a penchant for porridge, the Fomorians dug out a massive hole in the ground and filled it with the Dagda's breakfast of champions. They handed him a spoon and let him know that if he failed to clean his bowl they would be so badly insulted that they would have to kill him. The Fomorians

"The Dagda" by Sarah Lindstrom

thought they had devised a plan to kill him off, or at the very least, had pulled off a prank that would leave the Dagda humiliated. They deeply underestimated his appetite and overestimated his capacity to feel embarrassed for it. He successfully emptied the porridge reservoir, bloating his already portly belly to comic proportions, and offered up an earth-shaking belch before laying down to a post-porridge nap.

Unconventionally handsome though he may have been, the Dagda was no stranger to romantic trysts. Perhaps the reason he was so popular with the ladies was because he was a musician and with his harp could influence both the emotions of his listeners and control the seasons. Or maybe it was the fact that he had an enormous penis that dragged on the ground. Maybe some of both. When he had an illicit affair with the married goddess Boann, he used his magic to conceal the resultant pregnancy. Causing the sun to stand still in the sky for nine months, Boann conceived, carried, and bore a child[1] in one very long day, and her husband Elcmer was none the wiser. Another sexual foray for the Dagda brought about an even greater result than the birth of a child. When the Dagda put the moves on death and war goddess the Morrigan, he earned her guarantee that she would be on the side of his tribe of Tuatha de Danann in their next battle. Their triumph over the Fomorians was due in no small part to the Morrigan's aid and the Dagda's smooth moves.

Cu Chulainn

a.k.a.: Setanta, Cu Chulaind, Cuhulin, "Culann's Hound"
Pantheon: Celtic (Irish)
Spouse/Lovers: Emer, Aife, Fand
Parents: Deichtine and Lugh
Offspring: Connla

One of the great Celtic heroes, Cu Chulainn is the star and protagonist of the mythological text known as the *Ulster Cycle*. Ulster, the northernmost county of Ireland, is especially fond of this legendary warrior and it's not hard to see why.

As with all great heroes, Cu Chulainn had a spectacularly complex birth story. The princess Deichtine was out looking for magical birds with her father the king when they took shelter in the home of a couple of peasants. That night, Mrs.

---

[1] Angus, a god of love.

"Cu Chulainn" by David Manderville

Peasant gave birth to a son. The next morning, however, Mr. and Mrs. Peasant were gone and so was their home. All that remained was the newborn babe. Deichtine brought the baby home and cared for it. Apparently, though, she didn't do very well because the baby died. That night, the god Lugh came to her and told her that the dead baby had been his son and that Deichtine was now pregnant herself with the same baby thanks to having swallowed a tiny person who was taking a swim in her drink. When the unwed princess's pregnancy became common knowledge, speculation spread about who the father might be. Most fingers pointed toward the king, her father. Deeply wounded by such rumors, she quickly found a man to marry her. Wanting to be able to go to her marriage bed as "a full virgin" she aborted her demi-god baby and then, after getting married got pregnant again and gave birth to a child named Setanta who, beyond all reason, was still the same baby.

As a child of about six years old, the already mighty Setanta gained the new name of Cu Chulainn. After killing his father's friend's watchdog (either by accident or in self-defense), Setanta offered to raise a new watchdog and in the meantime, promised to act as the guard dog himself. And thus, as the guard of Culann's home, the little boy began a fresh life as the Hound of Culann a.k.a. Cu Chulainn.

Cu Chulainn was trained by the war goddess Skatha in order that he might prove himself to his would-be wife Emer. Along the way, he defeated and impregnated Aife, another war goddess, leading to the birth of his only child, a son named Connla, whom Cu Chulainn later killed in battle when Connla came looking for his deadbeat dad.

The most significant conflict of the Ulster Cycle is not the deep personal tragedy of Cu Chulainn killing his only begotten son, though. Rather, it is the story of a cattle raid. Queen Medb of Connacht, was jealous that her husband was one bull richer than her, so she sent her men to steal the much-lauded Brown Bull of Cooley. Cooley was in Ulster, the homeland of Cu Chulainn and, coincidentally, the site of a curse that left all other men in the area writhing on the ground like women in labor any time it was attacked by outside forces. Cu Chulainn alone was not affected by this curse because he did not have a beard and so did not meet the technical specifications of manhood at the time. In a wild and woolly battle, Cu Chulainn took on Medb's forces all by himself and was largely successful, if you don't count the wholesale slaughter of the children of Ulster and the theft of the Brown Bull of Cooley as failures. In the end, even the Brown Bull died and all was for nought, but that in no way demeans the tremendous heroic efforts of Cu Chulainn.

Cu Chulainn would finally meet his match years later when he did battle with the Children of Cailidin. Cailidin was one of Medb's men killed during the Cattle Raid. When Medb learned of Cailidin's death she had his three sons and three daughters sent to wizard school.[1] Cu Chulainn refused to fight them again and again, explaining that he had killed their father as part of a larger battle and that it hadn't been personal and so he had no reason or desire to fight the children. Through their magic, they eventually convinced him to do battle. Though the Morrigan tried to warn him again and again, he nonetheless engaged them and in doing so met his final fate. True fightin' Irish hero that he was, even when his abdomen had been torn open and his guts were dangling in the open air, he strapped himself to a rock so he could remain on his feet and keep fighting even as he died. And as further proof of his badassery, after he died, one of the children of Cailidin cut off his head, causing the lifeless Cu Chulainn to drop his sword which fell and chopped off the arm of his beheader.

Occasionally, when engaged in battle Cu Chulainn would experience a "warp-spasm" that transformed him into a terrifying monster. Kind of like the Incredible Hulk if, rather than turning green, Bruce Banner's hair lit up like sparklers, his bones spun around inside his skin, one of his eyes fell out along his cheek and the other got sucked back into his head, and his mouth opened so wide that you could see his lungs and liver at the back of his throat. In order to be restored to his normal, handsome-in-a-beardless-sort-of-way self; Cu Chulainn had to be dunked in three barrels of cold water by naked women.

Finn McCool

a.k.a.: Fionn mac Cumhaill, Fingal
Pantheon: Celtic (Irish)
Spouse/Lovers: Sadhbh
Parents: Muirne and Cumhall
Offspring: Oisin

---

[1] They were all House Slytherin, in case you're wondering.

"Finn McCool" by Ashley Campos

A supremely Celtic figure with a name that launched a thousand Irish pubs, Finn McCool has echoes of both Beowulf and Arthurian legend with a bit of Paul Bunyan tossed in for good measure.

Born of two star-crossed lovers, Finn's very conception led to a civil war. Raised by druids and war goddesses, once Finn was of an age, he traveled the world (or probably just Ireland) and studied under a variety of teachers. Most notable was the druid Finnegas who spent seven long years trying to catch a fish. Not just any fish, of course, but the legendary Salmon of Knowledge. After finally nabbing it, Finnegas asked his student Finn to cook the Salmon for him, being very clear that Finn was not to eat any of it. Finn listened and tried to obey, but as he was cooking a tiny droplet of fish grease spattered and landed on his thumb. To ease the pain, Finn stuck his thumb into his mouth and that one tiny speck of fish oil was enough to transfer the boundless knowledge of the Salmon of Knowledge into Finn. From that point forward, any time Finn was confronted with a puzzle or problem all he needed to do to access his vast wisdom was suck his thumb. A truly heroic pose if ever there was one.

The thumb-sucker went on to become the leader of his father's tribe, the Fianna. He did this by killing a Grendel-like monster who had a habit of inducing sleep in, and then killing all the Fianna men every twenty-three years. Finn kept himself awake by cleverly poking himself with a spear and then using that same spear to shish kabob the monster.

The great and tragic love of Finn's life was a woman named Sadhbh[1] whom Finn met while out hunting. And, as with many great love stories, Finn's courtship of Sadhbh began with him nearly killing her. At the time, Sadhbh had been transformed into a deer and, as he was hunting deer, Finn was ready to take the kill shot when his hunting dogs stopped him. His hunting dogs had also once been human and so they recognized the human soul within the doe and somehow communicated that to Finn. When Finn brought the deer home, she became a human woman and so they married. Tragically, one day when Finn was out, Sadhbh was tricked into leaving the Fianna encampment and instantly transformed back into a deer. To make matters worse, she was pregnant with Finn's only child at the time. Finn and Sadhbh would never see each other again. Sometime later a baby was found in the wilderness who turned out to be Finn's son whom he named Oisin or "Little Fawn." Oisin, as these things often go, would be the poet credited with first telling the tale of Finn.

---

[1] Rhymes with "five" because in Celtic languages sometimes the letters used are not actually indicative of how to pronounce a word.

Later in life, Finn took a decidedly Arthurian turn. As an aging king, Finn was promised Grainne, a beautiful young woman, to be his wife. He sent Diarmuid, one of his best men, to go pick her up and bring her to Finn. Just as Lancelot and Guinevere fell in love, so too did Diarmuid and Grainne. Eventually Finn forgave the couple and they lived happily ever after. Until, that is, Finn 'accidentally' let Diarmuid die from a hunting injury.

There is no single narrative of the death of Finn McCool but there are various allusions to possible endings to Finn's tale. He may have drowned, he may have been killed by his own men, or, once again echoing Arthur, Finn may simply be sleeping in a magical land and when his people need him most he will return and defend them. For Arthur, it was the island of Avalon. For Finn, it is a cave deep below Dublin. Either way, if neither the Blitz, Brexit nor the Potato Famine was enough to awaken either of these men, it is hard to imagine what the English or Irish will have to endure before their heroes step in.

There is also a rich tradition that depicts Finn McCool as a giant. These Finn the Giant stories are generally played for comedy and have the trappings of folk tale rather than myth. As Paul Bunyan accidentally carved out the Grand Canyon, Finn created "The Giant's Causeway," a chain of small islands connecting Ireland to Scotland -- for anyone with a large enough stride to walk across them. There's also a story where Finn scared away a rival giant by dressing up as a baby, which may or may not be a subtle joke about Finn's penchant for thumb-sucking.

Brigid

a.k.a.: Brigit, Brighid, Brigind, Breo Saighead, Brigantia, Ffraid
Pantheon: Celtic (Irish)
Spouse/Lovers: Bres, Tuireann
Siblings: Cermait, Aengus, Midir, Bodb Derg
Parents: Danu (or another unidentified goddess) and the Dagda
Offspring: Ruadan, Creidne, Luchtaine, Giobhniu
Deity of: fire, poetry, the hearth, the forge, fertility, healing, childbirth
Symbols: fire

The goddess Brigid and the Catholic St. Brigit are interwoven in a veritable Celtic Knot. Possibly the finest example of syncretization in the Celtic world, Brigid began as a triplicate pagan goddess and ended up as an Irish Catholic saint.

"Brigid" by Mallory Heiges

The Celtic Brigid was a member of the Tuatha de Danann. Her father was the Dagda and her mother may be the titular mother of the Tuatha, the goddess Danu. Of course, that is if she is not actually just another form of Danu herself. What we do know for sure is that she was a member of the Tuatha de Danann. Or three of them. Brigid may have been the collective name of three sisters, or the name of one of three sisters. She seems to have, at the very least, three jobs: that of poet, keeper of the hearth, and goddess of the forge. All three roles are associated with flames[1], a facet that carried over into her Christianized form.

The real drama in the tale of Brigid began when she married the handsome Bres. Bres became king of the Tuatha de Danann after Nuada was forced to abdicate his throne because he lost his arm in battle. Bres ruled the Tuatha as a selfish and cruel king. It is surprising to find the much-beloved Brigid as the wife of such a malignant man, but his fall from power may hint at whose side Brigid was really on. You see, Bres was forced to step down from the throne because a satirical poem made him the laughing stock of his people.[2] Did Brigid lend her flame of inspiration to the poet who ended her husband's abusive reign?

After Bres' fall, he went to his mother for answers about his parentage. She informed Bres that, much to her embarrassment, her baby daddy was one of the monsters of the deep and dark, the Fomorians. Bres joined with his paternal family and the Fomorians raised up an army to destroy the Tuatha de Danann. Tragically for Brigid, her son Ruadan fought and died on the side of the Fomorians. The loss hit her so hard that she invented a new form of mourning called *keening* which is a combination of crying and singing. The mythic Banshees of Ireland eventually made keening infamous, but it was Brigid who invented it.

According to Roman sources, Brigid may have been known as Brigantia to the Celts of mainland Europe. The Romans called her Minerva because they were great anthropologists who cared deeply about portraying their enemy's culture with understanding and respect. But not really. They played it pretty fast and loose with the way they connected Celtic deities with the Roman ones. Lugh, for example, was called Mercury because, um, they were both gods of diverse talents. Vesta, the goddess of the hearth is a closer parallel to one of three aspects of Brigid, but ultimately it is a gross over-simplification to try to lump deities of one culture into categories created by another culture.

Speaking of people who were totally respectful of others' religions: Christianity eventually made its way to Ireland. The older, pagan gods were driven

---

[1] The "flame of inspiration" for her poetic aspect.
[2] If only it were still that easy.

out of Ireland like so many snakes. It was only after the influx of Christianity that the most significant accounts of Irish Celtic myths were written down and those versions were burdened with a thick Christian lens. One early Christian leader in Ireland was a woman named Brigit, who may have been a priestess of the pagan Brigid in the pre-Christian era. She eventually became St. Brigit and was associated with healing and was regarded as the keeper of the flame. Whether St. Brigit was based on a real historical figure or was simply a Christian attempt to hold on to the popular Celtic goddess in a gospel-friendly form, we may never know for certain. What we do know is that Brigid, in one form or another, was a fan favorite in the Celtic world and the later St. Brigit, who is associated with many of the same images and deeds, is now regarded as one of the three great saints of Irish history. Coincidence? Possibly. Syncretization? Almost certainly.

"Among Giants" by David Manderville

179

Norse Mythology

It is possible that the Norse mythology of the Viking Age was quite different from what we have today. The received form of Scandinavian myths was written down hundreds of years after Christianity had become the religion of the land. While there was clearly a rich oral tradition that kept these stories being passed down even after the shift in religion, we cannot say for certain what details, be they great or small, may have been changed in the process. The written sources that we do have are mostly from two categories: Sagas and Eddas. The Sagas tell stories of historical and pseudo-historical heroic figures like Egil Skallagrimmson, Ragnar Lothbrok, Fafnir, and others. They are not strictly mythic, but do contain numerous references to the Norse gods and their activities. The most direct mythic sources for the Norse are the Eddas.

What is an Edda? We don't actually know what the term "edda" originally meant. Possible explanations are that it refers to Oddi, the Icelandic location where some of their contents may have been written down, or that it meant "grandmother" and thus contextually means something like "The Stories of Grandmother." That could be a bit like "Mother Goose" or simply an acknowledgement that these stories belong to older generations. Whatever it means, the only two things to bear the label of "edda" are the *Poetic Edda* and the *Prose Edda*.

The Poetic Edda is a collection of poems about the gods and heroes of Norse myth. There are two manuscripts from 13th century Iceland which generate the composite text of most modern translations. One is called the *Codex Regius* (King's Book) and the other is known as AM 748 (because it is found in the manuscript numbered 748 in the Arnamagnaen Collection). The organization of the two manuscripts is different, with *Codex Regius* featuring more poems in a deliberate order, whereas AM 748 is shorter and seemingly ordered at random. It does, however, feature some poems not found in the *Codex Regius*, most notably *Baldrs draumar* ("Balder's Dream").

The poems in the *Poetic Edda* were set to vellum[1] in the 13th century, but most (if not all of them) were likely composed much earlier. The Scandinavian poets (or *skalds*) who did the composing are largely lost to history because, of course, their

---

[1] Paper wouldn't come into use until later and, if we're being honest, writing on calfskin is way more 'Viking' than tree pulp ever could be.

craft was presented and passed down orally. Because they weren't set down in ink until after the Norse world turned Christian, we will never know how close to the original versions of the poems the received forms are.

The *Poetic Edda* is also referred to as *The Elder Edda* or *Saemund's Edda*. Calling it "elder" is accurate to the extent that when the other *Edda* (Snorri Sturluson's *Prose Edda*) was composed, the poems of the *Poetic Edda* already existed, but as far as the written forms are concerned it is Snorri's that is the elder. As for the label of *Saemund's Edda*, that's simply wrong. Saemund the Wise was a notable fellow from Icelandic history but nothing at all connects him to the composition of the *Poetic Edda*. Apparently, at some point in the late Middle Ages, someone found the name of Saemund and decided that since he was reputed for his wisdom and was from Iceland, he was probably the guy who wrote these poems.

The poems of the *Poetic Edda* that are primarily focused on stories of the gods, rather than of legendary heroes, include: *Voluspa* ("The Wise Woman's Prophecy"), *Havamal* ("Words of the High One"), *Vafthruthnismal* ("Ballad of Vafthruthnir"), *Grimnismal* ("Ballad of Grimnir"), *For Skirnis* ("The Ballad of Skirnir"), *Harbarthsljoth* ("The Poem of Harbarth"), *Hymiskvitha* ("The Lay of Hymir"), *Lokasenna* ("Loki's Wrangling"), *Thrymskvitha* ("The Lay of Thrym"), *Alvissmal* ("The Ballad of Alvis"), *Baldrs draumar* ("Balder's Dreams"), *Rigsthula* ("The Song of Rig"), and *Voluspa en Skamma* ("The Short Prophecy of the Wise Woman").

The *Prose Edda* is the most important written source for Norse mythology. Written by Snorri Sturluson in the early 13th Century, it quotes heavily from earlier skaldic poems, including some that are not otherwise preserved. It also includes a few stories that don't show up in any other sources.

Snorri Sturluson came from one of the wealthiest and most powerful families in Iceland. He was twice elected Law Speaker (the highest office in Iceland at the time) before making major political missteps that led both to Iceland falling under Norwegian rule and Snorri himself falling before a Norwegian blade. More importantly, though, he was a great big fat fella who liked to hang out in his hot tub reading and writing about mythology.[1]

There is some debate as to just how much of the *Prose Edda* (also called the *Younger Edda* or *Snorri's Edda*) Snorri wrote, but as his name is the only one connected to it since early on, and other examples of Snorri's writing are extant, I'm just going to err on the side of crediting him with too much. He knew the

---

[1] #Goals.

older skaldic poems, quoted and referenced them often, but the structure and compilation is all Snorri's.

The Prose Edda is broken into four sections: the prologue, *Gylfaginning*, *Skaldskaparmal*, and *Hattatal*. The latter does not include any mythic material and is therefore often omitted in modern publications.

The Prologue offers a Euhemeristic explanation for Norse myth. In a nut shell, Snorri (writing in the Christianized Iceland) explains that, years and years ago, there was a warrior of Troy named Tor (possibly even the *Iliad's* Hec*tor*) who saved a bunch of people from the fall of Troy and became a hero to his people. After his death, his legend grew to where his descendants would call upon him when going into battle. Generations later, there came a new leader named Odin who led the people from Turkey (part of Asia, in Snorri's reckoning) up into the Scandinavian lands. From there, the legend of the Asian (Aesir) warriors expanded and they came to be worshipped as gods. Of course, Snorri points out, we know that there is only one real god and these are just the tales of our pagan ancestors (subtext: "please don't kill me for being a heretic"). The historical evidence for this idea is scant (read: non-existent), but it was a good way for Snorri to cover his ass.

Gylfaginning includes the entire arc of Norse mythology from creation all the way to the world-ending battle known as Ragnarok. The framing of *Gylfaginning* ("The Deluding of Gylfi") is the Norwegian king, Gylfi, attempting to learn about the Aesir people by talking to three kings named High, Just-as-High, and Third— all three of which happen to be part of an elaborate illusion crafted by the top god Odin. Gylfi asks questions about history, the gods, and the future and the disguised Odin answers him. This section of the *Prose Edda* provides us with most of the real meat of Norse myth in a fairly concise package.

Skaldskaparmal ("The Language of Poetry") gives further myths, mostly those involved with the creation of poetry or explanations for mythic references made in other Norse literature.

The content of *Snorri's Edda* is second to none when it comes to our understanding of Norse myth. And, quite possibly the reason that the other most significant collection of Norse myths, *The Poetic Edda*, was ever set down was because of renewed interest generated by Snorri's work. It's even possible that Snorri served as editor for the thing we call *The Poetic Edda*. However you slice it, without Snorri Sturluson's work, we would have significantly less information about Norse myth, if any at all.

One of the most idiosyncratic aspects of Norse literature is the use of *kennings*. Possibly a term coined by dear old Snorri himself, a kenning is a poetic phrase used in conjunction with or in place of the common name. For example, one kenning for the sea would be the phrase "the whale road." The sun is "the sky candle." Arrows are "war-needles." Those are all examples of simple kennings and simple kennings are generally easy to work out and can be delightfully clever. Kennings can get much more complex and at times in Norse literature you will encounter long strings of kennings piled on top of other kennings until the actual meaning is so obscured that by the time you suss it all out you'll find that it was not really worth the effort. But, because kennings are used so prolifically and are uniquely Norse, I have included *some* of the kennings used for each of the characters profiled herein.

"Yggdrasil" by Zhangrui Zhou

Yggdrasil

a.k.a.: World Tree, World Ash, "Mount of Ygg"
Pantheon: Norse

Yggdrasil is the Norse World Tree. Generally thought to be an ash tree, Yggdrasil is at the center of the nine worlds and is "the holy place of the gods." It has three roots: one that goes to the Well of Mimir, one that goes to the Well of Urd, and one that goes to the Well of Hvergelmir. The Well of Mimir is owned by the wise Mimir who allowed Odin to have a drink for the price of one of his eyes. The Well of Urd (Fate) is where the gods make their final judgments and the Well of Hvergelmir is occupied by a dragon who gnaws on the root. That all sounds more or less straightforward, but it becomes much less so when you account for the fact that Hvergelmir is said to be in Niflheim, Mimir is said to be in the home of frost giants (which is generally identified as Niflheim), and Urd is in "heaven" (presumably Asgard). Most depictions of the Norse cosmology put Asgard in the upper branches of Yggdrasil, which even your most inexperienced of arborists would recognize as a lousy place to put a root. The written sources don't give us much more as far as a map of the World Tree goes, but they are quite clear on one thing: there are nine worlds. What they aren't clear on is what those nine worlds are.

The most commonly identified worlds that adorn Yggdrasil are: Asgard (home of the Aesir), Vanaheim (home of the Vanir), Midgard ("Middle Earth," home of us), Niflheim (dark and icy primordial world), Muspelheim (hot and fiery primordial world), Jotunheim (home of Jotun), Alfheim (home of elves), Helheim (dark and icy home of the dead), and Svartalfarheim (home of dark elves). But this list is far from consistent. There's also Utgard/ Utangard (which may be the same as Jotunheim or a catch-all term for the outskirts), Niflhel (which combines the virtually identical worlds of Helheim and Niflheim), and Nidavellir and Nithafjoll (both of which are identified as the home of dwarves). Given that Svartalfar ("Dark Elves") do not appear in Norse myth at all, and that the only time Svartalfarheim is referenced it is as the home of dwarves, we may be safe in assuming that "dark elf" and "dwarf" are synonymous and possibly that

Svartalfarheim, Nidavellir, and Nithafjoll are identical as well, which then leaves us with a list of nine worlds that is one world short.[1]

Other than the frustratingly inconsistent nine worlds held together by Yggdrasil, the World Ash is also home to a menagerie of beasties. In the upper branches, Snorri tells us, is an eagle who has a hawk named Vedrfolnir sitting between his eyes. The unnamed eagle apparently serves no purpose but to give the hawk a unique setting for his home. Vedrfolnir creates wind by flapping his wings—why there are two birds instead of just one is unclear but may simply be explained by a mistranslation or misunderstanding somewhere along the route from oral to written tradition. Elsewhere in the branches are four stags who live off the tree's foliage. Down at the bottom is the dragon, Nithhogg, gnawing on the root(s). His name is Nithhogg and he apparently nibbles on corpses in Helheim as well. Finally, Yggdrasil is home to a squirrel named Ratatosk who spends his time acting as an insult courier, running up and down the tree between Vedrfolnir and Nithhogg.

Yggdrasil literally means "Ygg's Mount" or "The Steed of Ygg" which is a direct reference to the story of Odin (Ygg being one of his many other names) being hanged from the World Tree for a span of nine days so that he could learn powerful runic spells.

Aesir & Vanir

Pantheon: Norse

In Norse myth, there are two distinct groups that are identified as "gods." One is the *Aesir* which includes characters like Odin, Thor, and Loki.[2] The second is the *Vanir* whose most prominent members are Njord, Freyr, and Freyja.

Mythologically speaking, there was a war between these two factions of gods. The exact whys and wherefores are mostly absent from the recorded myths, but we do know that there was a conflict between the two camps. The poem *Voluspa* tells us of the first war which was triggered by an enchanting goddess identified as both Gollveig and Heith[3] entering the world of the Aesir. She used some kind of evil or dirty magic and was thrice burned to death for it. What happened after that

---

[1] (1) Asgard; (2) Vanaheim; (3) Midgard; (4) Niflhel/Helheim/Niflheim; (5) Muspelheim; (6) Jotunheim/Utgard; (7) Alfheim; (8) Svartalfarheim/Nidavellir/Nithafjoll; (9) ?
[2] Kind of.
[3] Both of whom might simply be names for Freyja.

"A Peaceful Resolution" by Clayton Prell

187

is mostly lost to the ages; the crucial lines between the start of the war and the rebuilding effort afterward are not included in any extant Eddic source. What we do know is that neither group succeeded in wiping out or conquering the other so a peace was forged through a deity exchange program. The Aesir gave the Vanir the strong, well-meaning but generally not very bright Hoenir and the super-wise Mimir. The Vanir handed over their best and brightest: Njord, Freyr, and Freyja. The foreign gods assimilate into the Aesir well and became some of the most beloved and powerful gods of Asgard. The rest of the Vanir exist only in the foggy periphery, unnamed, and undiscussed for the rest of the mythic cycle.

Why two groups of gods? The belief amongst scholars is that the myth of a conflict between two groups of gods with a peaceful resolution via a swapping of deities probably reflects some actual culture clash. Two civilizations, one that worshipped the Vanir gods and one that worshipped the Aesir gods, interacted with each other and ultimately, rather than one wiping out the other, they came together. Clearly the Aesir group was the more dominant (or at the very least their traditions held out longer) but they welcomed in some of the most important gods of the Vanir as a way of forging peace. The exact nature of the clash between the groups, and which parts of which myths were original to which culture, is not known, but a historical merging of cultures seems a reasonable explanation for the presence of the two groups of gods.

There was a secondary way the two groups solidified peace that Snorri tells us about in his *Skaldskaparmal*. After the Aesir and Vanir held a meeting, they wanted to have some physical representation of their treaty and so they all spat into the same pot. Then they took the spit of all the gods and formed it into a man. Kvasir was his name and he was filled with the collective wisdom of all the gods. After traveling throughout the worlds for a time, Kvasir ran into a couple of dwarfs who wanted his knowledge for themselves. They killed him, collected his blood, and mixed it with mead. When the gods came looking for Kvasir the dwarfs told them that he had literally "choked on his own wisdom" because there was no one around to ask him smart enough questions. Points to the dwarfs for being creative. Eventually the blood-mead was taken by a Jotun named Suttung and later, Odin managed to steal it from him by sleeping with Suttung's daughter Gunnlod. He escaped by turning into a snake and then a bird and flew back to Asgard with the mead carefully hidden in his own belly. When Suttung pursued him, Odin vomited up the mead into several Asgardian vats and then blew the rest out of his butt to throw Suttung off the scent. The barrels full of Odin vomit are the source of a particular form of wisdom: poetry. The mead that Odin shot out of his ass is the source of bad poetry. So next time you go to a poetry slam, you can tell the bad poets that their breath smells of Odin shit and congratulate the good poets on having drank an extra helping of Odin vomit.

Odin

a.k.a.: Odin, Othin, Wotan, Woden, Hropt, Ygg

Pantheon: Norse

Spouse/Lovers: Frigg, Grid, Jord, Rind, Billing's Daughter

Siblings: Ve, Vili, Lodur, Hoenir

Parents: Bestla and Bor

Offspring: Balder, Hermod, Thor, Vali, Vidar, Hod

Deity of: death, battle, wisdom, gallows, magic, poetry

Symbols: ravens, wolves, spear, one eye, ash tree

Kennings: All-Father, Valfather, Old One, Father of Victory, Delight of Frigg, Lord of the Aesir, Friend of Wealth, Blind, Bor's Son, Journey Empowerer, Gallow's Burden, Wise One, Father of Magical Songs, Wanderer, Dangler, Riddler, Hooded One, God of the Hanged, Grey Beard, Father of Hosts, War-Merry, One Eyed, Raven God, Horse Hair Moustache, Yule Father, Long Beard, Red Moustache, God of Runes, Broad Hat, Slain God, Terrible One, Flame Eye, Wavering Eye, etc.

To know Odin is to know Norse mythology. While Loki may be the most dynamic figure, and Thor the most heroic, Odin is the icy grey heart of the Nordic pantheon. He embodies the themes of wisdom, sacrifice, and the impending doom of all. Odin appears as one of the central figures and/or as the titular character of six poems (which is more than any other god) in the collection we call the *Poetic Edda*. Thor is a central figure in four poems[1], and Loki takes center stage only in one. *Voluspa, Vafthruthnismal, Grimnismal,* and *Baldrs draumar* are all structured

---

[1] One of which, *Harbarthsljoth* is a verbal sparring between Thor and Odin and is named for the guise of Harbarth ("Grey Beard") that Odin adopts. Another of the Thor-centric poems is the nearly incomprehensible *Alvissmal* wherein Thor plays at being Odin and sets his wits against those of the dwarf Alvis ("All-Wise"). The two remaining Thor poems include him dressing in drag and him going fishing – both highly entertaining, but ultimately not worth much more than that.

"Odin" by Amanda Zylstra

around Odin proving his wisdom or forcing others to try to prove their own. The Norse answer to the Biblical book of *Proverbs* is called the *Havamal* ("The Counsel of Odin") and contains not only practical advice ('always check for enemies when entering a room,' 'don't trust women,' 'don't trust men' etc.) but also some truly poetic and inspirational sentiments and, conversely, some rather upsetting stories of Odin's love life. He's no Zeus, but Odin has his share of 'romantic' (read: rapacious) dalliances.

A great deal of Odin's character and story can be gleaned from the various names or *kennings* used to denote him. Snorri Sturluson tells us in the *Gylfaginning* that Odin has twelve names, but within the rest of the text of his *Prose Edda* and in the *Poetic Edda* (to say nothing of innumerable sagas and other Norse texts), he is given many more names beyond that. A handful of them refer to his prowess in battle[1], others describe his physical appearance[2], a few refer to how loud he is[3], many attest to his predilection for deception and disguises[4], and still others speak of his wisdom[5].

Odin was not simply born with his vast wisdom. He had to work to get it. One of the ways he did so was by sacrificing himself by hanging from the World Tree, Yggdrasil, for nine days—which is referenced in many of his names, including Vofudr ("Dangler"), Vingnir ("Swinger"), and Hangi ("Hanged One"). Conversely, the World Tree itself gets its name from this same incident—Ygg ("Terrible One") is a name for Odin and Yggdrasil means "the mount of Ygg" or more loosely, "the steed of Odin." Odin 'rode' the World Tree and thus it is called Yggdrasil. Hanging from a tree for nine days was not the only way Odin gained knowledge—aside from picking the brains of wise dead people, Odin was taught eight spells by his maternal uncle (whose name and any actual story about this event are now lost), he stole poetry (i.e. wisdom) from a Jotun by seducing his daughter and, perhaps most crucially, Odin sacrificed one of his eyes to obtain a drink from the Well of Knowledge. Losing an eye would be difficult for most anyone, but imagine how debilitating it would be for a warrior to be strutting

---

[1] Including: Atridi ("Attacking Rider"), Biflindi ("Spear Shaker"), Geirvaldr ("Gore Master"), Herjan ("Warrior"), Vidur ("Killer"), etc.

[2] Including: Harbard ("Grey Beard"), Langbarthr ("Long Beard"), Rauthgrani ("Red Mustache"), Sidhott ("Broad Hat"), Hrossharsgrani ("Horse hair moustache"), etc.

[3] Including: Gollnir ("Yeller"), Hjarrandi ("Screamer"), Hrjothr ("Roarer"), etc.

[4] Including: Skillvaldr ("Ruler of Treachery"), Ginnarr ("Deceiver"), Glapsithr ("Tricker"), Grimr ("Mask"), etc.

[5] Including: Fjolnir ("Wise One"), Gagnrad ("Advantage Counsel"), Haptasnytrir ("Teacher of gods"), etc.

around the field of battle with no depth perception and a spear as his primary weapon. Odin's sacrifices for knowledge are not trivial. All of which shows us just how large a premium Odin, and the Norse people, placed on wisdom.

One of the most popular and important attestations for Odin is Alfodr or "All-father." He is the literal father to key figures like Thor and Balder, he acts as paterfamilias to all the gods, and, because he and his brothers created the first humans, he is a father to all of us. His fatherly duties don't end at birth, nor do they stop at death. Instead, Odin is also called the Valfodr ("Father of the Slain") because he reigns over the dead. The worthy dead (those who die in battle, mostly) are taken up to Valhalla ("The Hall of the Dead") by the Valkyries ("Choosers of the Slain") where they become Einherjar, Odin's army of undead warriors who will fight with him in the final battle. Snorri makes the distinction between the worthy dead and the others who end up in cold, dark, boring Helheim but, it is not necessarily clear that such a distinction existed in Norse minds before or during the Viking Age. But, thanks to Snorri[1], it has become the popular take on the Norse afterlife so I won't quibble.

Odin's legacy lives on in myriad ways. Each Wednesday we acknowledge him (the Romans called him Wotan which is the namesake of the third day of the week), and thanks to Cambridge professor of Norse literature, J.R.R. Tolkien, the popular image of the wise old wizard is dripping with Odinic imagery. From Gandalf (a name which appears in the infamous list of dwarfs in both Eddas) to depictions of Merlin, right down to Dumbledore, we have nods to Odin, his broad hat, grey beard, avian familiars, and walking stick. Another place we find echoes of Odin is in the bushy-bearded, all-seeing, gift-giving visitor who is celebrated at the winter solstice: Santa Claus. Even the terms "Yule" and "Yuletide" are derived from Yulnir (or Jolnir), which is yet another kenning for the All-father himself. Add in the fact that he sacrificed himself by hanging from a tree in order to save the world and Odin has strong ties to both primary figures associated with Christmas.

Not everything about Odin's modern legacy is as exciting as wizards, Christmas, and Hump Day. Many modern worshippers of Odin (and yes, there are modern worshippers of Odin) are very nice, well-intentioned people but others

---

[1] Snorri Sturluson himself had a notably inauspicious death. He was killed by forces sent by the King of Norway whom he had unsuccessfully tried to suck up to. They reportedly found him hiding in his cellar and killed him on his knees while he begged for mercy. The poet Jorge Luis Borges immortalized the scene in a brief poem that beautifully encapsulates the bitter irony of Snorri dying with his "insides churning/ [. . .] A shame never to be forgotten."

are, well, Nazis. From xenophobic gangs in Scandinavia who hope to purge their native land of foreigners, to neo-Nazi groups who imagine that lessons of racial purity can be found in skaldic and Eddic verse, there is no shortage of deplorable people in Odin's fan club. Even the OG Nazi movement used Norse gods, symbols, and tales almost as much as they used Christianity to bolster their rhetoric and justify their unjustifiable deeds.

The ancient worship of Odin was often bloody business. Animals and even humans were killed in ritual sacrifice to Odin. Human sacrifice in the name of Odin was not a daily occurrence by any means, but it did happen, especially when his followers were desperate to get his attention. In fact, the bloody nature of Odin worship is probably one of the reasons that many Norse preferred Thor or Freyr as their go-to god.

It is largely thanks to Snorri that Odin is so prominent in our view of Norse myth—as a lover of knowledge and a scholar, Snorri was drawn to the wisdom-seeking tales of the All-father. Thor embodies the axiom that "when all you have is a hammer, all your problems look like nails," and so Snorri mostly employs him as a blunt instrument to crush enemies, or as a joke. Odin, on the other hand, provides the framework of the *Gylfaginning* and is discussed at length and with a degree of reverence and awe by Snorri.

Of course, a discussion of Odin would be incomplete without mentioning his inevitable doom. His fate is no secret and is, as you might have guessed, referenced in several kennings. Whether he is called Bagi ulfs, or Vadi vitnis, he is the "enemy of the wolf"—namely Fenrir, the enormous canine spawn of Loki. In the final battle of Ragnarok, the Valfodr himself will ride into battle wielding his peerless spear Gungnir atop his eight-legged horse Sleipnir and will very quickly be eaten by a great big doggy. A fate more befitting a bowl of Kibbles & Bits than the All-Father, Odin's death will not be terribly auspicious, but it is a very important part of the trajectory of Norse myth. Odin, as well as Thor, Loki, Freyr, and nearly everyone else, will die in the battle of Ragnarok. But that is not the end of the story.

After Yggdrasil itself has burned up and fallen away, a new world will emerge. This new world will be a place of peace, beauty, and reconciliation—such a world has no room for the Smith of Battle, Ruler of Treachery, or Inciter. Odin's time will have ended and the new world will be ruled over by the Quarrel Breaker, Odin's beloved son Balder. Odin and his ilk must die for the new world to be perfected. Being consumed by Fenrir is the ultimate sacrifice Odin will make to provide a better world for his children.

"Thor" by Clayton Prell

Thor

a.k.a.: Þor, Tor, Asa-Thor, Hlorridi

Pantheon: Norse

Spouse/Lovers: Sif, Jarnsaxa

Siblings: Balder, Hermod, Hod, Meili, Vali, Vidar

Parents: Jord (Earth/Fjorgyn) and Odin

Offspring: Magni, Modi, Thrud, Ull (step-son)

Deity of: thunder, battle

Symbols: Mjolnir (hammer), goats

Kennings: Thunderer, Hurler, Warder of Earth, Foe of the Midgard Serpent, Redbeard, Destroyer of Trolls, Mjolnir's Wielder, Wyrm Bane, Slayer of Giants, Skull Splitter of Hrungnir, Lord of Goats, Whetstone Skulled, Lone Rider, Meili's Brother, etc.

While Thor may be one of the best known mythic figures in pop culture today, the traditional Norse version of the thunder god is a bit different from the super-hero one. Rather than a handsome, super-buff dude with long blonde hair, the old school Thor is a ginger with a big, bushy beard, who dresses like a vagrant and smells of goat pee. Despite the differences, the old Norse Thor is also something of a super-hero in his own right.

As Odin sought knowledge and Loki sought whatever it was that Loki wanted at the moment, Thor wanted nothing more than adventure. Driven by a strong, if not particularly nuanced, desire for justice, and a pair of goats named Tanngrisnir ("Gap-Tooth") and Tanngnjostr ("Tooth-Grinder"), Thor ventured into the east[1]. He crushed Jotun's heads and maidenheads, and returned to Asgard to brag to the gods and Einherjar about his conquests. All the while, he defied the axiom by speaking loudly and carrying a small hammer.

The stubby-handled Mjolnir is Thor's weapon of choice and there is no distance it can be thrown that it won't return to the hand of the Hurler. Except, of course, when it was somehow stolen by the Jotun Thrym. *Thrymskvitha* is a rare and riotous narrative poem that tells of the lengths Thor was willing to go to to retrieve his precious hammer. Upon waking and finding Mjolnir absent, Thor

---

[1] East, for the skalds who told the tales, represented the vast, untamed wildlands of what we now call Russia. Viking explorers made their way to Russia, established trade with the Russians and the Rusk Vikings may in fact be the source of the word "Russia."

raised Hel in Asgard, demanding the gods help him find it. While Freyr searched his pockets and Tyr looked behind the couch cushions, Loki borrowed Freyja's cloak so that he could turn into a bird and scout the other eight worlds. He tracked down a self-satisfied Jotun named Thrym, who happily admitted to stealing the hammer and burrying it eight miles deep.[1] He informed Loki that he would only return the hammer if he could marry the goddess Freyja. However, Freyja was all too familiar with being used as a bargaining chip in disputes with Jotun and thus she refused to be sold for a hammer. Strangely, it was not the crafty Loki or even the wise Odin who came up with a solution, but the ever-watchful Heimdall who suggested a plot that would impress Odysseus and RuPaul alike. Days later, Loki, disguised as a handmaiden, rode up to Thrym's home along with a surprisingly bulky-looking Freyja in full wedding garb, veil and all. Thrym had a feast laid out for the nuptials and 'Freyja' sat down and began gobbling down all the food in sight. When Thrym wondered aloud why the dainty Freyja ate like a hungry dog, handmaiden Loki explained that she had been so excited to get married that she hadn't eaten in days. Still suspicious, Thrym asked to see what was under the veil. Loki insisted that that would be a no-no but, Thrym insisted louder. Finally, 'Freyja' agreed to give him a peek at 'her' eyes. Rather than the bewitching eyes of the goddess, Thrym was faced with a pair of bloodshot eyes. "You see," Loki explained, "she has been so excited to get married that she hasn't slept in a week and it is that and not a deep and abiding hatred for you that causes her eyes to look thusly." "Oh, ok," Thrym replied, flattered and eager to get the wedding underway. He called his servants to bring out the bride price: Mjolnir. 'Freyja' snatched it up, tore off her veil, and revealed that it was really just Thor in disguise! And then Thor killed Thrym and all the other Jotun present, including Thrym's elderly sister.

While being pulled around by goats with silly names may not be the sexiest way to get around, Thor's mode of conveyance does offer some advantages. Whenever Thor gets hungry on his journeys, he can kill the goats, skin them, butcher them, cook them, eat them, and then restore them back to life. If the real Viking explorers had an ever-replenishing supply of goat meat, their already impressive coverage of the map may have gone global. Apparently, the only limitation to the regenerating goats is that their bones can't heal themselves. When Thor took up with a peasant family for the night and offered them goat meat as thanks, the unthinking father broke a leg bone to suck the marrow out of it. When

---

[1] Given a depth deeper than the Mariana Trench, I don't suppose we can fault Mjolnir too much for not being able to return to Thor on its own.

Thor restored his goats, one of them was walking with a limp and Thor threatened to kill the man. By way of apology, the man gave him his son Thjalfi to be Thor's slave.

Many of Thor's exploits are more comic relief than comic book action. There is his unfulfilled fishing expedition to snare the Midgard Serpent, or the time he successfully killed a Jotun but ended up trapped with the corpse of said Jotun on top of him and half a whetstone stuck in his head. One tale that Snorri gives us is successful in simultaneously humiliating Thor and reinforcing his amazing prowess. In it, Thor, Loki, and Thjalfi were tricked by the Jotun Skrymir/Utgardaloki[1] into attempting seemingly simple tasks that proved nearly impossible. Thor was told to chug a horn full of drink and after three attempts managed to only guzzle down a tiny amount. Then he was told to pick up a kitten and succeeded in only getting a single paw off the ground. And finally, he wrestled and lost to an old woman. But, as it turns out, the drinking horn was connected to the ocean and Thor had successfully put a dent in the water supply of the entire world, the kitten was really the earth-encircling Midgard Serpent, and the old woman whom Thor almost wrestled to a standstill was Old Age itself. Thor ultimately proved himself more formidable than even the Jotun trickster had imagined.

Thor may not be a terribly deep thinker, but he was always the go-to guy when swift and brutal justice was called for. Not only did he save the day for the gods again and again, but he was also regarded as a savior of humanity. Going back at least three decades, there is not a single reported instance of a human being killed or even injured by a Jotun. Faced with that kind of data, one must admit that Thor is doing a spectacular job of keeping us safe.

---

[1] With a name that equates to "Jotun Trickster" or "Outside Deceiver," it's surprising that Thor, or at least Loki, didn't catch on to the trick earlier.

"Loki" by Ian Sedgwick

Loki

a.k.a.: Lopt, Hvedrung, Lodur (?)
Pantheon: Norse
Spouse/Lovers: Angrboda, Sigyn, Svadilfari
Siblings: Byleist, Helblindi
Parents: Laufey (Nal) and Farbauti
Offspring: Fenrir, Hel, Jormungand, Nari, Vali, Sleipnir
Deity of: fire (?), magic, trickery
Kennings: The Slanderer of the Gods, Source of Deceit, Disgrace of All Gods and Men, Sleipnir's Dam

Popular notions to the contrary, Loki is not the brother of Thor. A more accurate conception, based on the poems collected in the *Poetic Edda*, would be to view Loki as a brother of Odin, at least in bond if not in blood.

In the poem *Voluspa,* one of Odin's brothers and a co-creator of the first humans is identified as Loth (or Lod, Lothur, Lodur), which some scholars think might be another name for Loki. Maybe. It's kind of a stretch but people who know Old Norse languages far better than I do think it might be a thing, so maybe it is. That aside, in the poem *Lokasenna,* which is the finest poetic example of Loki being the antagonist that we imagine him to be, Odin himself says that he has vowed never to take a drink unless Loki is there to drink with him. This reveals an important (if not particularly well-explained) bond between the All-Father and the trickster. For someone who tosses back horns of mead the way Odin does, that's significant.

By most accounts, we can conclude that Loki's parents are Jotun. But that's true of Odin as well, so Jotun parentage doesn't exclude one from being counted among the Aesir gods. Truthfully, if we're to think of Jotun and Aesir in terms of taxonomical identification, they are at most two different races of the same species. They frequently intermarry and interbreed so, if there are biological differences between them, they are very minor. Blood is no barrier to Loki being one of the cool kids.

Most of the stories involving Loki in either Edda put him amongst the gods rather than in opposition to them. Sure, he creates a lot of trouble for them, but it's usually less malicious and his actions are more about saving his own ass. He doesn't try to overthrow Asgard, and he doesn't try to bring down Thor, Odin, or anyone else; he simply makes selfish or short-sighted decisions and then must twist and trick to fix the mess he has wrought. In poems and in *Snorri's Edda,* we repeatedly see Loki as a traveling companion and helper to both Odin and Thor. The only time Loki is linked directly with the Utgard is in accounts of the ultimate battle of Ragnarok. Of course, several of Loki's children are tied to the deaths of the gods, including Jormungand, who will one day kill Thor and Fenrir, who is destined to eat Odin. On the other hand, Loki is the mother[1] to Odin's renowned steed Sleipnir—so there is even ambiguity surrounding Loki's offspring.

In the aforementioned *Lokasenna,* Loki was tossed out of a party because he killed a servant. Apparently, he couldn't bear to hear nice things being said about servants so he killed him. Pretty lousy behavior, but given that Thor and Odin repeatedly brag about 'seducing' (a euphemism that really amounts to nothing more than raping) women, and Freyr won over his wife by having his servant threaten to beat her and make her drink urine, Loki killing a servant is far from

---

[1] You read that correctly. For more on that see *The Children of Loki.*

the worst thing a Norse god does. Still, he was tossed out of the party and then came back itching for a fight. Or a *flyt*—a Norse contest of verbal sparring wherein two men insult each other . . . it's basically a rap battle, if we're being honest. Regardless, Loki returned and then proceeded to insult each of the gods present, right up until Thor showed up and Loki decided he has pressed his luck far enough. The coda of the poem is a brief narrative describing how Loki was then bound and would remain imprisoned until the beginning of Ragnarok.

"Whoa, whoa, whoa!" you say, "I thought Loki killed Balder! Isn't that why he gets chained up? Isn't that a clear, unequivocal example of Loki being in opposition to the gods?" An astute question. And yes, you're right. Kind of. Maybe. Yes, Snorri Sturluson in his *Prose Edda* very clearly says Loki is responsible for the death of Balder, the god of light, reconciliation, and everything else beautiful and good. But, here's the thing: that might just be Snorri's version. Most of the poems, which were written before Snorri's work (though likely not written down or at least collected until after), do not make it explicitly clear that Loki is involved at all. Other than *Lokasenna*, where Loki taunts Frigg by claiming to have been the one who brought about Balder's death, it is never stated. In fact, in *Baldrs draumar*, the poem about the forthcoming death of Balder, it is said that Hod will be his killer and makes no mention of Loki's role. Since *Lokasenna* is generally dated much later than many of the poems it is possible that it and Snorri's depiction of Loki are the result of the influence of Christianity taking over the Norse world.

Snorri was a Christian. Since Iceland was the last Nordic country to go Christian and even it had been Christian for over 150 years before they were written down, presumably whoever compiled the written forms of the *Poetic Edda* was also a Christian. That means that when the main written sources of Norse mythology were set down, it was done by people who didn't really believe them. These were the stories of their pagan ancestors, not their personal, contemporary religious tales. Because Christianity had been the religion of the land for generations before these texts were written down, it is impossible to study them without considering the lens of Christianity. But what does any of that have to do with Loki?

As you may know, Christianity draws much clearer distinctions between good and evil than the skaldic writers of old Norse poems did. Rather than a pantheon of complex beings capable of both moral and immoral actions, Christianity offers an inherently, morally perfect god and an inherently immoral devil. So, the Christian Snorri found (or created) a pagan equivalent of the devil in the figure of Loki. Loki became the architect of Ragnarok. Loki became the deceiver. Loki became the reason for the death of the good god who would return one day to rule over a new, perfected Heaven and Earth.

And so, we have two different yet overlapping versions of Loki. The first is the tricky companion and advisor to the gods who shows up in the earliest versions of the stories. The second is the more malevolent, occasionally violent, and ultimately evil figure who comes to the fore in *Snorri's Edda*. We could also argue that there is now a third form of Loki that we find in popular culture. Thanks to his role as the evil brother of Thor in Marvel Comics and the even more culturally penetrative Marvel Cinematic Universe, audiences are familiar with the handsome, charming Loki driven by a lust for power. Perhaps it is only appropriate that the quintessential trickster figure has proven to be so protean and adaptable to audiences for well over a thousand years.

Children of Loki

Pantheon: Norse
Parents: Angroboda and Loki, Sigyn and Loki, Loki and Svadilfari
Members: Fenrir, Hel, Jormungand, Narfi, Sleipnir, Vali

Loki has six known offspring: Hel, Jormungand, Fenrir, Sleipnir, Narfi, and Vali. None of his offspring are very much like Loki in character or in appearance. A group shot of House Loki looks more like a nightmarish zoo than a traditional family photo.

Narfi and Vali are both the least important and most puzzling figures in the group. Snorri himself cannot be sure if the name is "Narfi" or "Nari" and when it comes to Vali, he (or another equally as forgettable character with the same name) is elsewhere identified as the son of Odin and the otherwise unknown woman named Rind. The only story connected to these mysterious sons of Loki is when Loki is captured after killing Balder[1] and Vali is turned into a wolf so that he can kill and disembowel Narfi (or Nari) so that his intestines can be used to strap down Loki. It's brutal, surprisingly graphic, and really unfair to both Vali and Narfi (or Nari). I'm not sure what crime would justify such treatment for either of them, but possibly there is a lost tradition wherein they do deeply evil things like killing babies or pronouncing the word as "fustrated."

"Loki and the Kids" by Christian Sitterlet

Despite sharing Loki and Angrboda as their father and mother, Hel, Fenrir, and Jormungand are all three different species of monster. Hel, like her parents, is a Jotun, but she's far from a run-of-the-mill giantess. Half of Hel is living and the other half is dead. Sources disagree on whether she is bisected vertically or horizontally. A vertical split makes her more visually interesting (kind of like Batman's nemesis Two-Face) but the horizontal split is stronger symbolically. Her top half is alive but her lower half, the half from which life is normally produced, is rotting and horrific. She is the source of death rather than of life.

Hel, like many other afterlife gods and goddesses, lives in a realm that shares her name. Helheim ("Hel Home") is the dark, dank, cold, and generally boring destination for those not selected to join the ranks of the Einherjar in Valhalla after death. It is either a city within the icy world of Niflheim, a neighbor to Niflheim, or simply the same thing as Niflheim (some sources call it "Niflhel"). It's not a place of torture like Dante's *Inferno*, but there are some corners of Helheim you'd do well to avoid. At the gate, there's the guard dog Garm with his spittle-and-blood-spattered coat and, somewhere near the back, there's Nithhogg, a dragon who munches on corpses. For the most part, Helheim's real charm comes from the psychological torture of knowing that you're missing out on all the fun being had by the Einherjar, and, of course, from the fact that you are now part of the army of the unworthy dead who will fight on behalf of the forces of evil during Ragnarok.

Jormungand is more commonly known as The Midgard Serpent. He spends most of his time at the periphery, acting as the physical border around the distance edge of Midgard. He encircles the world with his serpentine body which is just another example of what the Greek's called the *ouroboros*. The snake forming a circle with his tail in his mouth is a prolific symbol in many cultures in the world and paradoxically represents both the eternal (snakes are often thought to be immortal since they shed their skin and seemingly become young again) and the finite (the snake will one day consume itself). Jormungand appears in a couple of myths where he is a more-or-less accidental adversary of Thor. In one, Thor was tricked by Utgardaloki through an optical illusion to attempt to pick up Jormy who had been disguised as a kitten. In lifting this massive creature even a little bit, Thor caused earthquakes that threatened to rip the world apart. After the ruse had been exposed, Thor vowed revenge not on Utgardaloki, but on the Midgard Serpent. In another apparently very popular myth, Thor went fishing and almost reeled in Jormy before the Jotun Hymir cut him loose. The score left unsettled, Thor and

Jormy will have to wait until Ragnarok to square off again—a battle that will leave both of them dead.

The third child of Loki and Angroboda, Fenrir plays one of the most important roles of anyone in the battle of Ragnarok: he will eat and kill the All-Father himself. And while he grew to be a colossal, god-eating wolf, Fenrir started off as a cute little puppy. When the Aesir caught wind of Loki and Angrboda's horrifying brood being raised in Jotunheim, they broke up the family. Hel was cast away to her namesake realm, and Jormungand was banished to the ends of the earth, but Fenrir was just too gosh-darned adorable for Odin not to bring him home to Asgard. Which raises a thorny question: If Odin knew the future and knew that Fenrir was destined to eat him, why not save himself and take out Fenrir while he was a tiny, easily drown-able pup? Yes, Odin did know his and Fenrir' fate. Yes, Odin was capable of doing way worse things than puppy killing (if such worse things exist). This leaves us with two possible explanations: (A) Odin thought that by taking in the wolf pup he could raise it 'right' and change the future; or (B) Odin knew and accepted his fate, and even took direct action toward ensuring that the prophesied future came to pass. Trying to find motivation for characters in myth is often a frustrating and fruitless pursuit, and certainly there is no real answer to the question but the latter possibility is more thematically sound. The Norse had the word *feigr* which meant something along the lines of "doomed to die" and they often referred to the fated day of one's death with a sense of acceptance. 'If this is the day of my *feigr*, so be it.' With Odin, it isn't a question; he knows the day of his doom and knows either that he cannot or should not try to avoid it. Yes, Fenrir will kill Odin, but then Vidar will kill Fenrir and the death of god and wolf alike will eventually give way to a better, peaceful, post-Ragnarok world. So, ultimately Odin's death is not only fated, but is a good and necessary event. Or maybe Odin just has a soft spot for puppies.

Loki's final child has very little in common with his half-siblings. In fact, he doesn't even have the same father as the others because Loki is his mother. In a culture so driven by masculinity,[2] the fact that Loki was impregnated and gave birth was a real source of embarrassment for him and amusement for everyone else. The whole circumstance was the result of Loki's cleverness getting the better of him. Under Loki's advice, the Aesir had agreed to pay a man the sun, the moon, and the goddess Freyja in exchange for him building a wall around Asgard. Loki argued that if they set certain restrictions on the builder, he would never be able to complete the wall by the due date and, thus, they wouldn't have to pay him anything but they would get a chunk of wall built for free. However, as the deadline approached, the gods couldn't help but notice that the work was nearing completion. They let Loki know that he would be held personally responsible if the builder finished the wall and had to be paid the sun, the moon, and Freyja. Knowing that the threat on his life was one promise the gods would happily keep, Loki took drastic action to prevent the completion of the wall. In an effort to distract the builder's horse from hauling the construction material up to Asgard, Loki took the form of a sexy lady horse and coaxed the male horse into abandoning his work to go and play. His horse busily making the beast with two backs, the builder was unable to finish the wall and revealed his true identity as an angry Jotun. In no time flat, Thor crushed the head of the Jotun, and the Aesir ended up having their fortifying wall built pro bono. Meanwhile, Loki dropped off the map only to re-emerge a year or so later with his newborn offspring: an eight-legged horse named Sleipnir. He presented the octo-horse to Odin, and Sleipnir came to be known as the fastest and finest of all horses.

While none of his offspring seem to have inherited the dynamism of Loki, many of them become incredibly influential figures in the overarching story of Norse myth. Without Loki and his kin, the events of Ragnarok would play out very differently, if indeed Ragnarok would even occur at all without Loki at the helm and his children joining the fray.

Freyja

a.k.a.: Freya, Gefn, Horn, Mardoll, Syr
Pantheon: Norse
Spouse/Lovers: Od, Freyr, Dvalinn, Alfrik, Berling, Grer
Siblings: Freyr
Parents: ? and Njord
Offspring: Hnoss, Gersemi
Deity of: fertility, death, love, battle
Symbols: Brisingamen (necklace), Valkyries, cats, birds
Kennings: Od's Girl, Owner of Cats, Owner of Brisingamen, Flax, Sister of Freyr

Freyja is one of the most powerful and popular goddesses of the Norse. Originally of the Vanir tribe of gods, Freyja was traded to the Aesir along with her brother and father as part of the peace treaty between the two pantheons. None of the

"Freyja" by Amanda Zylstra

full-blooded Aesir goddesses come anywhere near Freyja in terms of prominence. In fact, many of the minor goddesses that are referenced in the literature are believed to be little more than additional names for Freyja herself. Just as Odin has a bevy of names, so too might Freyja. Some even argue that Odin's wife Frigg is just another facet of Freyja.

Freyja may also have been the spark that started the very first war in Norse myth. According to the Eddic poem *Voluspa*, a goddess showed up in Asgard who possessed some type of depraved magic. In bewitching many of the men she roused their anger and, as one does when one finds a witch, they burned her alive. But she didn't die. Three times they burned her and still she survived. At that point, *Voluspa* gets a bit sketchy and there seems to be a stanza or ten missing from the extant form of the text, because it suddenly shifts from the build-up to a war to the rebuilding that took place after the war. The mysterious goddess was called Gollveig ("Gold-Might") when she first appeared, and then after attempting to kill her several times the Aesir named her Heith ("Shining One")—since neither name appears again and because they carry distinct echoes of many kennings associated with her, it is generally believed that this character is none other than Freyja herself.

Combining beauty and power, love and death, Freyja is a complex figure. Because of her exemplary beauty, many stories in the received mythology involve various men trying to wed or bed her. When the builder arrived in Asgard and offered to rebuild the wall around the city, the price he asked was the sun, the moon, and Freyja. When Thor's hammer was stolen, the Jotun Thrym said he would give it back only if he could have Freyja's hand in marriage. Four dwarfs (Dvalinn, Alfrik, Berling, and Grer) crafted a necklace of unparalleled beauty and offered it to Freyja if she slept with each of them. Both the wall builder and Thrym ended up getting their skulls caved in by Thor, whereas Dvalinn, Alfrik, Berling, and Grer were paid in full and Freyja was given the Brisingamen necklace. It is a bit refreshing to see a sexually liberated goddess who isn't judged or diminished because of her sexual liaisons.[1] Interestingly enough, Freyja had a husband, but he never seemed to be around. While many were vying for a chance to marry Freyja, the one person who did marry her, (a rarely referenced god called Od) was constantly going off on long trips and possibly even abandoned Freyja altogether.

---

[1] In the poem *Lokasenna,* Loki does scold Freyja for her sexual dalliances, alluding to a time when the gods discovered Freyja in a coital embrace with her own brother. When they were discovered, Freyja was reportedly so embarrassed that it caused her to fart. She isn't the only one that Loki lobs these types of insults at, however. Loki 'slut shames' every woman present including Idunn, Gefjun, Frigg, Skadi, Sif, Beyla, and Freyja. Aside from Loki's attacks, there is no extant myth involving sexual misdeeds by any of these women.

Ultimately, Norse myth is one big build-up to the events of Ragnarok and Freyja has one of the most important parts to play. When Norse warriors died in battle, the Valkyries would whisk them off to Valhalla where they joined the ranks of the Einherjar and had daily battles in preparation for the battle of Ragnarok. By necessity, there were a lot of Einherjar, far too many, in fact, for Odin to oversee them all. It is Freyja, both a foreigner and a female, who is given command of a full half of Asgard's undead army. This is not a job tossed about casually—the fact that it is Freyja's job suggests that she is not only a superlative combatant in her own right, but also has what it takes to lead. Thor is unquestionably powerful and he will play a very important role in the last battle, but he's not a commander. Only Odin and Freyja (as the Lafayette[1] to Odin's Washington) have the military brilliance to lead the charge against the combined forces of evil.

Many of the Norse gods have companion animals. Freyja's brother Freyr has a golden boar, Odin has his ravens and wolves, and Thor has goats. Freyja has a chariot pulled by cats. Not just regular domestic house cats but something more along the lines of Norwegian Forest cats, which are like domestic house cats but slightly bigger and less domesticated. It's not the most intimidating image, perhaps, nor are cats the most practical choice to get you where you're going but, you've got to admit, it is kind of adorable. And maybe it is another testimony to Freyja's leadership abilities: she and she alone in all the worlds can herd cats.

Freyr

a.k.a.: Frey, Ingunar-Frey
Pantheon: Norse
Spouse/Lovers: Gerd, Freyja
Siblings: Freyja
Parents: ? and Njord, Skadi and Njord
Deity of: fertility, sun, weather, wealth
Symbols: boar (Gullinbursti), light, grain
Kennings: Adversary of Beli, Son of Njord, The Fruitful, Most Famed of the Gods

---

[1] America's favorite fighting Frenchman.

"Freyr" by Ashley Campos

As god of success, prosperity, fertility, the sun, the rain, and peace, it's easy to understand why Freyr was so popular amongst the Norse. Despite being one of the most worshipped gods of the Norse, Freyr is all but absent from the mythic tales. He gets a mention here and there and is reputed as being "the most splendid" of the gods, but his role in the myths themselves is minor at best. What we know of Freyr can be boiled down to four things:

(1) Freyr was of the Vanir. Along with his father Njord, and his sister Freyja, Freyr was traded to the Aesir as part of the peace treaty between the two feuding pantheons. What this means anthropologically is that Njord, Freyja, and Freyr were the most popular of the Vanir gods and so when the Vanir-worshipping culture was absorbed by the Aesir worshippers, these three were intentionally retained—either as a sort of cultural acknowledgement to the other group or simply because the Aesir thought these three were neat.

(2) Freyr was awesome. We don't have a lot of stories to attest to his awesomeness, but Snorri likes to remind us that, for whatever reason, Freyr is considered one of the best of all the gods. Freyr was probably on par with Thor and Odin as far as most worshipped gods of the Viking Age and, in many ways, Freyr was the most important for daily life since he was the one who made sure you had good crops and fertile land.

(3) Freyr had awesome stuff. He had a boar with golden hair named Gullinbursti, a boat called Skidbladnir that was big enough to hold all the gods and all their gear but could also be folded up and carried around in Freyr's pocket, and a magic sword that would do all his fighting for him. According to the Eddic poem *Grimnismal*, when he was but a baby, Freyr was given Alfheim by the gods to have as his home. That may mean he was the ruler of the world of light-elves (Alfheim) who, (despite getting a lot of ink from Tolkien) are rarely even referenced in Norse myth, or it may mean that Alfheim was the name of his hall, just as Valhalla is the hall of Odin.[1]

(4) Freyr married Gerd. Snorri briefly tells the tale that Freyr fell in love with a beautiful Jotun named Gerd and sent his servant Skirnir to woo her for him. Skirnir was successful, Freyr got Gerd, and Skirnir was paid with Freyr's magic sword.[2] For want of his sword, Freyr is doomed to die during Ragnarok at the hands of the primordial fire Jotun Surt. That's all Snorri really has to say on the subject, but, in the *Poetic Edda*, we get a full account of just how Skirnir got Gerd

---

[1] Almost all of the gods had halls with names; some gods had more than one.
[2] Man gives up his 'magic sword' when he gets married, which will ultimately bring about his unhappy end. Honestly, it's amazing that Freud didn't reference this myth.

to agree to marry Freyr. And it is not pretty. In fact, it may be the most singularly upsetting poem of the *Edda*. In *For Skirnis*, Skirnir goes to Geri, who rejects Freyr's request of marriage immediately. So Skirnir launches into a brutal, misogynistic, violent, and disgusting tirade, threatening Gerd with everything from being raped by monsters to having to drink goat urine if she does not agree to marry Freyr. Gerd politely acquiesces and the match is set.

Beyond those elements, the *Eddas* don't have much to say about Freyr aside from: (5) a tradition that claims Freyr as a historic figure who was the ancestor of the kings of Norway, and (6) a claim, made by Loki, that Freyr and his sister Freyja were caught having sex with each other once.

Heimdall

a.k.a.: Heimdoll, Heimdallr, Hallinskidi, Rig
Pantheon: Norse
Parents: Nine Sisters
Offspring: The Races of Men
Deity of: guardian, boundaries
Symbols: Bifrost (rainbow bridge), horn
Kennings: White God, Golden Toothed, Foe of Loki, Owner of Gjallarhorn

The ever-watchful watchman of Asgard, Heimdall has a relatively rotten job when you get right down to it. He stands atop the Bifrost Bridge (the rainbow walkway that connects the home of the Aesir to the other eight worlds) and will sound the alarm horn when the events of Ragnarok begin to unfold. Until the Doom of the Gods shindig kicks off, he's mostly just standing around being bored. In the poem *Lokasenna*, Loki mocks Heimdall for having such a horrible job saying: "a miserable fate was assigned to you:/ You have to stand all the time, / stay watchful all the time, / as the guardian of the gods." Sure, Loki's opinions do not necessarily reflect those of the Norse or their godly affiliates, but he's not the only one to acknowledge Heimdall's less than enviable occupation. In the poem *For Skirnis*, Freyr's servant threatens Gerd, saying that he'll humiliate her and make her "More famous than Heimdall." Apparently, Heimdall was viewed less as a stalwart guardian and more as the Asgardian equivalent of a Walmart greeter.

Heimdall was uniquely suited for his position. Snorri tells us that "[Heimdall] needs less sleep than a bird, and he can see equally well by night or by day a distance of a hundred leagues." Along with having superlative vision, Heimdall

"Heimdall" by Tyler Space

also possesses the ability to hear "grass growing" and the sound of "wool on sheep." So, he has to stand all day *and* he has to listen to grass gossip and wool whispers.

While well known for his watch as warden at the wall, there is more to Heimdall than just his vocation, much of which is severely puzzling. Even his parentage is unclear. In one poem, it's said that he can see the future because he is of the Vanir, but he is nowhere else connected to the Vanir. The ability to see the future is frequently associated with Aesir gods like Odin and Frigg, and Snorri tells us outright that Heimdall may be referred to as the "son of Odin" so tying him to the Vanir is a bizarre choice. Whether Aesir or Vanir, we do know that Heimdall was the son of "nine mothers." What does that mean? How? Why? Huh? We have no idea. He was also called "the father of the races of men." This really meant "social classes" more than it did "races," though, and Heimdall's connection is tentative. In the Eddic poem *Rigsthula*[1], a brief prose introduction explains that Heimdall also went by the name Rig. This may simply be an attempt to link the unknown protagonist of the poem to a better-known figure. It has also been suggested that Rig is more likely to have been another name for Odin. The story in *Rigsthula* wherein "Rig" uses magic words and impregnates a series of women is much more characteristic of Odin than it would seem to be of Heimdall.

Regarded as "the whitest" of the Aesir gods, Heimdall is not necessarily lacking in rhythm or ability to jump. In Norse lit, "white," "bright," and "shiny" are terms used to denote beauty (for example, Freyr falls in love with Gerd in part because of her blindingly white forearms), so it would seem that Heimdall is a good-looking fellow. And to cap it off, he has a mouthful of gold teeth, which is as impressive an example of bling as it is impractical.

A strongly adversarial relationship exists between Heimdall and Loki.[2] In some ways, opposition between the two is not all that surprising, given how diametrically different their roles are: Heimdall stands in one spot, waiting, and watching for something to happen, while Loki is inside, outside, and all around causing things to happen. Heimdall is border security and Loki is a serial boundary breaker. Perhaps the greatest Norse myth that we don't have is a tale from an unretained poem that Snorri alludes to wherein, disguised as seals, Heimdall and

---

[1] This is the one poem that actually uses the word "edda" within it. Edda is the first of a series of women that "Rig" knocks up.

[2] In *Thrymskvitha*, Heimdall is the one to suggest that Thor should dress in drag in order to get his stolen hammer back. Normally, one would expect a suggestion that goofy to come from Loki. Perhaps Heimdall and Loki are more alike than they appear.

Loki fight over Freyja's lost necklace. The next time Loki and Heimdall meet in battle, they won't be seals and neither one of them will survive.

Tyr

> Pantheon: Norse
> Parents: Hymir's wife and Hymir
> Deity of: battle
> Symbols: wolves, one hand
> Kennings: Fosterer of the Wolf, God of Battles, Feeder of the Wolf, One-Handed God

The Norse god Tyr is about as exciting as his namesake day of the week: Tuesday. He's not aggressively annoying like a Monday, nor does he offer the weekly milestone of Hump Day, or even the excitement of the approaching weekend found in Thursday and Friday—Tuesday is just kind of there. Tyr is present, but for the most part he doesn't do a whole lot for better or for worse.

He is a war god, but he's only a shadow of the greater war god: Odin. Tyr possibly began as a regional variation of Odin and, rather than being absorbed into the Odinic tradition, he was preserved as a separate character. His lineage within the mythology is not entirely clear either. In the poem *Hymiskvitha*, Tyr's parents are identified as the Jotun Hymir and Hymir's wife but, nowhere else is his parentage referenced nor is there any other reason to associate him with any group aside from the Aesir. But, of course, both Loki and Odin have Jotun parents and that doesn't prevent them from being active, card-carrying Aesir. Snorri praises Tyr for his courage, wisdom, and prowess in battle, but there's almost no surviving myths from which to draw that characterization. In *Hymiskvitha*, Tyr is Thor's traveling companion and despite most of the story taking place in and around his parent's home, Tyr doesn't have much to say or do in the poem. Tyr is destined to kill and be killed by Garm, the watchdog of Helheim, in the events of Ragnarok, but the two are matched up for no apparent reason. The most important story about Tyr by far is the tale of the chaining of Fenrir.

Fenrir, the gigantic wolf and son of Loki, grew too big and strong for the Aesir to keep him under control. The gods attempted to leash the hound with bigger and stronger chains only to have him break even the sturdiest of bonds in

"Tyr" by Ian Sedgwick

a matter of seconds. With the help of some innovative dwarfs, the Aesir came to Fenrir with a thin thread. The only way they could get Fenrir to agree to having the magic ribbon placed on him was by the Aesir swearing that if it proved unbreakable, they would remove it and use it only when completely necessary. To solidify their pledge, the bold and courageous Tyr placed his hand in the wolf's mouth as a sign of mutual trust. When Fenrir was unable to break the thread, the gods decided to leave it on him. Fenrir, in retaliation for the broken promise, bit down and relieved Tyr of his hand.[1] While Tyr was not necessarily the one to blame, he paid dearly for the god's unfulfilled promise. Not only was one-handedness a less than optimal situation for a war god, but it also posed another problem because the best way to seal a contract was with a hardy handshake. Tyr was thus rendered unable to make a pledge and was therefore seen as untrustworthy, which is both unfortunate and unfair.

Sif

Pantheon: Norse
Spouse/Lovers: Thor, unnamed father of Ull
Offspring: Ull, Thrud, Magni, Modi
Deity of: crop fertility (?)
Symbols: golden hair, grain (?)

The most important myth featuring Sif involves her only tangentially. The story goes that, for some reason known only to himself, Loki snuck up on the sleeping Sif and cut off her hair. When Thor discovered his hairless wife, he threatened to break every bone in Loki's body if he did not correct the situation. Knowing full-well that Thor was both willing and able to live up to his threats, Loki sought the help of some dwarfs known as the Sons of Ivaldi. Presumably in an attempt to get out of the god's doghouse, Loki commissioned a couple of additional projects to curry favor. When all was said and done, the Sons of Ivaldi produced golden hair for Sif that would grow just like real hair, Skidbladnir, an enormous ship that could be folded up and carried in a pocket, and Gungnir, a spear that would never miss its mark. With the problem resolved, Loki could very easily have brought these gifts to the gods and the whole matter would have been settled. But Loki didn't want to simply break even -- he wanted to win.

---

[1] Because of this story, "wolf joint" was a popular kenning for the wrist.

"Sif" by Sarah Lindstrom

Loki took Sif's hair, Skidbladnir, and Gungnir, and went to talk to a rival dwarf smithy. He showed off the work of the Sons of Ivaldi. "Aren't these the finest objects you've ever seen?" Loki asked them. "I bet you couldn't make even a single object to rival these, let alone three that surpass them. In fact," Loki went on, "I will wager my head on it!" The dwarfs, Brokk and Eitri, took the bet and set to work.

Brokk worked the bellows while Eitri started smithing. As Eitri smithed away[1], a fly landed on Brokk's hand and bit him hard. Undeterred, he pumped the bellows until Eitri finished and had crafted a living boar covered in golden hair. As Eitri worked on the next item the same fly returned and, this time, bit Brokk twice as hard on the neck. Undeterred once again, Brokk pumped away until Eitri was done crafting a magical golden ring. Eitri began working on a third and final project and the fly, now desperate to ensure that he not lose his head, bit Brokk between the eyes. The blood flowed into both his eyes and blinded him. Brokk wiped the blood from his eyes and in doing so neglected the bellows for the briefest of moments—it was enough to create a single flaw in Eitri's work. He had been forging a hammer and the momentary interruption somehow led to the hammer ending up with a short handle. Despite the stubby handle, this hammer and their other work would become the stuff of legend.

Loki, Eitri, and Brokk went to present their presents to Thor, Odin, and Freyr. To Odin, Loki gave the spear Gungnir, and Eitri and Brokk gave Draupnir, a magical ring that would self-replicate every nine days. To Freyr, Loki gave Skidbladnir while the dwarfs gave him the golden boar named Gullinbursti. And finally, Thor was given the magical golden hair for Sif, and Eitri and Brokk offered him the stumpy-handled war hammer Mjolnir. While the gods admitted that the work of the Sons of Ivaldi was very good, they agreed unanimously that Eitri and Brokk had outdone them. Thus, Loki would have to forfeit his head. Loki, brave as ever, ran away as quickly as his legs would take him. Of course, Thor (always a big fan of justice) grabbed Loki and demanded the dwarfs be paid their due. When they came at him with a knife the quick-thinking Loki cried, "STOP! The bargain was for my head, don't you dare take any of my neck!" Unclear on precisely where the neck ended and the head began, the dwarfs were stymied and unable to claim their prize. Instead, they took a consolation prize, and rather than removing Loki's head, they sewed his lips shut.

---

[1] It should be noted that extensive research into the art of smithing was not done in preparation for this book.

While that story gives us the origin of many important items in Norse myth, Sif is little more than a plot device to get the ball rolling. It has been argued that Sif's hair, which is harvested and then replenishes[1], is a symbol of crop fertility. If that's the case, she joins several other Norse gods already associated with seasonal fertility. In Snorri's *Skaldskaparmal*, we are told that "Sif's hair" is a kenning for gold, which may simply be because the dwarfs made it out of gold or because crops provide the main source of sustainable wealth.

If the assumption that Sif is a harvest goddess is correct, then she surely played a crucial role in the lives of Scandinavians, most of whom were farmers. Though exciting explorations and Viking raiding parties occupy a larger share of the popular concept of the Norse and, indeed, of Norse literature and mythology, their daily lives were much more often dedicated to tending the flock and fields. In the marriage of Sif and Thor, we have the mundane though necessary parts of Scandinavian life joined with the high adventure and derring-do of the Vikings. Not surprisingly, it is the thrilling tales of Thor that fill the imagination while homebody Sif provided the daily bread for her followers.

Valkyries

a.k.a.: Choosers of the Slain, Shield Maidens, Disir (?)
Pantheon: Norse
Notable members: Brynhild, Sigrun, Thrud

The Valkyries do a lot of the heavy lifting in Norse myth but get very little of the credit. Their titular job as Choosers of the Slain is one of the most important aspects of Norse belief: after the hurly burly was done and the battle was lost and won, they would swoop in and carry off the souls of those who died bravely in battle. Those chosen slain then joined the ranks of Asgard's army of Einherjar. But the Valkyries' work was not done. From here to Ragnarok they spend their days tending to and training the Einherjar. Working under Freyja and/or Odin, the Valkyries are in charge of making sure that the Einherjar are ready to do their

---

[1] If we're being honest, that's not all that special. Most hair that is cut off regrows most of the time.

"Ride of the Valkyries" by Mandy Cantarella

part in the final battle. Sometimes referred to as "Shield Maidens," these spear-wielding women bestride flying horses are a force to be reckoned with.

The Aurora Borealis was well known to the Norse and is one of the most unearthly beautiful phenomena that can be witnessed with the naked eye. While they attributed the endless journey of the sun and moon to those celestial bodies being chased by ravenous wolves, the Northern Lights were given a much less menacing explanation. The ethereal shimmer in the sky is the result of light glinting off the Valkyries as they ride their winglessly flying steeds across the sky. Granted, they are coming to collect the souls of the worthy dead so their traverse is not without an edge of darkness to it, but their travel in and of itself is a dazzling sight to behold.

Of course, the Valkyries also take prominent roles in many of the sagas. Most famous of them all is Brynhild who appears in the *Volsung Saga*, which inspired Wagner's epic opera, the *Ring Cycle*, which in turn inspired one of the greatest cartoon shorts ever: *What's Opera Doc?* Yes, Bugs Bunny plays Brynhild. And the stereotypical obese opera diva wearing a horned helmet is a nod to Brynhild and thus in a circuitous route, the Valkyries of Norse myth gave us the expression "it's not over until the fat lady sings."

The Valkyries may have counterparts that gather souls for Hel, rather than Valhalla. The Disir are goddesses of fate like the Valkyries but seem to carry with them more negative connotations. It stands to reason that if Odin has the Valkyries to gather his dead, there would be a parallel role to help out Hel.

Popular depictions of Norse figures are a far cry from the reality of what people living in the Viking Age really looked like and what they likely pictured their gods to look like. The Valkyries are perhaps the most egregious example. Nearly naked women clad in horned helmets and metal bras would not be very well equipped to live, much less do battle in the often-frigid Scandinavian landscape. There is no evidence that the flashy horned helmets were ever worn by Norse warriors and with good cause—they are heavy, awkward, and would actually increase the likelihood of a deadly blow to the head. If such ornate headgear ever existed in the Viking Age, it would have been for ceremonial purposes only, never for battle. Metallic bras are, as I'm sure most any woman can attest, a bad idea on every level. Like the imagined helmets, armoring only your breasts is a greater liability than an asset since it not only leaves vital organs exposed but would help direct an enemy's weapon toward the heart. Also, they'd be super uncomfortable. Heavy Metal fantasies aside, real Norse women dressed for real Norse weather and real Norse fighting.

"Hyrrokkin" by Jerry Butler

Jotun

a.k.a.: Jotan, Jotunn, Jötnar, Giant, Troll, Frost Giant

Pantheon: Norse

Notable Members: Surt, Ymir (Aurgelmir), Angrboda, Aurvandil, Baugi, Beli, Bergelmir, Bestla, Bolthorn, Geirrod, Gerd, Grid, Hraesvelg, Hrungnir, Hymir, Hyrrokkin, Jarnsaxa, Laufey, Skadi, Skrymir/Utgardaloki, Suttung, Thjazi, Thrym, Aegir

The traditional translation of Jotun as "giant" is problematic at best. "Giant" suggests certain characteristics about the being being described, not the least of which is that they are gigantic (or at least taller than average). For instance, the biblical character Goliath was either 6'6 or 9'6, both taller than your average human of the time but only the latter would be considered superhumanly large today. Whereas the Marvel Comics character Giant-Man can be anywhere between 10 and 25 feet tall or however tall he needs to be for any given story. The Jotun of Norse myth are not gigantic, at least not all of them.

Skadi and Gerd, the wives of Njord and Freyr respectively, seem by all accounts to be roughly the same size as their husbands. Far from being hulking monsters who tower over those around them, both Skadi and Gerd are regarded as quite beautiful.

Ymir, on the other hand, seems to be impossibly large. The first of the Frost Giants, Ymir was killed by Odin and his brothers and his body parts were used to craft the world(s). Apparently, he was so big that the seas are filled with his blood and the sky is formed from his skull. But other frost giants, including his direct offspring, appear not to be on the same scale as Ymir. When Ymir's blood was spilled, it caused large-scale flooding, killing off all his descendants except one (possibly Bergelmir, who possibly had nine heads), who survived because he built a boat. If my father was killed and his blood drained out into a room, I would barely have to roll up my pant legs let alone build a boat or risk drowning. Ymir is clearly a giant amongst "giants."

Surt, who only gets mentioned in the context of the beginning and the end of the world, may or may not be Ymir-sized. He is a primordial being with no known genesis. He seems to simply exist in the fiery world of Muspelheim in the time before much of anything else existed. Because of this, we might assume that he is of significant proportions but we're never really told so. He is the lone-named Fire Giant but there are apparently more that will march with him when the battle of Ragnarok begins. As cool and scary-sounding as Fire Giants are, they are little more than a footnote in the whole of Norse myth.

Frost Giants aren't doing much better than their hotter counterparts. Ymir was the father of the Frost Giants, but other than his immediate offspring there's nary a mention of this race. An unnamed pair was born from his armpits and another child (possibly Bergelmir) was born from Ymir's feet having sex with each other. But outside the creation story, the race of icy Jotun exists only as background noise.

It is the type of Jotun that is neither fiery nor frosty that appears most often in the tales. Sometimes translated as troll, sometimes as giant, this class of Jotun presumably includes the character who built the wall around Asgard, Thrym who stole Thor's hammer, Hymir who went fishing with Thor (and possibly fathered Tyr), the trickster Utgardaloki/Skrymir, Hyrrokkin who was the only being strong enough to launch the boat used for Balder's funeral pyre, Hrungnir whose corpse pinned down Thor, Thjazi who kidnapped Idunn, his daughter Gerd, Gilling, Suttung, Gunnlod, possibly Aegir (the frequent host to the Aesir's parties), and a variety of other characters. They come in a variety of sizes as well as alignments. Odin, Loki, Tyr, and arguably others amongst the gods have one or more parent of Jotun lineage.

If we are to think in terms of genetics, there is less difference between a god and a Jotun than there is between any two types of Jotun. The Norse almost certainly did not concern themselves with the genetic diversity of their mythic beings but focused rather on the insiders vs. the outsiders. There were the opposing worlds of the Innangard ("Inside land") and the Utangard ("Outside land") that were not separated strictly by geography, but by status and mindset. The Innangard world was orderly and safe(ish) whereas the Utangard was wild and wooly. "Giantland" (which includes Jotunheim, Muspelheim, and Niflheim) was beyond the literal and proverbial wall that protected Asgard, Midgard, Vanaheim, Alfheim, and (maybe) Svartalfarheim, but individuals from the outside could find themselves part of the in-group. The core conflict of Norse myth was much less about race or geography and was much more about tribalism, or the cool kids vs. the weird kids.

"Balder" by David Manderville

Balder

a.k.a.: Baldr
Pantheon: Norse
Spouse: Nanna
Siblings: Hermod, Hod, Thor, Vali, Vidar
Parents: Frigg and Odin
Offspring: Forseti
Deity of: beauty, reconciliation, joy, innocence, peace, light
Symbols: mistletoe
Kennings: Slaughter God, The Good, God of Tears, Bright God

Balder is one of the most important characters in all of Norse myth and yet the only story connected to him at all is that of his death.

The poem *Baldrs draumar* ("Balder's Dream") tells us that the Aesir assembled to figure out what to do about Balder's bad dreams. Odin decided to travel down to Hel and forced a dead Volva to reveal Balder's fate. Compelled by Odin's power, she told him that Balder would die, Hod would kill him, and Odin would have a newborn son named Vali who would then kill Hod. And that's about it. At only 15 stanzas long, *Baldrs draumar* is the shortest of the poems in the *Poetic Edda* and despite being named after him, Balder doesn't so much as speak a word.

Snorri gives us a bit more about Balder in his *Edda*, but not much. In the *Gylfaginning*, the tri-faceted disguise of Odin tells the knowledge-seeking Gylfi that Balder is beautiful. He is super pale, white, and shiny—the height of sexiness to the Norse people. Beyond that, we're told that Balder is the best of the best: he is not only the sexiest, but also the "wisest," the most well-spoken, and the most merciful. Snorri lays it on thick, describing Balder as superlative in all things. Except, Snorri says almost off-handedly, as wise and merciful as Balder is, "none of his decisions are effective." Maybe it's that impotency that leads to Balder being left out of so many other narratives or maybe it's nothing more than an insight into the mind of a bitter author who struggles to find many examples of mercy in the world at large. Either way, we're left with a brilliant, beautiful man who can't do a damn thing.

Except for an odd reference here or there about his hall or about how beautiful his feet were presumed to be, we don't hear much about Balder until Snorri describes his death. Snorri fleshes out the tale well beyond what we're told in *Baldrs draumar*. He explains that in an attempt to save Balder from his fate Frigg asked everyone and everything to take an oath promising that they will never hurt Balder. Snorri also tells us of Loki having disguised himself as an old woman to learn from Frigg that only one thing in all the world(s) had not been asked to take the oath: the mistletoe. Loki gathered some mistletoe and set up the blind god Hod to take the fatal shot. *Baldrs draumar* leaves Loki out of the assassination completely. The only poem to reference Loki's role is *Lokasenna*, which is typically dated amongst the latest composed. Regardless, Balder died and Hod was killed without being given an opportunity to explain. Snorri tells us of the attempt to get Balder (but not Hod) out of Hel by getting everyone and everything to weep for him. And everything did, save for one cranky old lady called Thokk. Snorri quotes a poem on the point of Thokk not weeping for Balder, but the poem in question hasn't survived so all we have is Snorri's word to go on. Of course, he also lets us know that Thokk was really a disguise of Loki and thus Loki is responsible for Balder's death and preventing his resurrection.

For Snorri, the function of the story of Balder's death seems to be establishing Loki as the true antagonist of Norse myth and also setting us on the one-way trip to Ragnarok. Once Balder is dead and stays dead, Ragnarok bears down on us like a freight train. Odin and Frigg's one attempt to change the future (by preventing Balder's death) has failed and thus we are forced to conclude that the fate of the world(s) at large is unalterable. For scholars, the function of this myth is still a source of debate.

One popular idea is that Balder represents the sun. His death is, therefore, about the changing of the seasons. These types of stories show up all over and generally involve a god or goddess of fertility or light dying or otherwise descending into the underworld for the winter only to rise again in the spring. The Greek tale of Persephone is probably the best known of these types of stories. If that really is the function of this particular myth, there's the thorny question of why it only happened once. Usually the descents are annual and cyclical because, well, that's how seasons go, but Balder's death is a one-shot deal. But then, maybe that's just the way Snorri (or the Christian Norse in general) told the tale. The perfect son of god who died because of the machinations of an evil being have obvious Christian parallels. Add in the fact that Balder will return after the events of Ragnarok to usher in a new, idyllic world and he's a clear Christ figure. So how large a role did Balder play in pre-Christian Norse myth? We honestly don't know but somewhere along the line the story of his death became the pivot on which all of Norse myth swivels.

"The Last Gasp" by Andrew Zesiger

Ragnarok

a.k.a.: The Doom of the Gods, the Twilight of the Gods
Pantheon: Norse

Ragnarok will be the final, climactic battle of the Norse mythic cycle.

To say that all of Norse mythology is building toward the events of Ragnarok is an understatement. From the very beginning, the content of the *Eddas* reveals not just a fascination, but an obsessive preoccupation with the coming doom. One of the two worlds that existed prior to creation was Muspelheim, literally "Doomsday Home." Before we are even told about creation, we are told of Surt, a primordial being from the fiery realm of Muspelheim, who will set fire to the created world in the events of the final battle. Before the beginning, we are told that the end is coming.

The oncoming doom is the drumbeat that the Norse gods march to. It is never far from the thoughts of either the characters or their writers. Ragnarok is coming. It's not a maybe, it's not an "if this, then that"; it is as inevitable as death.

The broad strokes of Ragnarok are this: First, will be the Fimblvetr or the Winter of Winters. Brace yourselves. As three successive winters will follow each other with no Spring in between, Midgard will collapse into moral decay and civil war. Then will come the earthquakes. Loki and Fenrir will each break free of their imprisonments. The Jotun ship Naglfar will be released from the ice that holds it in dock. Jormungand will uncoil and head toward shore, poisoning the air and causing tidal waves and further earthquakes as he moves. The forces of Muspelheim will march across the Bifrost Bridge and shatter it. The unworthy dead of Helheim will pile into their ship made of the toenails of the dead. As the forces of evil mobilize, the Aesir watchman Heimdall will blow on the Gjallarhorn to alert the forces of good. The Aesir and their Einherjar and Valkyries, along with the Vanir, elves, and dwarves will mount up and head for battle on the Plain of Vigrid. An unparalleled battle will commence. Swordless Freyr and ancient Surt will kill each other as will Heimdall and Loki, Tyr and Garm, and Thor and Jormungand. Odin will be eaten by Fenrir who will, in turn, be killed by the silent but deadly Vidar. As Surt dies, he will toss fire throughout Yggdrasil and all nine worlds will burn. The World Ash will sink into the sea. Every world, every being will die.

The End

. . . Or is it?

No, it isn't.

After the events of Ragnarok unfold, there will be a new world. Two humans will emerge on the other side of Ragnarok completely unscathed. Their names are Lif and Lifthrasir ("Life" and "Life Raiser") and they will repeople the world. And it will be a very different world. Odin will be replaced as chief god by a reborn Balder. The top of the call sheet will change from a grey, brooding god of war and death to the light, bright, shiny god of reconciliation. If Ragnarok is the end, Norse myth wouldn't have a lot to offer beyond some fun stories and a nihilistic worldview. The quiet little coda that follows the events of the final battle gives Norse myth its real heart. The Norse looked at the world and saw that it was hard and brutal and ultimately fatal to all, but they strove and fought for the promise of something better on the other side knowing full well that none of them would ever see it personally. Ragnarok isn't the end, it is simply the last gasp of a vicious, violent world before everlasting peace takes over.

"Far, But Not Forgotten" by Ashley Campos

Indigenous American Mythology

Long before Europeans 'discovered' the 'New World,' people were living in this very old world all the way from the edge of the Arctic Circle down to the Strait of Magellan. And those people didn't beat Columbus by just a few years, they predate that genocidal maniac by tens of thousands of years. And yet, much of the received mythology from peoples indigenous to the Americas was not written down or seriously studied by the rest of the world until the 19th and 20th centuries. By that time, many of the indigenous mythologies had been irreparably altered, if not completely erased by the cultural imperialism and religions of people of European descent. Since people have been living in the Americas for somewhere between 15,000 and 130,000 years, there are doubtless many cultures with their own deities and mythic traditions that are simply lost to history. What we do have is an array of tales from hundreds of different tribes from dozens of different language groups.

The Maya hold a unique position in the annals of indigenous peoples of the Americas. Though, to be clear, there was no unified group known as the Maya. That blanket term was first used by 20th century scholars who decided it was easiest to lump together a variety of people who lived in and around what is now Mexico, Belize, Guatemala, El Salvador, and Honduras. They shared a language group but they were no more unified than, say, the Romance languages. What we think of as simply "the Maya" are as diverse a group as "the Europeans" and linguistically even more so. Some people falling under the blanket term of Mayan (specifically the Quiche) had a written form of their creation and foundation myth, something that is incredibly rare amongst people indigenous to the Americas. Even rarer still, relatively early written versions of this story have survived to this day. This text is known as *Popol Vuh* ("Book of the Community").

It is with good cause that the *Popol Vuh* is referred to as "The Mayan Bible." Like the Hebrew Bible (or the Old Testament if you prefer) the *Popol Vuh* contains a creation story, a foundation myth, and instructions on how to live the right way.

Unlike the Old Testament (or the Hebrew Bible, if you prefer), which is chock full of lists of rules of what you can and cannot eat, what you can and cannot wear, what you can and cannot do, and what you can and cannot have sex with, the *Popol Vuh* avoids direct orders. Rather, it includes instructive tales from which we are meant to derive lessons on how to behave. The *Popol Vuh* gives its readers a lot of credit, allowing them to suss out for themselves the best way to live one's

232

life. Time and again, the message seems to be that the most important attributes one should display are cleverness and sacrifice for the greater good. The characters who are proud, showy, or self-centered are brought down by the cunning of characters like the Hero Twins. Being wealthy or powerful means nothing compared to having real merit and a sharp intellect.

Unlike the Hebrew Bible (or Old Testament, if you prefer), which is a compilation of pieces written by many different writers over a stretch of time, the *Popol Vuh* is consistent in its tone, style, and objective. It's also significantly shorter.

As much as European settlers are to blame for the destruction of indigenous cultures, we do have to thank at least one European for the preservation of the *Popol Vuh*. In the 18th century, a Dominican friar named Francisco Ximenez saw the value in retaining the mythic tales of the Maya and so he made sure to record the contents of the *Popol Vuh* in Latin with the help from one or more native speakers. If not for one European who showed respect for the culture, all the other Europeans may have succeeded in destroying all vestiges of the *Popol Vuh*. The received version that comes to us by way of Ximenez' Latin translation is clearly not 100% unadulterated as it has clear nods to the Christianization of Mayan peoples, but even with that caveat, it is one of the oldest and most reliable mythological texts from peoples indigenous to the Americas.

The so-called Mayan civilization had been in decline long before the Spanish showed up in Central America, but the Aztec were still flourishing. Perhaps because of the adversarial relationship between the Aztec and Spanish, our earliest references to Aztec myth don't seem to be too concerned with doing the culture justice. The early Spanish accounts tell of the Aztec practice of ritual human sacrifice with seemingly inflated numbers. That is not to say that the Aztec didn't do tons of human sacrifices, but that the Spanish simply exaggerated the exact number a bit. Archeological evidence proves that sacrifices were a huge part of the Aztec way of life, but also that the Spanish ideas about the Aztec deities was not always accurate.

In North America, we have myriad different indigenous tribes stretching across tens of thousands of years of time and millions of square miles of land. No single volume could do justice to the array of gods, goddesses, culture heroes, tricksters, and beasts that can be found amongst the peoples indigenous to the continent. We won't pretend to even scratch the surface in this text, but rather will discuss and celebrate a few of the most prominent, most entertaining, or most unusual figures.

A note on terminology: the terms "Indian," "Native American," "American Indian," and others have been used to label the people whose myths are touched on in this chapter. All of those terms are (shall we say?) imperfect. "Indian" is a relic of the genocidal maniac Christopher Columbus who thought he was in India. But, on the upside, it means "beautiful people" which is a nice thing to be called, generally speaking. "Native American" has the stink of manifest destiny, as if this land had always been America, even if the people living here for thousands of years before the formation of the United States didn't know it. And "American Indian" is a great term if you want the baggage of both of the other terms. Of course, there are various other terms that have been used over the years that are just flat-out racist and are therefore now only in usage amongst the ranks of racists and sports teams. Why it is still acceptable on any level to have team mascots that demean a group of people, I will never understand. Aside from the overtly racist, dehumanizing terms, it is not my place to tell anyone what they should be called. Many people who belong to these groups identify themselves as Indian, Native American, American Indian or whatever label they like. And in fact, the correct answer about what to call them (or anyone for that matter) is whatever they prefer to be called. In an effort to be as inclusive as possible I have chosen to use the terms "Indigenous American" or "peoples indigenous to the Americas" when referring broadly to those groups of people who are indigenous to the continents now known as North and South America. If you are a member of that broad group and object to that terminology, I apologize. When possible, the groups being discussed are identified by their particular tribe or larger linguistic group.

"The Hero Twins and the heads of One Death (left), Seven Macaw (center), and Seven Death (right)" by Darian Papineau

The Hero Twins

a.k.a.: Hunahpu and Xbalanque
Pantheon: Quiche Maya
Parents: Blood Moon and One Hunahpu (and Seven Hunahpu)

Hunahpu and Xbalanque, better known to the Maya simply as "The Hero Twins", were skilled athletes and magicians. Before they came along, though, there was another pair of Hero Twins who were less talented, less clever, and less heroic. The first Hero Twins, named One Hunahpu and Seven Hunahpu, got themselves humiliated and killed by a group of death lords.

The trouble began with a simple pickup game of the Mayan national pastime: The Ball Game. The Ball Game was a bit of a cross between football (soccer), basketball, and hacky-sack and was the first sport to use a rubber ball. In Europe they were still inflating goat bladders and such while the Maya had mastery over the rubber arts. One and Seven Hunahpu played too near the entrance to Xibalba, the subterranean afterlife realm, and annoyed the Lords of Xibalba. They were called to answer for their crimes of irritation and to test their mettle against the death gods on the ball court. Unfortunately, One and Seven Hunahpu never even made it to the match because, on their way there, they faced a variety of mental and physical challenges, each of which they failed miserably. For what would prove to be their final challenge, they were given torches and cigars and left alone for the night. When the gods returned the next morning, they asked where the cigars were and our not-that-heroic Hero Twins said, "Uh, we smoked them. Duh." And so, they were killed.

The Xibalbans put One Hunahpu's head in a calabash tree overlooking the field where his body and his brother's everything were buried. It was meant as a warning to anyone else who might be tempted to play too rowdy a game too close to the entrance to Xibalba, but it ended up leading to the defeat of Death itself.

One day, a young woman named Blood Moon was walking by the aptly named "Place of the Ball Game Sacrifice" when the severed head of One Hunahpu called her over. He asked her to hold out her hands and, for some reason, she listened to the animate head in a tree, held up her hands, and the head promptly vomited blood into them, which caused her to become pregnant. Which is why, when handling bloody vomit, one ought to wear rubber gloves. When her father, a Xibalban Lord named Blood Gatherer, found out about her pregnancy, he tried to kill Blood Moon. She escaped and eventually gave birth to a new and improved set of Hero Twins named Hunahpu and Xbalanque.

Hunahpu and Xbalanque picked up the work of their father and uncle and they too annoyed the Death Lords with their ball playing. And because the shortest distance between two points in a myth is always a labyrinthine path, they were called to Xibalba by way of their Grandmother, who told a flea, who was swallowed by a toad, who was swallowed by a snake, who was swallowed by a falcon, who vomited out the snake, who vomited out the toad, who vomited out the flea, who told the Twins they were cordially invited to attend their own tragic end in the lovely land of Xibalba.

Far cleverer than the previous generation, Hunahpu and Xbalanque succeeded where their dad and uncle had failed. One challenge they faced was to address the Lords of Xibalba by name, a feat which they accomplished with guile and some help from a friendly mosquito. The mosquito went on ahead of them and bit the first death lord who promptly said, "Ow!" to which the second death lord replied, "What's wrong, Scab Stripper?" And then the mosquito bit the second death lord who promptly said, "Ow!" to which the third death lord replied, "What's wrong, Demon of Pus?" and on down the line until the mosquito had learned each of their names, which he then passed on to the Twins.

When the Hero Twins were given their torches and cigars, they made sure to avoid the fate of their predecessors. Rather than lighting the cigars, they stuck bright red feathers to the ends so that, from afar, it looked like they were lit. The next morning, they produced the intact stogies and astonished the death lords.

Hunahpu and Xbalanque then faced Xibalba's Dream Team on the Ball Game court. One Death, Seven Death, Scab Stripper, Demon of Pus, Demon of Jaundice, Bone Scepter, Skull Scepter, Bloody Teeth, Bloody Claws, Blood Gatherer (the twin's maternal grandfather), Wing, and Packstrap[1] took on the Hero Twins. Despite the Xibalbans managing to rip off one of the Twin's heads and use it as the ball for a brief time, Hunahpu and Xbalanque still managed to win the match. And so, they were killed.

Following the advice of a couple of double agents who were friends of the Twins, the death lords burned their bodies, ground up the ashes, and threw them into the river. Of course, this was the exact recipe required to bring them back to life, first as salmon and then a day later as themselves once again.

---

[1] Clearly, Wing and Packstrap were late to the "handing out of scary sounding names" party.

And then the Hero Twins became traveling magicians. Since humans didn't yet exist at this point in the narrative, it is a natural question to ask: for whom were they performing? If you're looking for a satisfying answer, you are bound to be disappointed. What we do know is that they became so well-renowned for their magic shows that they were eventually invited to do a show in Xibalba.

In their performance, the Hero Twins (presumably wearing false mustaches or some other clever disguise) killed a dog and then brought it back to life. Then they killed a human[1] and brought him back to life. Then they killed each other and came back to life. By this point, the death lords were loving the show so much that they practically begged the Twins to bring them into the act. One Death and Seven Death were brought up on stage, and the Twins killed them. And left them that way.

Thus, the Hero Twins heroically vanquished Death itself, which is not to say that no one else had to die. Everyone dies, the Quiche Maya knew, but because of the Twins' actions it meant that death was no longer the end. They had paved the way for an afterlife.

Somewhere along the line, the Hero Twins also made it possible for the sun to rise. Like a Tarantino movie, the *Popol Vuh* is told out of order and so the story of the Twins' birth and triumph over death comes after the story of their defeat of the false sun, Seven Macaw.

Seven Macaw, a rich and richly-colored bird, took to a perch in the sky and assumed the role of the sun before the actual sun could make an appearance. The Hero Twins were so disgusted that this being with no virtue, no talent, no qualifications, and with weird discolored spots around his eyes had taken the highest position in the land simply because he was rich and entitled, that they decided to take him down a peg. Using a blowgun, they shattered his beak and sent him tumbling to the ground. They pummeled the strangely-colored, wealthy creature who, for his part, managed to rip off one of Xbalanque's arms and escape to his home. The Twins then disguised themselves as doctors and went to Seven Macaw's house to offer their services. They were invited in, but rather than repairing Seven Macaw's bloody face, they killed both him and his wife. With the fall of the brazen bird, the Twins paved the way for the true sun to rise. So, it is only thanks to the Hero Twins that we have a real sun and a promise of life after death.

---

[1] Just go with it.

"The Plumed Serpent" by Trevor Plaggemeyer

Quetzalcoatl

a.k.a.: Kukulcan (Maya), Gucumatz (Quiche), Ehecatl (Huastec), Tlahuizcalpantecuhtli (Nahuatl), "Feathered Serpent"

Pantheon: Mesoamerican (Aztec, also Olmec, Teotihuacan, Toltec, Maya etc.)

Siblings: Tezcatlipoca, Xolotl, Huitzilopochtli, Xipe Totec

Parents: Omecihuatl & Ometecuhtli; Tonacacihuatl & Tonacateuctli,

Deity of: wind, rain, creation, agriculture, arts and crafts

Symbols: Venus/the morning star, the evening star, snakes, opossums

The Plumed Serpent god appears not only amongst the Aztec, but also among their predecessors the Olmec, the Teotihuacan, and the Maya. The Aztec themselves had a variety of traditions featuring Quetzalcoatl, but the one commonality they all share is that Quetzalcoatl is an important and beloved god.

Often, Quetzalcoatl was a creator god to one degree or another. Sometimes he and his brother Tezcatlipoca worked together to kill an all-devouring goddess by turning into giant snakes and ripping her in half. Half of her body was used to form the earth, the other half the sky. The fact that the bisected goddess remained angry and hungry was used as justification for the impressive number of humans that were sacrificed by the Aztec. Gotta keep that hungry, hungry goddess happy with fresh blood and hearts.

In other versions, Quetzalcoatl and Tezcatlipoca had an adversarial relationship. Their wrangling back and forth for the seat of cosmic power resulted in the four ages of the world, each beginning with the creation of a new sun and ending with the destruction of humanity by flood or other means.

Quetzalcoatl was also credited with creating humanity in its modern form. After the slate had been wiped clean in the previous age, Quetzalcoatl ventured down to the land of the dead, Mictlan, to retrieve some bones. The dual underworld god/goddess Mictlantecuhtli/Mictlancihuatl offered to let him have the bones if he blew on a conch shell while making laps around Mictlan. Of course, they tried to trick him by giving him a holeless conch. Luckily, Quetzalcoatl had some helpful worm friends who bored holes for him, and some bee buddies who amplified the sound. Outraged that he had outsmarted them, the death gods tripped Quetzalcoatl on his way out and he fell, shattering the bones. No biggie, though, as Quetzalcoatl brought the broken bones to a goddess who mixed them with some maize and blood from Quetzalcoatl's penis[1] to fashion the first humans.

While he was most often portrayed in serpent form, some traditions paint him as much more human. In one tale, possibly derived from a historical king who later adopted the name of the god as his own, Quetzalcoatl served as a mortal king. While he devoutly worshipped the gods, King Quetzalcoatl did not believe in human sacrifice. Instead he offered up cattle and, when necessary, his own blood. Bleeding yourself again and again is not, as pre-Edwardian doctors would have you believe, the road to wellness. And so, Quetzalcoatl grew weak, much to the delight of his brother Tezcatlipoca, who in this tale was an evil sorcerer. Tezcatlipoca sent a mirror as a passive-aggressive gift to his brother. When the king saw his reflection, he was horrified by how gaunt and ill he appeared. So, he asked his people to make him a mask (because covering it up is the same thing as getting better, right?). He was given the mask and was so pleased by the bright colors that he celebrated with a drink. And when you are low on blood supply it doesn't take much to get too drunk. And Quetzalcoatl got too drunk. Way too drunk because he ended up having sex with his own sister. When he woke up, he was so horrified by what he'd done that he built himself a funeral pyre and jumped on to it. Or maybe he just left on a boat made of snakes. Either way, the story suggests that he would one day return to help his people. This myth may reflect a real cultural shift that brought human sacrifice to the forefront.

Made infamous through a slanderous propaganda campaign by the Spanish, Quetzalcoatl has been used as the symbol of the gullibility and backward thinking of pre-Christian "savages." Decades after the Aztecs had been all but obliterated by small pox blanket-wielding Spaniards and the lightest of anthropological work had given the conquerors a peek at the Aztec pantheon, some a-hole concluded that the reason the Spanish had so soundly defeated the Aztec was because the latter believed the former to be gods, specifically, Quetzalcoatl finally returning to his people. "What a bunch of uneducated rubes!" the Spanish laughed, "Those fools were so taken aback by our horses, shiny armor, and general awesomeness that they thought we were gods and thus, they laid down their arms and died for us." What a neat story to show off the supremacy of European intellect and guile! Except that it is completely untrue. The Aztec did not believe Cortes to be the returned god Quetzalcoatl. Cortes, for all his flaws, never made that claim nor did any of his men. But more importantly, the Aztec did not give up as easily as the

---

[1] Because, of course, penis blood is the most powerful thing on earth.

Spanish account would have us believe. Yes, they invited Cortes and his men in when they showed up on their shores. But they didn't do that because they thought they were gods; they did that because that's what decent people do when a guest shows up. When the Spanish made their real intent known, the Aztec rose up and kicked their asses so hard that Cortes had to swim[1] all the way back to Spain to get more men. The Aztec fought back hard, but ultimately, they had two things working strongly against them: (1) they were accustomed to a very different form of warfare; and (2) they had no immunities to the various viruses the Spanish brought over to the New World.

In traditional Aztec combat, much of the focus was on being able to capture enemies so that they could later be sacrificed to the gods. If you kill them on the battlefield, their deaths are much less helpful than if you, say, maimed them and brought them back to use as fodder for your rituals. The Aztec had an impressive pile of weapons and certainly were capable of killing, but the Spanish sought only to kill and that put the Aztec at a disadvantage.

The greatest weapon Europeans brought with them was the one they didn't even know they had. Having already been exposed to and survived small pox, the Spanish were safe from the disease, but the Aztec were anything but. Not only did disease plague the Aztec, killing or weakening many, but it also delivered a strong mythological message. Here they were, being ravaged by an illness they'd never seen before, and meanwhile the Spanish were healthy as horses[2], leading to the only logical conclusion: the gods were not on the side of the Aztec. Talk about a morale killer.

Tezcatlipoca

a.k.a.: Ehecatl, Telpochtli, Yaotl, "Smoking Mirror"
Pantheon: Mesoamerican (Aztec, Toltecs)
Siblings: Quetzalcoatl, Huitzilopochtli, Xipe Totec
Parents: Omecihuatl & Ometecuhtli
Deity of: creation, death, slaves, war, the night sky, obsidian
Symbols: jaguars, horned owls, Great Bear constellation, skulls, obsidian mirrors, turkeys

---

[1] Ok, he probably took a boat, but still.
[2] Horses, not being native to Central America, offered a variety of advantages as well.

"Tezcatlipoca" by Christian Sitterlet

Each year, one handsome young Aztec man was cast in the role of a lifetime: he would play the god Tezcatlipoca. For a year, this young man would be treated not as a king, but as a god. Whatever he desired would be his, including four women who were at his disposal. At the end of the year of pampering, Tezcatlipoca's human representation would climb to the top of the temple and four priests would hold him down while a fifth stuck an obsidian blade under his ribs, reached in and yanked out his heart. A year of being worshipped, followed by a few minutes of brutal murder; what more could a guy ask for?

Tezcatlipoca is a swirl of contradictions. He is a creator god who brought about mass death and destruction. A god of darkness and night who is sometimes manifest as the sun god. Brother and adversary to Quetzalcoatl, who is also an aspect of Tezcatlipoca. In fact, this Dark Lord was viewed, at times, as a near monotheistic god, all other gods being simply different forms in which he interacted with the created world.

It is easy to paint Tezcatlipoca as a figure of evil. One of his favorite forms was the jaguar, the bane of the existence for many in Mesoamerica, and another was a disembodied skull. Along with his often-frightening appearance, Tezcatlipoca offered up cold, darkness, sickness, and the aristocracy[1] to make humanity miserable. The rise of ritual murder in Mesoamerica may be linked fairly closely to the rise in worship of Tezcatlipoca.

Despite all that, Tezcatlipoca also did some really nice things. Like that time he created dogs by decapitating the only two human survivors of a worldwide flood and then reattaching their heads to their butts. Yes, that is where dogs come from. Tezcatlipoca was also responsible for bringing music to Earth, his favorite instrument being the flute. He was known, too, for protecting slaves and punishing their masters when they treated them too cruelly. The ultimate punishment Tezcatlipoca could give to an abusive master was to bring about their ruin until they were forced into slavery themselves. Poetic justice was apparently something that the Aztec could appreciate. While he was a god of warriors and the patron of the schools where young men were trained to become warriors, he would also stir up conflicts for them to fight and die in. He was, in many ways, a god of change and opportunity, both for good and for ill. How could a warrior ever achieve greatness if there were no wars to fight in? Tezcatlipoca made sure that his followers always had a way to change their status, allowing the lowly to raise

---

[1] Truly the most evil of all of his creations and much more difficult to get rid of than darkness.

themselves up by their bootstraps and for the rich and powerful to be brought low by their arrogance and ignorance.

Obsidian, the shiny black volcanic rock, was closely associated with Tezcatlipoca. Sharp and durable, the stone was used to make a variety of weapons for the Aztec. Most significantly, of course, were the deadly blades that were used by priests (who often wore jaguar masks as an additional nod to Tezcatlipoca) in the execution of ritual sacrifices. His name (literally: "Smoking Mirror") is a direct reference to the obsidian mirrors he used to reveal dark truths. Tezcatlipoca is the dark reflection of humanity that pervades Aztec culture.

Tezcatlipoca managed to outlive the Aztec Empire itself. His legacy lives on in the stunning *calaveras* (or sugar skulls) featured in Day of the Dead celebrations and, more insidiously, in the 'black mirrors' we carry around with us every day. Stare into the black mirror and Tezcatlipoca stares back into you.

Coatlicue

a.k.a.: Teteoinnan, Toci, Tonantzin, "Skirt of Snakes"
Pantheon: Mesoamerican (Aztec)
Offspring: Huitzilopochtli, Coyolxauhqui, the Centzonuitznahua
Deity of: earth, childbirth, motherhood
Symbols: snakes, earth

Coatlicue has the distinction of being so terrifying in appearance that when her statue was discovered by archaeologists in the late 18th century, they immediately reburied it. Eventually it was re-unburied and can now be seen in all its glory in the *National Museum of Anthropology* in Mexico City. A hulking, nine-foot-tall behemoth, the statue features Coatlicue in her titular attire, a skirt made of writhing, interwoven snakes. She also wears a necklace made of human hands and hearts with a skull in the middle. Her hands and feet have eyeballs on them, as well as long, talon-like claws. Rather than a head, the statue has two massive snakes rising from her neck and facing each other. The snakes may not literally be her head but may be an artistic representation of blood spurting from the stump where her head used to be. Apparently, that was a thing the Aztec did to indicate flowing blood. Considering that the statue would have originally been painted in those bright colors the Aztec loved so much, it would have been even more striking centuries ago. In some ways, the most interesting detail of this massive figure is that Coatlicue is depicted with a pair of sagging breasts to indicated that she had

"Coatlicue" by Chloe Stewart

mothered and nursed many. The juxtaposition of this bizarrely realistic detail mixed with the other grotesque aspects makes the statue all the more fascinating. One final, startling find was that this massive statue stood atop and fully covered a depiction of the hungry, hungry deity of the earth. The Aztec must have gone to extraordinary effort to craft the image of the devouring earth deity, and then they covered it up with Coatlicue's clawed feet, indicating that this was not a showpiece, but a piece of deep spiritual significance.

A motherly goddess, Coatlicue was both loving and fearsome. She represented fertility, stability, and nourishment, but she also had carnivorous appetites and would feed on the corpses of the victims of ritual human sacrifice. She was mother to the stars, the moon, and the sun, but her children didn't do a beautiful celestial dance so much as they were engaged in mortal combat with the very fate of the world on the line.

When Coatlicue was impregnated by a clump of feathers, her four hundred and one pre-existing children were appalled for some reason, and they decided to kill her. They chased her up Snake Mountain (Coatepec) and just as they were about to kill Coatlicue, her son, the sun, (Huitzilopochtli) erupted from her abdomen, armed and spoiling for a fight. Or, in another interpretation, Coatlicue's shoulders had already been unburdened of her head and Huitzilopochtli arrived from her neck stump to take his vengeance. Either way, her son/sun killed her one daughter, casting her body down a mountain and tossing her head into the sky where it became the moon. The four hundred other sons (the stars, which technically are suns for other planets) were killed or ran away. Each morning Coatlicue relived this heinous birth story, at least metaphorically. This was such an important story for the Aztec that the temple in their capital city of Tenochtitlan (which was dedicated to Huitzilopochtli) was modeled on Snake Mountain and decorated with snake imagery. It was also the site of the massive statue of Coatlicue and, oh yeah, thousands of human sacrifices. While the exact number of people killed is unclear thanks to Conquistadors' relatively unreliable · accounts, archeological evidence is clear that Coatlicue was provided with plenty of snacks.

Despite losing her head, Coatlicue went on to have an illustrious career as a soothsayer. The story goes that Moctezuma II[1] sent some priests on a pilgrimage to speak with Coatlicue. On the way, they got caught in some sand and began to sink. This, apparently, was a sign from Coatlicue that the Aztec cities would soon fall. As luck would have it, the Spanish were already heading across the sea with

---

[1] He's the one who gets revenge on your digestive system if you drink water that your stomach bacteria are not equipped to handle.

their weapons and their small pox. This tale has all the stink of a post-Spanish invasion re-imagining. It is possible that this was a real myth that the Aztec happened to tell just before the Spanish showed up (Moctezuma II was still on the throne when they got there) and that they truly could predict the future, but applying Occam's Razor, it is more likely a later invention of either the remaining Aztec people or the Spanish themselves. Conquered and colonized people often post-date their doomsday predictions as if to suggest that the invading forces were an inevitability. Had the Aztec not been subjected to European warfare and disease, we may have inherited an even richer tradition of their myths.

Huitzilopochtli

a.k.a.: Uitzilopochtli, Xiuhpilli, Totec, "Hummingbird Left"
Pantheon: Mesoamerican (Aztec)
Siblings: Coyolxauhqui, the Centzonuitznahua
Parents: Coatlicue
Deity of: sun, warriors
Symbols: hummingbird, eagle, feathers, sun, *xiuhcoatl* (flaming serpent spear)

Many cultures throughout the history of the world have looked to the sky and concluded that our two most prominent celestial orbs, the sun and the moon, seem to not get along with each other very well. Some have imagined the two as siblings who are holding an eternal grudge against each other and so as soon as Sun shows up at the party, Moon makes a hasty exit. The Aztec took the idea of feuding siblings and turned it up to eleven with their sun god Huitzilopochtli.

The story goes that the goddess Coatlicue had one daughter and hundreds of sons. When she became pregnant again, her children decided it was time for Mom's womb to close up shop and that they needed to kill her. They chased her up a mountain, her one daughter, Coyolxauhqui, leading the charge. As they closed in on Coatlicue, her abdomen burst open and her child emerged like a xenomorph popping out of John Hurt. He was no normal newborn though: he was fully formed, fully grown, and fully armed. He was dressed in battle regalia worthy of an Aztec warrior, and was covered in brightly colored flowers and feathers. The only thing the preemie Huitzilopochtli lacked was skin, but that oversight was more than made up for with a layer of blue paint. He even came with accessories, the most noteworthy being a spear made out of a living, blue, flaming serpent.

248

"Huitzilopochtli atop Serpent Mountain" by Jerry Butler

After erupting from his mother like the most metal tattoo Ed Hardy ever imagined, Huitzilopochtli's first act was to decapitate Coyolxauhqui while simultaneously ripping the heart from her chest. He took her head, stuck it on top of the mountain, and then killed or, at the very least, scared away his four hundred or so brothers. This battle, the Aztec believed, was re-enacted every day. All we mortals see is the sun coming up over the horizon as the moon and stars disappear, but what's really happening is that Huitzilopochtli (sun god) is bursting out of Coatlicue (earth goddess) and killing Coyolxauhqui (moon goddess) and his hundreds of brothers (the stars).

Despite Huitzilopochtli's staggering degree of badassery, his most important symbol (other than the sun itself) was the lovely and dainty hummingbird. Egyptian sun gods got to have a cool, predatory birds as their symbols, but who would be afraid of a hummingbird? First, the correct answer is: everyone should be afraid of hummingbirds. Even knowing the science of hummingbirds doesn't make them seem any less other-worldly. The way they move is so unlike any other bird that it's unsettling. Add in the fact that they have beautiful plumage and are attracted to colorful flowers and you can start to understand why the Aztec were drawn to them. Not only is Huitzilopochtli often dressed as a hummingbird, but the Aztec believed that fallen warriors spent their afterlife in the form of the bizarrely beautiful birds.

Whereas regular hummingbirds feed off flowers, Huitzilopochtli had different nectar that kept him going. The Aztec believed that the gods were sustained by an elixir called *chalchihuatl* which could only be found in human blood. To make sure Huitzilopochtli arrived every morning to kill the envious moon and keep the eternal night in check, sacrifices had to be made. Human sacrifices. A possibly unparalleled level of human sacrifices took place during the Aztec empire. While many of the accounts of the sacrifices come from slightly (read: very) biased sources such as the 16th century Spanish who killed more Aztec people than the Aztec did, archeological evidence proves that it was an undeniable and important part of the Aztec world.

As is often the case, their sun god took a prominent (if not *the* prominent) position in the pantheon. Huitzilopochtli was central to the Aztec worldview and was, in fact, the literal center of the Aztec calendar.[1] And while much human blood was shed in the name of Huitzilopochtli, one big part of his job was to make sure that the other gods didn't get too greedy. Yes, they were entitled to some

---

[1] The easiest way to find a picture of the Aztec calendar online would be to search for the "Mayan calendar" since way too many people can't seem to tell the difference between the two.

chalchihuatl, but Huitzilopochtli was there to cut them off when they'd had their share.

Xipe Totec

a.k.a.: Xipetotec, Tlatlauhca, "The Flayed Lord"
Pantheon: Mesoamerican (Aztec, Toltec)
Deity of: spring, rebirth, agriculture, disease, seasons
Symbols: flayed skin

Xipe Totec was the Buffalo Bill of the Aztec world, if, Buffalo Bill imprisoned, tortured, skinned, killed, and wore the skin of his victims as a fertility ritual.

The Aztec were no strangers to ritual bloodshed. Thousands, maybe even hundreds of thousands of people had their still-beating hearts ripped from their chests in sacrifice to the gods at sites like the temple of Tenochtitlan. Even with that backdrop, Xipe Totec's celebrations were intense. Each spring, living human beings would be skinned, while still living, in homage to Xipe Totec, whose name means "The Flayed Lord." The priests would then wear the recently-removed skins and dance around in them. While that is a horrifying spectacle to imagine, it might actually be more insulting if they *didn't* use the skin after peeling it off. At least this way it looked important. The suffering, however, must have been excruciating, and it is no accident that Xipe Totec was associated with the color red.

Just as corn kernels shed their outer layer in preparation for their rebirth, so too did Xipe Totec. If his priests had wanted an accurate representation of the annual process Xipe Totec went through, they would have to skin themselves. But they were apparently not all that concerned with verisimilitude. The Flayed Lord removed his own skin, revealing beautiful gold flesh underneath. He would then wear his old skin like an ill-fitting Halloween costume. The Aztec depictions of him are both horrifying and fascinating.

Why and how human sacrifice rituals came to be is a complicated issue. Not relegated to any particular area of the globe, human sacrifice can likely not be linked to a single origin. Many cultures who partook in human sacrifices would do so only in times of dire need or on special occasions. The Aztec seem to have been operating at a level beyond other cultures in this regard, and the particularly grizzly

"Xipe Totec" by Alayna Guza

forms their rituals took reveal an intense form of sadism. Were these brutal acts linked to religious ceremonies in order to justify an ancient leader's personal taste for cruelty? Did they begin as less extreme or more symbolic acts that became more elaborate over time? No matter what the inception of these rituals may have been, one cannot overlook their significance to the Aztec and one should not overlook the horrors humanity is capable of committing in the name of belief.

Tlazolteotl

a.k.a.: Ixcuina, Tlaelquani, Toci, "Filth Deity"
Pantheon: Mesoamerican (Aztec)
Offspring: Centeotl, Yum-Kax
Deity of: filth, vice, disease, sexually transmitted infections
Symbols: snake, broom, moon

It has been said that confession is good for the soul. In the case of Tlazolteotl, it is also good for the stomach. As the Aztec goddess of purity, Tlazolteotl fed on confessions. Especially tasty to her were confessions of a sexual nature—nothing was quite as delectable as someone telling her about their fetish for jaguar masks or admitting to performing a sex act known only as the 'Conquistador.' She made sure there were always plenty of tawdry tales of sexual liaisons to feed off of because she was also the patron goddess of adulterers. In a pinch, though, any vice would do, not just sexy ones. And, worst-case scenario, if no one was available to share their torrid tales, Tlazolteotl would also feed on literal filth. So yes, that expression on her face is truly a "shit-eating grin."

Perhaps more of a commentary on children than anything else, Tlazolteotl was a goddess of childbirth as well. To be fair, birth can be a messy business so it's nice to have her around to help with the cleanup.

Tlazolteotl is the goddess you didn't know you knew. Few would be able to identify her by name, but she plays a central role in one of the most iconic scenes in film history. The opening sequence of *Raiders of the Lost Ark* where Alfred Molina gets impaled[1] and Indiana Jones is chased by a giant boulder is all in thanks to Tlazolteotl. The booby traps are set off when Indy tries to swap out a golden

---

[1] Spoiler.

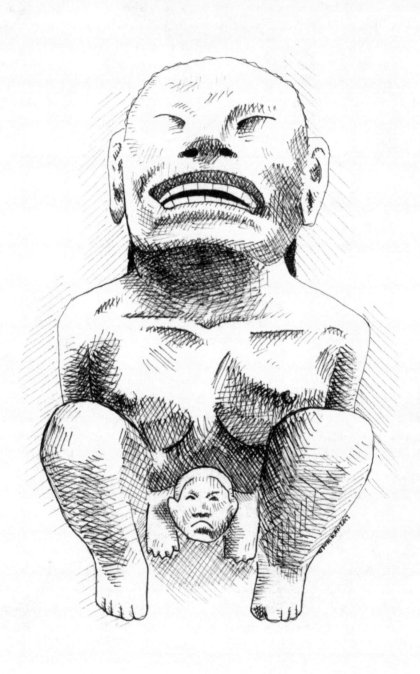

"Tlazolteotl" by Whitney Ruhlman

idol with an equally weighted bag of sand. That little gold statue with the broad grin/sneer on her face is none other than Tlazolteotl.

Sedna

a.k.a.: Sanna, Arnakuagsak, Sassuma Arnaa, Nerrivik, Nuliajuk, Mother of the Sea
Pantheon: Inuit
Spouse/Lovers: a smelly seabird
Parents: Anguta
Deity of: sea, sea creatures, underworld
Symbols: seal, walrus, whale, fish

Sedna appears in a variety of native groups along the Arctic Circle. She goes by many names and the set-up to her story varies a great deal from culture to culture, but the end result is essentially the same: Sedna becomes a moody, fingerless goddess of the deep.

Most versions of her tale identify her as a beautiful young woman who ended up in an unhappy marriage. Anguta, her father, had tried to marry her off, but none of the suitors he offered her were up to her standard. Sometimes she was portrayed as being haughty and stubborn for refusing all the men that were tossed in her direction. I mean, what kind of monster would demand a say as to with whom she would spend the rest of her life? Such a nasty woman. In one version, her stubborn insistence on marrying someone that she wanted to marry was enough to warrant her father tossing her into the sea then and there. In the more complex narrative version, a suitor finally arrived who was to her liking. He promised her a nice home, plenty of food, and impeccable treatment and so, Sedna settled for him and they went off to his distant home. The twist was that this suitor was not the handsome young man he appeared to be, but was really a smelly fulmar[1] and his home offered such amenities as slimy fish-skin blankets, drafty walls, and a closet full of clothes that look like they came from a Goodwill run out of a trash heap. She tried to contact her father immediately, but since it was a particularly harsh winter, her dear old dad couldn't make it out to her until spring.

---

[1] Think arctic seagull.

"Sedna" by Allie Wass

She suffered the long winter months[1] in the stinking hovel until her father came for a visit. Rightly upset for his daughter having been conned by the seabird, Anguta beat his odorous son-in-law to death, which was about the closest Anguta ever came to doing anything good. When they hopped in a kayak to go back home, Sedna and her father were set upon by a flock of funky-smelling fulmars. They were so pugnacious and pungent that the kayak threatened to capsize. The ignoble Anguta grabbed Sedna and tossed her into the sea to save his own ass. When she tried to climb back into the boat, Anguta[2] grabbed a knife and started slicing off his daughter's fingers so she couldn't hold on. As her severed digits tumbled into the sea, they transformed into seals, whales, walruses, narwhals, and fish. Fingerless, Sedna fell into the sea and drowned. Or, in an even darker version of the tale, she managed to pull herself into the boat by her bloody stumps and, after making land, she commanded dogs to eat her father, whose cries were so horrifying that the earth opened up and swallowed Sedna and Anguta both.

In yet another alternate form of the tale, Sedna was not a young woman refusing to marry, but was an anthropophagous[3] monster. She was so horrible to look upon, and her cravings for human flesh so unquenchable, that her parents tossed her into the sea. When she tried to get out, they cut off her fingers and we come back around to the digit-less deity of the dark.

By land or by sea, Sedna found herself in the underworld and became the ruler of the creatures of the sea. Since fishing and hunting sea beasts were so important to the Inuit and other northern peoples, Sedna (in her various iterations) was regarded as one of their most important deities. Because she very directly affected prosperity, as well as who lived, and who died, priests would take a spiritual journey to her realm to ensure that she was happy and that sea resources would be abundant. The priests did the one thing for Sedna that she couldn't do herself: they brushed her hair. Because, of course, that's the only real inconvenience for a lady missing her fingers, apparently.

Already a popular figure in some of the coldest regions on Earth, Sedna has now also taken a seat in one of the coldest regions of our solar system. In 2004 a large trans-Neptunian minor planet was named 90377 Sedna, after the fingerless goddess herself. An appropriate name for an object found between the Roman gods of the sea and underworld.[4] Significantly, with the naming of Sedna,

---

[1] Which, I believe, is roughly 11 months.
[2] Fun fact: Anguta is *not* the Inuit word meaning "World's Greatest Dad."
[3] People-eating.
[4] Neptune and Pluto, respectively.

astronomers have established a precedent for other trans-Neptunian objects to be named after other deities from the arctic. While our solar system has been dominated by Greco-Roman figures for centuries, now we may start to see more deities from the Great White North getting their place in the sun, be it ever so distant.

Coyote

a.k.a.: Maii' (Navajo), Chirich (Arikara), First Coyote (Mandan), Isily (Caddo), Jamul (Achumawi), Old Man (Blackfoot), Old Man Coyote (Crow), Sinawava (Chemhuevi), Talapus (Chinook), Yelis (Coos) etc.

Pantheon: Apache, Navajo (also Achomawi, Arikara, Blackfoot, Caddo, Cahuilla, Chemhuevi, Chinook, Chippewa, Comanchi, Coos, Costanoan, Crow, Flathead, Ho-Chunk, Hopi, Karuk, Klamath, Maidu, Mandan, Mayan, Menominee, Miwok, Mohave, Nez Perce, Nlaka'pamux, Ohlone, Pomo, Popluca, Sanpolis, Shasta, St'at'imc, Syilx, Tongva, Tohono O'odham, Tsilhquot'in, Wasco, White Mountain Apache, Wintu, Yakama, Yana, Zapotec, Zuni and more)

Spouse/Lovers: Various
Siblings: Various
Parents: Various
Offspring: Various
Deity of: creation, rain, mischief
Symbols: coyotes

There is no single "Indigenous American Mythology." There are thousands of different cultures throughout the American continents and each has its own pantheon of deities and stories associated with them. That being said, the character of Coyote is nigh-ubiquitous in tribes from all over North and Central America.[1] Though the stories vary from place to place, there is a lot of commonality in this particular figure. Though his motives may range from benevolent to malevolent, and are most often simply selfish, Coyote remains one of the most widely discussed tricksters in the world.

One feature that is consistently inconsistent is Coyote's appearance. Almost always male, Coyote may appear in human form or as an anthropomorphic coyote (to varying degrees) or as a 'normal' talking coyote. Ultimately, his shape is

---

[1] Only in the areas where actual coyotes may be found, coincidentally.

"Coyote" by Malena Salinas

259

determined by the necessity of the narrative—he has hands when hands are called for and a tail when one is needed.

Coyote, in very typical trickster fashion, often ended up the victim of his own tricks. He pushed just a little too far, or wanted just a little bit more and because of that, everything fell apart. When he was taught how to take out his own eyes so that he could throw them into a tree and survey the land, he ignored the part of the instruction that said if he did it too often his eyes wouldn't come back. When he tried to get a buffalo to feed upon, he inadvertently released all buffalo into the world. When he stole a box of light so that he could hunt in the dark, he ignored the advice to only open the box so far—and thus the sun escaped from the box and out of Coyote's control. The release of the sun was just one of the many times Coyote unintentionally helped create order in the universe. Just as often as we have stories of Coyote trying to get more than his share, we have tales of Coyote paving the way for human beings to exist, or bringing living creatures into the world. In the Navajo emergence creation myth, Coyote was one of the first beings. He was joined by First Man and First Woman as they climbed from one world to the next until finally emerging into the world we live in now. Coyote 'helped' the process along by kidnapping the children of the water serpent Tieholtsodi in the third world, leading to the massive flooding that pushed them into the fourth and even the fifth and final world. The world would reap the benefits of Coyote's mischief, leaving him the only real victim. As Joseph Campbell would say, Coyote is "the giver of all great boons" from life to language to creation itself.

That being said, there is also an enormous number of stories of Coyote's sexual appetite. While a lot of the stories have the feel of a dirty joke told around a campfire, there is some real darkness there, too. Coyote, more than once, encountered the phenomenon of *vagina dentata*. The toothed vagina that tried to, and sometimes succeeded in, biting off part of Coyote's penis suggests some real, primal fears of female sexuality. Often, the stories reached a 'light-hearted' resolution after Coyote performed a form of genital mutilation and/or rape. This gives us insight into not only the specific cultures from whence these stories come, but about human psychology.

Of course, Coyote may be best known to the masses as the inspiration for the *Looney Tunes*' Wile E. Coyote. Like his Indigenous American namesake, Wile E. Coyote is too clever for his own good. His elaborate schemes (enhanced with help from the Acme Corporation) to catch that cursed Road Runner invariably fell apart as his reach exceeded his grasp.

"White Buffalo Calf Woman" by Emily Luyk

White Buffalo Calf Woman

a.k.a.: White Buffalo Woman, Pte Ska Win
Pantheon: Lakota
Deity of: culture, ceremonies, buffalo
Symbols: ceremonial pipe, white buffalo

White Buffalo Calf Woman is the culture-bearer goddess of the Lakota Sioux. Though she only made a brief appearance to the Lakota people, she left an enduring mark.

The story goes that the Lakota people were in a time of crisis. Food was scarce, the people were hungry, and there was little hope to be found. In a desperate attempt to save the tribe, scouts were sent out far and wide. Two of these scouts observed a figure in the distance. As they got closer, they saw that it was a woman with a red dot on each cheek and clad in white buckskin. The scouts were struck dumb by her beauty, which only grew the closer she came to them. One of the men decided that a woman had no right to walk around freely and without fear of harassment or assault and so he tried to rape her. This was a poor choice on his part. As he reached for her, a thick mist swirled around him and, when it dissipated, a bare skeleton clattered to the ground. Another version of the story says he was struck by lightning and reduced to a smoking pile of blackened bones—either way he got what was coming to him. The other scout showed the woman respect, not just because she scared the living shit out of him, but because he was genuinely a pure-hearted fellow. The woman told him to go back home and have his people prepare a feast because she would be stopping by for a visit. In some tellings, they prepared a feast for her, which is directly antithetical to the issue of famine that began this whole adventure; in other telling, they had nothing to offer her but some grass dipped in water. Either way, it's the thought that counts, and since they treated her with all due respect the magical woman imparted to them sacred knowledge.

White Buffalo Calf Woman taught the Lakota how to use a pipe, which represents much more than just a way to kick back at the end of a long day. The red bowl of the pipe represented the work of men, and the wooden stem was crafted by the women. The smoke rising from the pipe represented a connection to the spiritual world. The flame, bolstered with dried buffalo poo, was the torch of knowledge and tradition passed down from generation to generation. The bowl of the pipe further represented the buffalo, which itself represented the four directions as well as the plentiful gifts offered to people who live in concert with nature. She gave them seven ceremonies altogether that would connect the earth, humanity, and the divine. When she was done, she walked off into the sunset, stopping and rolling on the ground four times. The first time, she became a black buffalo, and then a brown buffalo, a red buffalo, and finally a white buffalo. Lakota lore holds that the most sacred animal of all is the white buffalo.[1] From that time on, the Lakota flourished by following the teachings of the woman whom they call White Buffalo Calf Woman.

As the institutor of much of their rituals and traditions, the Lakota people revered and still revere White Buffalo Calf Woman, even after much of the old religion has been syncretized with Catholicism. Along with genocide and disease, Europeans brought with them other 'gifts' like cultural imperialism and, of course, religion. Many of the Lakota converted to Roman Catholicism[2] and for reasons that are not overtly clear, they likened Mary, the mother of Jesus, to White Buffalo Calf Woman.

The story of White Buffalo Calf Woman carries a lasting and remarkable legacy. In 1977, a non-profit organization dedicated to helping victims of abuse and sexual assault called the White Buffalo Calf Woman Society was founded and it became the first women's shelter on an Indian Reservation in the United States. While so many atrocities have been committed in the name of deities around the world, it is heartening to see something so important and so beneficial being done under the banner of this truly badass goddess.

Blue Jay

a.k.a.: Blue-Jay, Jejejiniga
Pantheon: Chinook, Mohawk, and others
Spouse/Lovers: Dead Girl
Siblings: Ioi
Deity of: trickery
Symbols: blue jays

---

[1] Though rare, they do exist and often change color somewhat over time.
[2] Including Black Elk whose 1932 account *Black Elk Speaks* is one of the most significant recordings of Indigenous American culture and myth to date.

"Blue Jay" by Malena Salinas

Like his namesake, Blue Jay is more often annoying than he is destructive. He's not a trickster in the model of Loki or Coyote, but is more in the vein of Bart Simpson. He's a brat who intentionally misinterprets instructions and does what he wants to do rather than what he should be doing.

In Chinook tradition, the primary target for Blue Jay's special brand of annoyance is his sister Ioi. Once, to keep him occupied, Ioi gave Blue Jay the task of putting out five fires and gave him five buckets of water to do so. A poor listener, Blue Jay used up all the water on the first fire and was then burned to death by the second. For some reason, many Blue Jay tales involve either the trickster dying or merely traveling to the land of the dead.

When Ioi told her little brother that it was time for him to get married, Blue Jay decided not to marry the woman she had picked out for him. To be fair, Ioi has selected a recently-deceased old woman to be her sister-in-law, so Blue Jay's objections are understandable. He would rather marry a recently-deceased *young* woman. Granted, there was no Match.com or Tinder around, but it still seems a bit bizarre to be looking for a love connection amongst the dead. Not to yuck his yum, of course. After selecting his corpse bride, Blue Jay had to bring her to a village where they could reanimate the dead. When he got there, the magic people informed him that they could only revive someone who had been dead one day and this girl had now been dead two days, so he would have to go to the next village for help. By the time he reached the next village, the girl had been dead for three days and so he was sent to a third village. On and on this went until finally he found a village that could reanimate the less than fresh wife he had picked out. When he and his zombie love came back home, the family of the young girl were ecstatic to see their little girl alive again, because now they could exact a bride price from Blue Jay. It was in an attempt to avoid this very situation that Ioi had recommended to her brother an elderly woman with no living relatives. The price the young woman's family asked was Blue Jay's hair. Though it'd be a bargain at twice the price, Blue Jay was unwilling to part with his lovely locks. The girl's family came after him and Blue Jay transformed into a bird[1] and flew back to the magical village of the dead. The moment he abandoned his wife, she once again fell dead and so they reunited in the land of the dead. And they lived (or didn't live) happily ever after.

In yet another Blue Jay-in-the-land-of-the-dead story, he went to visit his sister Ioi who had married a dead man. When he got there, he saw his sister talking

---

[1] Quite possibly a blue jay, but who can say for certain?

to the piles of bones lying around her. Ioi explained that these bones were those of her in-laws' and that the denizens of the land of the dead tended to fall apart when surprised. Blue Jay saw this as a great opportunity for mischief and so he made a game of scaring the dead and laughing as they tumbled to the ground, which no doubt sounded like a xylophone. When that got old, Blue Jay took to switching bones around from one pile to another so that when they reassembled themselves they would end up all catawampus with their heads on the wrong bodies, too many or too few appendages, and so forth. Eventually, Blue Jay got his comeuppance either by being driven mad by the dead or by becoming dead himself.

Unlike fellow indigenous trickster figures like Coyote, Blue Jay's exploits rarely result in either helping or harming the common good. Blue Jay stories, largely speaking, aren't etiological, but rather they are instructive. And it's a very simple, clear, but nonetheless important lesson that we learn from Blue Jay: Don't be a dick.

Windigo

a.k.a.: Wendigo, Widjigo, Wintigo, Wehndigo, Windgoe etc.
Pantheon: Algonquin, Chippewa, Ottawa, Potawatomi
Deity of: famine, greed, cannibalism

Windigoag[1] are enormous, insatiable, people-eating creatures feared by numerous groups indigenous to the Great Lakes Region. More than just a bogeyman, the Windigo speaks to some of the most primal fears of the human heart.

Imagine life in a hunter-gatherer society in the pre-climate change Great Lakes Region. Brace yourselves, winter is coming. Food is scarce and getting scarcer by the day. The local fauna has mostly tucked themselves away for the winter already, but you've still got a family to feed. Even in an agricultural society, one of the greatest challenges humans can face is famine. How do you keep everyone fed when there isn't enough food? When those around you are dying from lack of sustenance, what do you do to help as many people as possible survive until spring? You can only ration so much, and divvying up food only works so long as there's food to divide. You can't divide zero. So, what do you do? Do you let your loved ones die? Do you make a last-ditch effort to find food,

---

[1] The plural form of Windigo.

"Windigo" by Mandy Cantarella

knowing that if you fail you're all dead? Or do you look at Mitch who died just yesterday and think "I mean, Mitch is made of meat . . ."? What does it say about you if you are willing to eat another human being? What does that do to you? How do you live with it? What if it turns out that Mitch is really tasty?

Cannibalism is, even for people without any other options, a dark thing to contemplate, much less act on. Windigoag are the mythic embodiment of those fears. A Windigo is not a race of people-eating monsters like various yokai of Japan, but is the resultant punishment for humans who resort to cannibalism. If you eat the flesh of another person, even if it's for a really good reason and not just curiosity, Algonquin tradition holds that you may very well become a Windigo. Like to a potato chip, it's hard to eat only one human.

Rather than transforming as one would into a werewolf, a Windigo is more of a horrible monster suit worn over your human body. Windigo are large, sometimes just a little bigger than a human, sometimes as tall as a tree, sometimes they get bigger with each new person they devour. They may be described as being hairy, made of ice, covered in ice, or looking like a large, emaciated, rotting human, but the general consensus is that contained within the beast, like an icy heart, is the frozen body of the person who became the beast. Traditionally, the only way to stop a Windigo was to kill the frosty person inside—some have suggested that a person might be saved from Windigo possession but, let's be honest, that's probably just wishful thinking. Once you become a Windigo, you have but one goal in life: Feed.

Though it's a good idea to avoid cannibalism anyway, it may not be the only way to become possessed by a Windigo. There are stories of warriors who became Windigoag in order to save their people from a threat. Other times it is suggested that becoming a Windigo may be the price you pay for being exceptionally greedy. Or maybe you just spent too much time around a Windigo. Or maybe you're a precocious child who gets punished for learning to talk early by becoming a monster. Any number of things might result in Windigo-ism.

Windigoag are incredibly dangerous, but they can be defeated. Dogs, especially giant dogs whose previous owners were benevolent spirits, have been known to kill Windigo. In fact, the Ojibwa's etiological myth about domesticated dogs involves the first dog saving a couple of hunters from a Windigo. Even more extraordinary is the tale of a little girl who brought the smack-down to a Windigo. When her village was threatened, she gathered up two sticks and marched right up to the giant Windigo, growing taller with each step she took, until she could look the monster straight in the eye. With a blow from one stick, she knocked it to the ground; with the second stick, she crushed its skull. The Windigo melted away and all that was left was a dead, wet guy with a fractured skull. Admittedly, the myth of a little girl kicking the ass of a man-eating Windigo is just plain awesome. What's less awesome is when the world of myth bleeds over into the real world.

In 1906 a Cree shaman named Zhauwuno-geezhigo-gaubow, but better known as Jack Fiddler, was arrested for doing what other legendary figures had been commended for: he killed a Windigo. The key difference between Fiddler and the mythic killers of Windigoag is that Fiddler and his victim were both very real human beings. He claimed to have defeated fourteen Windigoag in his life, some of which had asked him to kill them before they transformed. In Fiddler's defense[1], all accounts indicate that he sincerely believed that he was helping people by stopping the evil possessing them, and quite possibly those he killed believed just as sincerely. That being said, killing people regardless of whether or not you or they think they are turning into a mythic anthropophagous[2] monster is still highly illegal[3] and, from an objective standpoint, immoral.

---

[1] Jack Fiddler escaped captivity and committed suicide before the trial even began. His brother Joseph, who was arrested along with him, was eventually convicted and sentenced to death. The verdict was appealed and he was due to be released, but died in prison before word of his pending release even reached him.

[2] Whereas cannibalism is the eating of human flesh by another human, anthropophagy is the eating of human flesh by anything, human or not.

[3] This case was part of a significant shift in Canadian law that ended up removing the rights of First Nations to govern completely independently.

"Filling the Earth" by Chloe Stewart

African Mythology

The continent of Africa has been peopled since before the rise of *Homo sapiens*. *Homo habilis*, humanity's ancestor and the first of our genus, lived in Africa over two million years ago. And yet, African cultures and their myths were largely ignored by the rest of the world until the 19th and 20th Centuries.

Why has African mythology been overlooked for so long? No small part of that is due to the fact that for many centuries the great empires of Europe (and later America) were too busy committing atrocities against African people to take the time to do anthropological studies. It makes it much harder to enslave, torture, and kill people if you see them as, well, people. By ignoring the cultures of Africa, and even taking pains to ensure that people were separated from others that shared a mutual language or belief system, it made slavery and genocide more palatable for the white folks involved. Proving the resilience of myth, some African gods and religious systems managed to survive the dark passage and took root in the Americas. The Voudon religion, for example, became Voodoo in the Caribbean and even syncretized with Catholicism to create Santeria. Popular African trickster figures metamorphosed into folk figures of the American south like Br'er Rabbit.

Because African myths have an incredibly long history prior to being written down, the received forms of the myths may often be quite different from their original versions. While I would argue that oral tradition is not as unreliable as is often assumed[1], it certainly leaves room for changes and corruptions. Many of the African myths we have bear clear markings of outside influence, such as direct references to white people and their gods. Many African myths are entirely lost because whole African languages and cultures have been wiped out by outside interference (to put it mildly) and so no matter how much African mythology we have accumulated (and continue to accumulate), there is even more that is completely lost to the ages.

What we do have of African mythologies is far from uniform but there are some broad commonalities that show up in many (but certainly not all) African cultures. Perhaps the most notable is the belief in a single, supreme creator deity who separates themselves from the world after creation has occurred. Beneath that creator figure is usually a wide array of other gods and goddesses who take part, to varying degrees, in the day-to-day workings of the world. We also find in

---

[1] See *Mwindo* for more on that.

many African traditions belief in a type of guardian spirits, typically ancestral figures, who keep a close eye on humanity. Oftentimes, an elder of the village will demonstrate special abilities or knowledge, a close connection to ancestral spirits, or the gods themselves. Another common feature of African mythologies is the prevalence of the trickster figures. There's Eshu, Anansi, and Hlakanyana who are all featured in this book, but there are (conservatively) dozens of others as well. Probably hundreds would be more accurate, and even that may be low balling. African cultures love their trickster tales and it's not difficult to understand why.

Because African mythology is far from monolithic, I have attempted to specify from which group within the continent each character comes. That's not always as cut-and-dried as one might hope, though, since the languages and myths of neighboring groups often overlap. For any and all omissions, you have my deepest apologies. And of course, the scope of African myth is widened and fractured even further when you account for the non-voluntary relocation of many African people. Or, to put it more bluntly: the slave trade. Over the course of the African slave trade, over 12.5 million people were taken out of their homeland and brought to Europe and the Americas. These parts of the world, particularly the southern United States and the Caribbean, wherein large populations of African people were 'forcefully immigrated' to, and where large populations of their descendants still live, is known as the African diaspora. In the diaspora, the languages and myths of continental Africa evolved over time into something unique. Many of the characters and stories found originally in Africa still echo in the diaspora, but they may be blended with figures from other religions, most prominently Catholicism. The syncretization of these very different traditions leads to some very fascinating and also very confusing new forms.

Astute readers of this text may have noticed that the first chapter of this book is, in fact, about an African mythology. Why has Egyptian mythology been separated out from the rest of the continent? Mostly because Egypt is an entirely different beast than the rest of Africa. Not only is it tucked away in a corner and more accessible from the Sinai Peninsula or the Mediterranean Sea than Sub-Saharan Africa, but the character of their culture and the form of their mythic record is completely different. Yes, they are all on the same continent, but that fact of geographic commonality does not supersede the vast cultural differences. To be fair, lumping all non-Egyptian African cultures together in a single chapter is, well, kind of shitty. Just as each Indigenous American group could and probably should get their own chapters, African cultures each deserve theirs. Partly due to the relative lack of scholarship on their myths, and in the interest of keeping this text to a manageable size while still including a taste of what African myth has to offer, I have opted to highlight some prominent figures from a variety of different African groups. It is not enough, to be sure, but it's a start and hopefully it will whet the appetite for further delving into African mythologies.

"Mawu" by Jon Alderink

Mawu

a.k.a.: Mawu-Lisa, Mahu[1]
Pantheon: Fon, Akan, Ewe
Spouse/Lovers: Lisa
Siblings: Lisa
Parents: Nana Buluku
Offspring: Xevioso, Gu, seven pairs of twins
Deity of: creation, wisdom, moon, motherhood, life, abundance
Symbols: moon, coiled serpent

Mawu, goddess of the moon, and Lisa, god of the sun, are lovers. Or twins. Or both. Or a single dual-nature entity named Mawu-Lisa. Then again, none of those things are mutually exclusive and so they might all be true at the same time. No matter which lens you want to look at this (these) figure(s) through, one thing remains constant: Mawu, the feminine half, always gets top billing. Lisa is almost completely overlookable—less of a figure in his own right, and more of a supporting player in the continuing adventures of Mawu.

Mawu and Lisa are the offspring of the supreme creator goddess Nana Buluku. Though the supreme deity of all deities in her pantheon, Nana Buluku doesn't do very much. Sure, creating the universe is nothing to sneeze at,[2] but it was really her daughter, Mawu, who did the heavy lifting (not literally; Mawu's snakey assistant literally does the heavy lifting, but more on that later). Nana Buluku made reality, made Mawu-Lisa, and then walked away to let them sort out the rest.

Mawu, either as an individual or as the feminine half of Mawu-Lisa, created the world and everything in it. Lisa was responsible for the sun and . . . well, that's pretty much it. Mawu, however, is a goddess of abundance—almost to a fault. She loaded up the world with so many mountains and rivers and plants and animals and people that she was afraid that this island earth might sink into the sea. To prevent a tragic end to the recently-begun world, she asked her serpentine servant, Aido-Hwedo, to coil up under the land to hold it in place.

---

[1] Interestingly, Māhū is the term used in some Polynesian cultures for people of the third gender (which is often equated with people who are transgender). It is a notable coincidence that Mawu (Mahu) has a dual gender nature but, ultimately, it is almost certainly nothing more than a false cognate. But still pretty neat, right?

[2] And it's a necessary step if you want to make an apple pie from scratch.

275

Aido-Hwedo (also called Ayida-Weddo or Da) is, like Mawu-Lisa, a dual-gendered figure. In Voudon, and especially in the African diaspora, this Rainbow Serpent is an incredibly important figure.[1] The male portion is red and the female aspect blue, which makes for a diversity of gender identities along the (visible light) spectrum. Aido-Hwedo is a perfect reflection of Mawu-Lisa in this way too, with Lisa as the fiery-red sun and Mawu as the calming moon.

The gifts of Mawu did not stop after creation was completed. Each night she brings sweet relief from the blazing African sun with the soothing night sky and the cooling temperatures that come with it. Mawu's gift of moonlight is a symbol of wisdom and maturity—possibly because the spirit cools as one grows older, or because in order to grow wise, one must study through the night, or just because when you get old you're awake all night getting up to pee. Whichever.

The greatest gift to the world, without question, must be the gift of life itself. Called *sekpoli*, the breath of life is bestowed on every living thing from the mother of us all, Mawu. And while she is generally a tender, patient mother, Mawu can get kind of riled up when she is not given due credit or respect. One story says that the first monkey, an obnoxious fellow named Awe, believed that he too was capable of granting life. When he bragged to the other living beings, Mawu caught wind of it and challenged him to prove it. Awe chopped down a tree and skillfully carved a human looking wooden figurine from it. "See! I made a person!" he proclaimed, proudly. Mawu asked Awe to bring his new person to life, so Awe blew on it as hard as he could. Nothing happened. He tried again. And again. And again. And while he had carved a neat looking statue, he found himself incapable of animating it with the breath of life. Mawu offered him a bowl of porridge as condolence for his failure. Awe ate it up and only after doing so did Mawu reveal that the Seed of Death had been mixed in with the porridge. Mawu sent a strong message: not only was she the only one capable of giving life, but she had no qualms about taking it away, too.

Because even an active creator like Mawu can't be bothered to help with every little thing, she sent her kids to do some of the day-to-day tasks. Gu (or Gun)[2], the heavenly handyman, was responsible for fixing up cracks in the earth's foundations (often resulting from Aido-Hwedo getting itchy and accidentally

---

[1] See the classic film *The Serpent and the Rainbow* starring America's greatest president: Bill Pullman.

[2] Likely a variation on the Yoruban god Ogun who serves essentially the same function and is also a major player in Voodoo and other religions from the African diaspora.

causing earthquakes) and other tasks. Her son Xevioso[1] brought thunder and the accompanying rains. Beyond that, she and Lisa birthed seven pairs of twins, each with their own domain. All the children begat by Mawu-Lisa were the result of the coupling together of the moon and sun in the ultimate display of celestial intercourse: the solar eclipse.

Cagn

a.k.a.: |Kaggen, Khaggen, Cang, Kaang, Kho Thora, Ngo, "Mantis"
Pantheon: San[2]
Spouse/Lovers: Coti
Offspring: Cogaz, Gewi, unnamed others
Deity of: creation, trickster
Symbols: praying mantis, caterpillar, eland

From the birthplace of humanity comes a god with a magic tooth and a fondness for elands.[3] Cagn's narrative adventures touch on many of the most prominent and widespread themes in African myth and, given that he comes from the staggeringly ancient society of the San of southern Africa, his stories may well provide insight into some of the earliest forms of mythology on Earth.

Cagn is said to have created the earth, the sky, and everything that fills them. The process seems to be your standard *ex nihilo* creation, using thought and speech for the most part. A few things get individual creation narratives including certain types of animals and the moon. There are at least two different versions of Cagn creating the moon: in one, the moon is an old shoe of his that he tossed into the sky; in another, the moon is the result of Cagn wiping mucus off his face with an ostrich feather after a gall bladder exploded and coated him in slime. The eland also gets multiple origin myths having either been born of Cagn's wife Coti or made from the discarded shoe of Cagn's meerkat son-in-law Kwammanga.[4] Either

---

[1] Likely a variation on the Yoruban god Shango who serves essentially the same function and is also a major player in Voodoo and other religions from the African diaspora.
[2] San (or Saan) is a problematic term, as are most of the other terms assigned to these particular people. Traditionally, Europeans used the term "Bushmen," which is rife with negative connotations and is not a name they applied to themselves. San was applied by rival groups and later Western anthropologists and can also a bit pejorative. A third label of Basarwa is no less problematic.
[3] A relative of the antelope.
[4] Married to Cagn's adopted porcupine daughter. Really.

"Cagn" by Matt Renneker

way, Cagn took special interest in the eland, hid it away, and gave it daily doses of honey to help it grow big and strong.[1] When his son, son-in-law, or grandson found the eland, they killed it. Cagn was enraged, not because he didn't want the animal to be killed, but because he didn't want it to be killed yet. Thus, the killing of the eland before it reached maturity was meant to teach the hunter-gatherer people to hunt game when it was in season and may have been a contributing factor to Cagn turning his back on humanity and leaving the earth behind. The figure of the creator god who leaves the earth to its own devices after becoming irritated with humanity is a common one throughout Africa.

The mythologies of Africa are rife with some of the most bizarre and delightful trickster tales from anywhere in the world. Along with playing the role of distant creator, Cagn was a trickster and yet again, the eland was woven into his stories. Though human in appearance, Cagn's name means "mantis," and the praying mantis was one of his favorite shapes to shift into; he was also known to disguise himself as a caterpillar, a snake, or an eland. Given that eland is one of the most coveted game animals of the region, it's not always a great idea to strut around looking like one. In one tale, while trying to covertly watch some dancing ladies, Cagn, in the form of an eland, was killed and butchered. Four of the five members of the family that had hunted him down each grabbed a chunk, leaving his head for the youngest daughter to carry. When the eland opened its eyes and asked the little girl why they had hurt him so badly, she, understandably, freaked the hell out. When her family came running to her, the bits of eland-Cagn wriggled back together and he bounded off, leaving the family with a new respect for the trickster's power.

Many of Cagn's adventures involve him using his children to do his work for him, only to have to step in later to save them. One of his unnamed daughters fell in with the wrong crowd when she literally fell into a pit of snakes and ended up married to the chief of the snakes. Rather than going himself, Cagn sent his son Cogaz to go retrieve her, and for protection, he sent him with one of Cagn's magical teeth. Cogaz escaped with his sister and then Cagn sent a flood to kill off the snakes. Fortuitously, the good snakes climbed high enough to survive the flood while the bad snakes were killed off. Cagn then struck the good snakes with his staff and they became the ancestors of humanity. In another tooth-bearing mission, Cogaz rescued a group of women from a pack of ogres and when the ogres gave chase, Cagn diced up an old shoe, the pieces of which became dogs

---

[1] In one, he feeds it honey; in another he rubs it with honey.

and chased the ogres away. Whatever powers of protection Cagn's tooth had to offer, it was apparently not enough to keep Cogaz from being killed by baboons. The baboons stuck his corpse in a tree, danced around it, and sang a mocking song about Cagn. When Cagn showed up, they literally changed their tune, but Cagn insisted that they sing the original one. As the baboons sang, Cagn walked around and drove pegs into each of their butts, stole Cogaz's body, and subsequently brought him back to life.

As creator god, Cagn's natural adversary was Gauna, the lord of the dead. Gauna's goal in life was to destroy that which Cagn created. Oh, and Cagn himself. Cagn, however, was hard to kill. Even when an ogre swallowed him, Cagn was vomited back up healthy and whole. Gauna's agents, the ants, once overwhelmed Cagn and picked his bones clean, but even from that Cagn somehow managed to bounce back. Death is powerful, but life will ultimately win out—or to put it another way: Cagn gets knocked down, but he gets up again, you are never gonna keep him down.[1]

Waka

a.k.a.: Wak, Wa'a, Waga, Waaq, Waq, Waaqa, Waaqa Tokkicha, Waaqa Gurracha
Pantheon: Oromo
Offspring: races of men, animals and demons
Deity of: creation
Symbols: *Faajjii Walaabuu* (tri-color emblem), black

To say that a majority of indigenous African cultures are or were polytheistic is, perhaps, an understatement. Nearly every native African religion is populated by numerous deities. Often there is a single, supreme god at the top of the heap, but that is still a far cry from anything resembling monotheism. The religion of the Oromo (or at least the received form of it) is a real outlier in that it features one and only one god: Waka.

Waka created the world and everything in it. After he created most everything he could think of, including a human man, he walked around the earth and realized that it was kind of flat and boring. He asked the man to build a coffin

---

[1] Apologies to Chumbawamba and further apologies to those of you who now have that song stuck in your head.

"Waka" by Caitlin Rausch

and seal Waka inside it. Once safely tucked away, Waka called down a rain of fire, which, like lava from an erupting volcano, made the topography more interesting by creating mountains and such. Climbing out of his coffin, Waka saw all that he had created and made and that it was good. The man approached him and asked why Waka had been gone for so long, which surprised the creator who had thought he had only been secluded for a few minutes. In fact, it had been seven years and Waka felt bad about how lonely the man had become in that time. To make it up to him, Waka took some of his own blood and crafted a woman to be a companion to the man. The man and woman noticed differences in each other's anatomy: namely, the man had a penis on his finger and the woman had a vulva in her armpit. Yes, you read that correctly. The first man had a literal dick finger and the woman bore her reproductive organs in her armpit. After fitting finger into armpit, the woman swelled up and eventually gave birth to either nine or thirty children. Somewhere along the line, Waka moved their reproductive parts to between their legs because the woman was embarrassed by having it in her armpit and because the man wanted his to line up with hers. It is unknown whether this move was made before or after she gave birth.

The differing accounts of the offspring of the first man and woman offer origins to very different types of creatures. In the version where the two had thirty children, the man was so embarrassed at the abundance that when Waka came by for a visit, he hid half of them away. You can't pull a fast one over on Waka, though, and he found the additional fifteen children and transformed them into animals and demons. This is likely the older version of the tale and connects humanity to the animals as well as the fearsome forces of evil that stalk us. The version of the story wherein they had only nine children is steeped in Biblical imagery, including the most beloved son being robbed of his inheritance because an ailing, near-sighted father is tricked into bestowing the blessings on a younger son, a la Jacob and Esau. The thieving son, blessed with great riches and power over other people, ran off and his descendants became the wealthy and oppressive people known as Europeans and Arabs. The beloved son who was the intended recipient of the blessing instead became the ancestor of the Oromo people. Another son became the ancestor of Muslims, so it's clear that this story came about only after some outside influences had shown up in the Oromo world.

Given that the region inhabited by the Oromo (Ethiopia, Somalia, and Kenya) has been influenced by Christianity since the mid-500s CE and Islam nearly as long, it is entirely possible that their monotheism is something more than coincidental. The worship of a singular, supreme god is very likely the product of the inundation of Christians and Muslims who came to the region with missionary zeal. The received form of the traditional religion of the Oromo[1] is probably a response to, or syncretization of, their old religion and the invasive Abrahamic religions. As such, many of their myths bear echoes of Biblical or Quranic stories or themes.

Not everything about this monotheistic religion is derived from outside influences, however. One significant difference in the traditional Oromo religion versus Christianity and Islam is that there is no real concept of an afterlife and, as such, rewards and punishments are doled out to the living rather than the dead. If you break *safuu*, the moral code handed down by Waka, throwing off the balance of the universe and inviting chaos[2], you will be dealt with in the here and now. We also find similarities to other African groups in their belief in ancestral spirits who keep an eye on them and in their physical and spiritual connection to nature.

Perhaps the most elegant and poetic image associated with Waka and the religion of his people is the *Faajjii Walaabuu*. Made up of white, red, and black, this tri-colored emblem is beautiful in its simplicity. White represents the past—the white bones of our ancestors, the white ash of an extinguished fire. Red represents the present—the blood coursing through us, the flames of a roaring fire. And black represents the future—dark, unforeseeable, unknowable, you cannot see the future until it is exposed to the light of the present. Like the future, Waka is black and therefore distant, unapproachable, and mysterious. And yet, he is always there on the periphery, just out of our grasp.

Itherther

a.k.a.: Ali Itherther Mskin
Pantheon: Kabyle
Spouse/Lovers: Thamuatz
Offspring: Achimi, unnamed daughter
Deity of: buffalo, game animals, fertility
Symbols: buffalo, rock bowl

Itherther is the primordial buffalo of the Kabyle people of Algeria. His story reads a bit like the story of Oedipus as told from the perspective of Oedipus' father—

---

[1] Most of their stories were not recorded until the 20th Century.
[2] A very similar worldview is found in Egypt, which is just north of the Oromo homeland.

"Itherther" by Naomi K Illustration

with an Indigenous American-style emergence myth and buckets of buffalo semen mixed in for good measure.

Itherther and a female buffalo called Thamuatz followed a river out of the dark and deep realm of Tlam and emerged into the bright and beautiful world above. There on the earth, they delighted in the sun and the warmth and light it provided. Even when the dark and cold of night fell, they were too pleased with this new world to even consider going back to Tlam. The two ran around for days until Itherther caught a glimpse of Thamuatz peeing. He was perplexed to find that she urinated backwards, while he urinated forwards. This discovery led him to notice the differences in their anatomies and it wasn't long before he learned how to make use of those differences.

After much putting together of opposing pieces, Thamuatz grew large and eventually a bouncing baby boy buffalo was born. Achimi was his name and when he was but a year old he tried to have sex with his own mother. Because she was already pregnant (and because incest is gross), she pushed Achimi away.

Achimi then went off into the world. He stumbled upon a village of humans. They had never before seen a buffalo and so they tried to kill him. Luckily for Achimi, their primitive hunting techniques proved not up to the task. Then he encountered an ant who explained the workings of the world to him and pointed out that, alone among the living beings, buffalo were allowed to have sex with their mothers and sisters. Whether that was true or whether the ant was simply an asshole trying to cause trouble is unclear. Bolstered by the ant's permission, Achimi returned to the place of his birth and found and raped both his newborn sister and his mother. When Itherther found out what had happened, he attacked his son but Achimi was far stronger and easily tossed Itherther away.

Now it was Itherther's turn to wander the earth. Separated from his beloved buffalo bride, Itherther experienced what can only be called a severe case of buffalo blue balls. Every time he thought of Thamuatz, semen welled up inside him but he had no place to release it. Until, that is, he came upon a large rock with a bowl-like depression in it. He filled the rock with his semen and then he left it to stew under the hot sun. When he returned to the bowl months later, seven different pairs of animals climbed out of the vat of baby batter. He raised them all and taught them how to find their own food before leaving them with a great commission to 'be fruitful and multiply.'

According to the Kabyle, Itherther was directly responsible for the abundance of game animals found throughout their region of northern Africa. They are quick to point out that one animal in particular was not from Itherther:

the lion. The first lion was once a human cannibal named Ihebill and from him, and not the potent buffalo, do all other cats come.

As a fun side note, the rock bowl which Itherther filled with ejaculate was a real object located in the real place called Wuahaithar where real people would make real sacrifices before going hunting.

Heitsi-eibib

a.k.a.: Heitsi, Haitse-aibeb
Pantheon: Khoikhoi (Khoi/Khoekhoe/Hottentots)
Spouse/Lovers: Various unnamed wives
Parents: a cow and magic grass or a young woman and magic grass
Offspring: Urisib
Symbols: cairns

It is a popular saying that: "whatever doesn't kill you, makes you stronger." In fact, that is not true as there are many things that can weaken without outright killing, but that is neither here nor there. The Khoikhoi have a saying, or at least they should have a saying, that: "whatever *does* kill you, makes you stronger." Such is the case with more than one Khoikhoi culture hero.

Heitsi-eibib is a culture hero and trickster who overcame great adversity and even the grave (repeatedly) to help his people. But, like all good heroes, Heitsi-eibib had humble origins. One tale of his birth says that he was born of a cow, another that he was born of a young woman; either way, the paternal half of his genetic code came from some magical grass that was consumed by either the cow or the young woman. In his bovine biography, he was a calf who very quickly grew to be very large. When the people came to slaughter and cook him, the bull ran off. His would-be killers followed the trail of his hoof prints until the tracks suddenly stopped. They asked a man whom they found at the end of the trail if he had seen any big, meaty bulls come by, but the man said no. And, technically, he hadn't seen any anything pass by because the bull hadn't passed, but had become the man. Heitsi-eibib's first words as a human were, ironically, a bit of bullshit.

Though primarily regarded as a hero to his people, Heitsi-eibib was not always a very good person to those closest to him. There's the tale where, while his mother was changing his dirty diaper, he grew to the size of an adult man and raped her, only to return to baby size so that no one would believe her when she told them what had happened. And then, of course, there was the time when

286

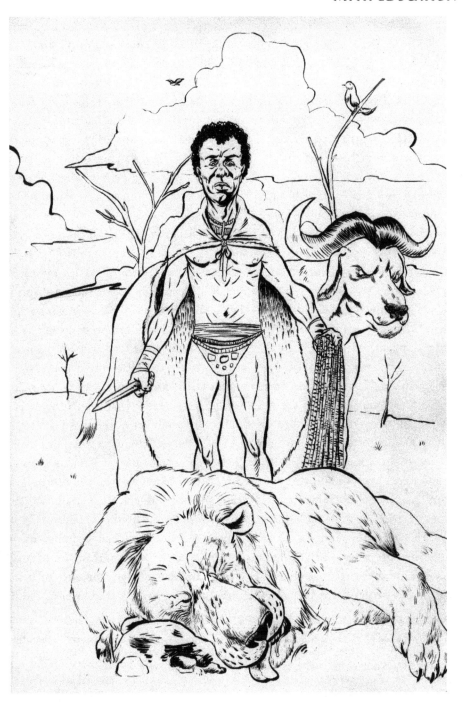

"Heitsi-eibib" by Christian Sitterlet

Heitsi-eibib got so sick of his responsibilities as a husband and father that he chose to die rather than spend time with his family. When he snuck out of his grave to go party, his son Urisib caught him and quite literally dragged him back to his family.

Of Heitsi-eibib's heroic feats, three are the most notable: (1) his battle with ‡Gama-‡Gorib[1]; (2) his battle with |Hau-|gai-|gaib[2]; and (3) his battle with Lion. ‡Gama-‡Gorib was a monster who menaced Heitsi-eibib's people by forcing them to compete with him in a match that was not unlike a game from *American Gladiators*.[3] They would grapple on the edge of a pit and the loser, which always happened to not be ‡Gama-‡Gorib, would get knocked into a video game-esque pit filled with spikes. Heitsi-eibib decided it was time someone took down the Khoikhoi equivalent of Gemini[4] and so he challenged ‡Gama-‡Gorib to a bout. Heitsi-eibib lost. As he fell into the pit, he asked the pit to heave him back up and, of course, it did. Again, he lost and again he was spat back out from the pit, each time emerging stronger than before. Finally, Heitsi-eibib struck ‡Gama-‡Gorib with a fatal blow right behind the ear. Heitsi-eibib then asked one last favor of the pit and all the people who had been defeated by ‡Gama-‡Gorib were resurrected. The set-up and, indeed, the bizarrely specific location of the fatal shot are identical in Heitsi-eibib's defeat of |Hau-|gai-|gaib. The only real difference is that |Hau-|gai-|giab fought with a stone that he removed from his forehead, rather than over a deadly pit. Whenever the stone was hurled at |Hau-|gai-|gaib it bounced off and kill the person who threw it. Only Heitsi-eibib knew to aim for the spot behind his ear to take him out. Not only did Heitsi-eibib defeat two villains by striking them behind the ear, but the other great hero of the Khoikhoi, their creation god Tsui||goab, also defeated his adversary ||Gaunab the same way. Tsui||goab and Heitsi-eibib both died multiple times, re-emerging stronger each time so apparently those type of stories really resonated with the Khoikhoi.

Heitsi-eibib's triumph over Lion is perhaps more significant than his other battles because it resulted in some major power shifts between man and nature. At one time, we're told, Lion lived in a tree and/or had wings. Because of that, Lion would swoop down and slaughter man, woman, child, and cattle all he liked

---

[1] Because the language of the Khoikhoi uses clicking sounds with no real equivalent in English phonemes, ‡ is one of the symbols commonly used to indicate their use.
[2] | also indicates a click, but a different click than the one indicated by ‡.
[3] Many of our younger readers may not remember *American Gladiators.* Suffice it to say, it was the pinnacle of televised athletic competitions.
[4] The American Gladiator who was nigh-invulnerable to pugil sticks, not the constellation of the same name.

and there was nothing the humans could do about it. Until, that is, Heitsi-eibib burned down Lion's tree and cursed him to live on the ground. Or Heitsi-eibib got Lion so fat that he couldn't fly and then carefully cut off Lion's wings. The net result was that the descendants of Lion could now be hunted and defeated by the descendants of Heitsi-eibib: namely, humanity.

Due to his frequent deaths, grave sites for Heitsi-eibib can be found throughout the Khoikhoi regions of southwestern Africa. Typically marked by cairns, it is still considered an important sign of respect for their ancestral hero to place a stone, flowers, or other objects on the grave when passing by. Though he doesn't use the graves, what with not staying dead and all, Heitsi-eibib is deeply touched by the gesture. As evidence for how beloved Heitsi-eibib is by his people, anthropologist Theophilius Hahn included a prayer to him in his 1881 publication *Tsui | | Goam: The Supreme Being of the Khoi-khoi*:

Oh, Heitsi-eibib,

Thou, our Grandfather,

Let me be lucky,

Give me game,

Let me find honey and roots,

That I may bless thee again,

Art thou not our Great-grandfather?

Thou Heitsi-eibib!

Hai-uri

a.k.a.: Bi-Bloux (female), Tikdoshe (Zulu variation), Chiruwi (Central African variation)

Pantheon: Khoikhoi (Khoi/Khoekhoe/Hottentots)

Deity of: underworld

The Hai-uri straddle the world of the living and the world of the dead. Because they are one foot in the grave (so to speak) they appear in this world as half a man bisected sagittally.[1] Here in the world of the living they have only one eye, one arm, one leg, one nipple, half a nose, etc. and yet they get around with surprising agility. Rather than running around obstacles Hai-uri bound over them like a living pogo stick. Though they are only half as scary as other mythic monsters, you would

---

[1] The fancy medical terminology that means cut in half vertically.

"Hai-uri" by Ashley Campos

do well to avoid their clutches[1] because if they do get a hand on you, they are more than happy to eat both sides of you. The same is true for the much less common female variety called Bi-Bloux.

Surprisingly, the specter of a one-legged, one-armed monstrous creature shows up in Celtic mythology as well. It would be an understatement to say that the Khoikhoi of southern Africa are distant relatives with Irish Celts, and yet they find common ground in at least one type of mythic monster. For the Celts, the forces of darkness are populated with a group called the Fomorians who are described (from time to time) as having only one leg and one arm. It is almost certainly nothing more than a coincidence, but it is still worth noting that from Africa to Ireland, the fear of a malicious mono-side is not unique.

Within Africa, there are variations on the Hai-uri. Both the Zulu and central African groups have similar boogey-men. For them, though, it is not a race of beings, but a single figure creeping about. For the Zulu, he is a dwarven half-man named Tikdoshe, and in central Africa he's called Chiruwi—both names apparently mean something along the lines of "mysterious creature." As scary sounding as "mysterious creature" may be, the term hardly conveys the distinctive appearance of these particular mysterious creatures, but a half-man by any other name is still just as fierce. Both Tikdoshe and Chiruwi are spoiling for a fight and will challenge anyone who stumbles across them. How a half person is able to fight with any prowess is difficult to imagine, but apparently, they are able to fight and they kill their mortal opponents more often than not. If you somehow manage to defeat[2] them, they have been known to impart vast medical knowledge to the victor.[3] Presumably it's an anatomy lesson since they have such easy access to extremely realistic visual aids.

Eshu

a.k.a.: Eleggua, Elegba, Legba, Esu-Elegba, Echu, Esu, Exu
Pantheon: Yoruba
Parents: Olorun or Orunmila
Deity of: crossroads, thresholds, misfortune, chaos and balance
Symbols: red and black (Santeria)

---

[1] Or should that be "clutch"?
[2] Or should that be "de-foot"?
[3] Perhaps you could use a half-nelson?

"Eshu" by Darian Papineau

Like all good tricksters, Eshu is an orisha[1] of the boundaries and crossroads. He is, what Homer Simpson would call a "crisitunity"[2] god and can be found at literal and metaphoric crossroads and even in doorways. The threshold, the border between two spaces, is the domain of Eshu. We've all experienced the phenomenon wherein you walk into another room and immediately forget what it is that you went there to do—in psychology that is known as the "Doorway Effect" but in mythological terms it is the work of Eshu. He can also take a simple decision and turn it into a quagmire of possibilities. That's also a psychological phenomenon known as the "Netflix Queue Effect."[3]

In one of his most famous tales, Eshu grew bored, which is the most dangerous thing a trickster can grow. And so, he decided to cause some mischief. He found two men, best friends and neighbors, and Eshu walked casually down the border between their properties. Both men were working their respective lands as the stranger walked by. Later, when the two friends were chatting, one said to the other: "Hey, did you see that guy walking between our fields earlier?" "Yeah," said the second man, "Never seen him before. I wonder who he was." "I don't know either," said the first man, "but that was an unusual hat he was wearing." "Oh yeah!" said the second man, "I've never seen a big black hat like that before." "Me neither," said the first man, "But I think you mean white." "No," said the second man, "his hat was black." "It was white," the first man explained. "It was black. I remember thinking how it was blacker than the night sky." "No, no," said the first man, "I distinctly remember thinking: 'that hat is as white as the clouds hanging overhead.'" "On my word," insisted the second, "it was black." "That hat was white, I tell you!" "Black!" "White!" It's unclear who threw the first punch, but soon the men were tumbling about beating each other viciously. Like a fist fight in a hockey match that clears the benches, the entire village was soon swept up into the melee. In the midst of it all, a fire broke out. Eshu, who had been watching from a distance, tossed away his two-sided hat (one white, one black) and went to the villagers to offer help. As their homes were burning, Eshu stood

[1] The term for a minor deity of the Yoruba and other African cultures. Though "orisha" is a more complex idea than the personified figures whom we usually associate with the terms "gods" or "deities," for our purposes here they are more or less interchangeable.
[2] According to Lisa Simpson, the Chinese have a word that means both "crisis" and "opportunity" but, shockingly, unlike all other facts learned from cartoons, this one is not strictly true. But it sounds like a neat idea. And "crisitunity" really should be a word.
[3] This effect has yet to be recognized by the psychiatric community, largely because I just made it up.

293

amongst them and said "Grab your possessions! Save everything you can! Bring it out here and I'll keep an eye on it for you!" And they did so. They laid their possessions before Eshu who kindly redistributed them any way he pleased, giving to one person something that belonged to another, sowing even further seeds of discord.

Eshu is an instigator. He didn't start the fire;[1] he simply reminded the people that they had matches. He doesn't cause the problems, but he opens the door to allow the problems to enter on their own.

Eshu also acts as a go-between. Since his realm is the crossroads, the highways, and byways, it is not surprising that Eshu is used by the gods to carry messages to humanity and vice versa. As the distance between the heavens and the earth can be vast, both physically and metaphysically, it is helpful to have a guy like Eshu to bridge the gap for us.

Appropriately, Eshu is a key figure in Santeria which is a syncretic religion popular in the Caribbean that straddles the intersection of Catholicism and the traditional Yoruban religion of Voudon. As complicated as a Catholic/Voudon hybrid is, Eshu fills an even more complex space in the religion. In Santeria, there are 201 Eshu who were spawned from their father cutting chunks off the original Eshu whose massive appetite led him to eat nearly everything in existence. Each of the 201 Eshu act as paths to the wise orisha Orunmila. But the Eshus are not simply messengers, they are also the manifestation of evil. Their ultimate goal, however, is not evil for evil's sake, but rather to create order and peace by providing misfortune and chaos that will draw people to the good. Rather than being comparable to the Devil of Catholicism, they are connected only to the form of the Devil who tempted Jesus during his time in the wilderness. It's a nuanced difference that is largely about motive: The Devil (who would lead the world to ruin) is not like Eshu, but the Devil who tempts Jesus so that Jesus may then choose against temptation is like Eshu.

Eshu's two-toned appearance is a reminder of the constant need for balance. He is neither all black nor all red but is bisected by the two. Eshu is a god of boundaries who at one moment walks the line between order and chaos, and the next moment shatters it. If you don't show Eshu proper respect, he will surely bring you to ruin. The best way to ensure your safety against Eshu is to offer him a standing invitation into your home and then hope he never takes you up on it. The only thing more dangerous than Eshu coming into your house is Eshu not

---

[1] It was always burning since the world's been turning.

being welcome in your home. It is a narrow edge for us to walk along and Eshu wouldn't have it any other way.

Oya

a.k.a.: Egungun-oya, Oia, Oya-Iyansan, Yansa, Maman Brigitte (syncretized with St. Bridget), "She Tore"
Pantheon: Yoruba, Voudon, Voodoo, Santeria
Spouse/Lovers: Shango (Chango)
Parents: Yemaya
Offspring: Egungun and four sets of twins
Deity of: change, wind, storms, death, rebirth, divination, women
Symbols: purple, rainbow, eggplants, buffalo, Niger River (Odo-Oya)

A powerful orisha, Oya is as popular in the Caribbean as she is in Nigeria. In the syncretized religions of the African diaspora she is linked with the likes of St. Brigit, St. Theresa, and Our Lady Candelaria, a manifestation of Mary, the mother of Jesus. And it's no surprise that Oya is so beloved, because there's a lot to love about her. She is a figure of change who helps ease the transition into death, and she's a fierce protector and defender of the rights of women and children. And she loves eggplants.[1]

Oya is a goddess of death in the way that the Egyptian Anubis is. She is not a bringer of death like the Grim Reaper; she, like Anubis, shepherds the newly-dead into the sweet hereafter. She, like Anubis, guards the burial sites of the dead and her most common haunt is the cemetery. Because of this, Oya is the one who facilitates communication between the living and their dead ancestors. Perhaps more importantly for our current cultural zeitgeist, Oya blurs the line between the living and the dead by employing zombies. Yes, long before George Romero created the modern zombie in *Night of the Living Dead*, Oya was doing that Voodoo that she do so well.

Voodoo zombies are not the same as your *Walking Dead* zombies. In fact, they don't always have to be dead, often a sleeping person can be controlled by Oya or one of her adherents. Yes, they can be the re-animated corpses of the recently deceased, but even in those cases they don't shamble about looking to eat flesh—Oya's zombies are given specific tasks to accomplish, like holding someone

---

[1] Because eggplants are delicious and if you disagree you can take it up with Oya.

"Oya" by Jerry Butler

captive or nailing Bill Pullman's genitals to a chair[1]. Oya is also the figure called upon to give power to the well-known but poorly understood Voodoo dolls.

Oya acts as the great arbiter of disputes. But, before you call on her to settle an argument between you and your spouse, you should first ask yourself one important question: "Am I a woman?" If the answer is "no," you'd best not invoke Oya since she is known for highly favoring women. Of course, it may not be that she is biased; it may simply be that women are most often right.[2]

In her native Africa, Oya is believed to be the goddess of the Niger River, known locally as Odo-Oya. The nine tributaries that feed into the Niger are said to be her nine children, eight of which are pairs of twins. While the river shows how she provides many gifts to her people, not every connection Oya has to nature is so beneficial.

Oya is not the goddess of gentle breezes and spring showers; she is the goddess of storms so violent that they change the landscape. Her power uproots trees, displaces villages, and sends farmhouses to Oz. Though her husband Shango is technically the storm god, Oya is the one who turns a regular thunderstorm up to eleven. It is not through marital cooperation that Shango and his wife generate such power. Rather, it is said that storms are the result of the two squabbling with each other.

When they first met, it was love at first sight. Nevermind that Oya was already married to Ogun, the god of workers. When she saw Shango, she fell hard for him. She ditched Ogun and went after the man of her dreams, only to find that poor Shango had been kidnapped. Oya found some of the magical items Shango left behind, one of which was a bowl of liquid that gave her the ability to breathe fire (i.e. shoot lightning out of her mouth). She saved Shango from his captors and basically terrified Shango so much that he agreed to marry her. In another version, Oya herself is the one who held Shango captive because she didn't want to share him with his other wives, Oshun and Oba. When Oshun helped Shango escape from Oya's zombie guards by dressing him as a woman, Oya took up the magical items he left behind and gained her lightning-spitting power expressly to get revenge on Shango rather than to save him.

Despite being a representative of all that is feminine and badass, Oya's story can also kind of undercut the very "girl power" message she promotes. She is as fierce a warrior as you're likely to find; her weapons include the machete, flywhisk,

---

[1] If you haven't watched *The Serpent and the Rainbow* since the mention in 'Mawu' it's your own fault for not getting that reference.
[2] Or so my wife and five daughters have informed me.

tornadoes, and lightning, but she must adopt a masculine appearance when she goes into battle. It is said that she wears pants and even grows a beard when she engages in battle, which seems to suggest that for a woman to really be a fearsome warrior she must look and behave like a man. Fiercer than any other orisha, much of her power seems to be drawn from her ability to be, at least partly, masculine. The myths around Oya frequently and very clearly establish that she is a superior warrior to her husband Shango but at the same time Shango is emasculated and Oya is defeminized. Shango dresses as a woman to escape when Oya has him imprisoned; Oya dresses as a man to fight. This betrays a not-at-all-unique dichotomous way of thinking: to be tough and aggressive is to be masculine, to be weak or passive is to be feminine. Is Oya an empowering symbol for women or is she one more example of a narrow-minded view of what it means to be feminine?

Oshun

a.k.a.: Ọṣun, Ochún, Oxúm

Pantheon: Yoruba, Ifá

Spouse/Lovers: Shango, Ogun

Deity of: love, sex, fertility, beauty, pleasure, fresh water

Symbols: Osun River, violin (Cuba), gold, pink

She is a living symbol of women's empowerment and is beloved the world over for the gifts she has bestowed on humanity. I am speaking, of course, of Beyoncé. And Beyoncé could not have picked a more fitting mythic figure to pay homage to than that of the Yoruban orisha Oshun.

Like Queen Bey, Oshun made her mark in a world often dominated by men. When Oshun was sent to earth along with sixteen other orishas to finish off the creation process, she was the only female. In a not-surprising-at-all turn of events, the men completely ignored Oshun, believing that a woman had nothing worthwhile to contribute to the discussion. While the myth doesn't say specifically, we can safely assume that some of the issues on the table included women's reproductive health and therefore, the men agreed, these were decisions best handled by the people who knew best what women need: men. Because the men refused to listen to the woman, she raised up a group of super-powered women called the Iyami Aje who prevented the men from getting any work done until the women's voices were heard. And the men heard the women roar in numbers too big to ignore. They stood up, refusing to be silent or overlooked. They persisted.

"Oshun" by Qing Zhu

And they won. The men learned that not only were women worth listening to, but that everyone was better off when all voices were heard.[1] Oshun then let the rivers flow, making the land flush and fertile with both flora and fauna.

While much of the earth's bounty comes from the gifts of Oshun, she wasn't afraid to use her powers to correct humanity when correction was called for. If humans neglected their duties to the gods, or abused the earth and its resources, Oshun might cause the river to either dry up or flood, depending on which was more likely to get us back in line at any given time. She gave life, and she could take it away. Part of keeping Oshun happy was the celebration held annually by the Osun River and the Osun-Osogbo Sacred Grove in her honor. Osogbo is held as the location of the site where Oshun first had direct interaction with humanity and is therefore one of the holiest of holy locations in Nigeria.[2] That annual festival was the best chance the Yoruba had each year to get the attention of Oshun and ensure that she would grant them wealth, health, and fertility for both their crops and themselves.

Oshun was one of the wives of the thunder god Shango. Out of Oshun, Oya, and Oba, Oshun was usually held to be the favorite wife. When Oshun first met Shango, though, the thunder god played hard-to-get. Oshun, who knew what she wanted and was determined to get it, seduced Shango with a dance and then, as she drew near to him, she slipped her fingers into a magic gourd and wiped the sweet juice from it onto Shango's lips. And from that point on, he was hers. A man having multiple wives is certainly not unheard of, but more unusually, Oshun seems to have multiple husbands.

When Oshun's sister wife Oya left her first husband Ogun[3] to be with Shango, it caused some real trouble. Dumped unceremoniously by the fiery-tempered Oya, Ogun went off into the wilderness to sulk. As the orisha of blacksmiths and laborers in general, Ogun's self-imposed exile was felt keenly amongst his people. Just as when the Mesopotamian goddess Ishtar was temporarily dead leading to a dearth of sex in the world, when Ogun was gone no work could be done. Various orishas tried to draw Ogun back to work, but all of them failed until Oshun took up the cause. Using her patented seductive dance and magic gourd juice combo, Oshun got Ogun back on his feet and landed herself

---

[1] "Nothing to see here, folks! This is just some ancient nonsense with no possible application to modern society," said Mr. Patriarchy.
[2] As of 2005 Osogbo has been designated an UNESCO World Heritage Site.
[3] Lots and lots of orishas have names that being with "O" including, but not limited to: Orunmila, Obatala, Olorun, and Olokun.

a second husband. Which makes for a very awkward arrangement wherein one of Oshun's husbands is married to the ex-wife of her other husband. That is some serious Jerry Springer-level family drama. In all the chaos, though, Oshun remains a woman who gets what she wants and suffers no men who try to tell her what to do.

Mami Wata

a.k.a.: Mamy-Wata, Mammy Water, Mother Water

Pantheon: various West, Central, and Southern African groups and African diaspora in the Americas

Deity of: water, healing, fertility

Symbols: fish, reptiles, snakes, precious gems and stones, red and white

Mami Wata is not the name of an individual being, but a pantheon of African water spirits. They can be male, but are most often female. They can appear fully human, but most often are half reptile or fish. They are popular figures in myriad African cultures as well as in the African diaspora in the Americas, especially in Haiti and other areas were Voodoo has flourished.

As with other mermaid figures, Mami Wata have a complicated relationship with humanity. They have been known, siren-like, to lure people out into the water and then pull them under. They have been blamed for causing the strong undertows that lead to drownings, but are also said to bestow great gifts upon those people they grab in the water. If a Mami Wata gets her hands on you and brings you to her underwater domain, you will leave richer, happier, healthier, and with a way more chilled disposition. Or they may kill you. But mostly they seem benevolent to those who treat them right. If you happen upon a Mami Wata brushing her hair and looking in her mirror, she is more than likely to flee. If you then take her brush and mirror, she may come to you in a dream, offering wealth and abundant sex1 if you agree to give them back and to be sexually faithful to her. If you don't give them back or if you cheat on her, she will bring terrible misfortune upon you.

---

[1] The cross-cultural theme of humans having or wanting to have sex with mermaids may be taken as proof that fish fetishists are far more common than most of us would like to believe.

"Mami Wata" by Annamarie Borowiak

Among the other gifts of Mami Wata are prophecy and the ability to heal most injuries and illnesses. When a Mami Wata priestess, known as a *mamaissii*, does an ecstatic dance, she may become possessed and then speak prophetically in tongues.[1] If you find a Mami Wata or one of her *mamaissii*, they are said to be able to cure almost anything that ails you, excepting only infertility, which they themselves suffer from. So, don't go to Mami Wata if you want a baby, but do go to Mami Wata if you want to be financially secure enough to have or adopt a child later. She is not stingy when it comes to giving out the many treasures of the deep that she possesses.

Depictions of Mami Wata vary. In some, they have the lower body of a snake or other reptile, in others they look more like the familiar mermaid with fishy fins. Some they have curly, black hair, and some long straight hair. The most common depiction is a woman with the lower half of a fish, and a snake (a symbol of divination) wrapping around her with its head between her breasts.

There is a fair amount of debate regarding the origin of both the figure of the Mami Wata and even the name. One school of thought says that the very image of Mami Wata was inspired by the mermaid figureheads on European slave ships. It has also been suggested that "Mami Wata" is nothing more than pidgin English for "Mommy Water," which, admittedly, sounds good when taken at face value. It is possible that one or both of these things are true, that the name and/or image of Mami Wata came about only as a result of the slave trade and the unquestionably enormous impact it had on African people both in Africa and in those regions they were taken away to. It's possible, but that theory reeks of European ethnocentrism and suggests that belief in Mami Wata (at least in the current form) began only after European incursions into Africa. It is conceivable that worship of Mami Wata began after the start of the slave trade and became so popular that it survived the transatlantic voyage to the Americas, but that hypothesis is far from a given. Why would creatures associated with slave ships become beloved figures of healing? If "Mami Wata" is pidgin English, why is it so widespread in non-English speaking parts of Africa?

Another school of thought argues that Mami Wata is a purely African creation from very old African traditions. Though "Mommy Water" may be the modern translation of the title, it seems more likely that it is something of a

---

[1] Scientifically this is known as *echolalia* and shows up in a variety of religious practices including forms of modern Christianity.

linguistic false friend.[1] Mamaissii Vivian Hunter Hindrew suggests that belief in Mami Wata amongst the Dogon people may go back some 4000 years and may stem from even older Egyptian and/or Mesopotamian roots. Rather than the facile translation of the name, she says that *mami* may derive from the same source word meaning "truth" or "wisdom" that gives us the Egyptian *maat* and the Mesopotamian *me*. *Wata* is pronounced similarly to the Egyptian word *uati* and the Khoikhoi word *ouata*, both of which mean "water" or it may come from words like *watoa* and *wat-watt* which mean "woman." Similar female deities connected to water and/or healing show up in other parts of Africa including the Togo goddess Densu, Olokun of the Yoruba, and, indeed, Egypt's Isis. We may never have a definitive answer on the origin of Mami Wata, but it seems entirely plausible that it is a very old African figure whose portrayal may have solidified into what we have now in part because of European influence.

Hlakanyana

a.k.a.: Uthlakanyana, Uhlakanyana, Ukcaijana-bogconomo, Mathlab'-in-doda-i-s'-emi, "Clever Little Boy"
Pantheon: Zulu
Symbols: mongoose, weasel

Many tricksters, either intentionally or unintentionally, have caused profound change in the world. Prometheus gave humanity fire. Coyote accidently gave us the sun. Anansi both intentionally and accidentally gave us stories. Other tricksters, however, primarily use their particular set of skills to get themselves into and back out of trouble. Such a trickster is Hlakanyana.

In the language of the Zulu, *hlaka* means "clever" or even "trickster" and *nyana* means "little boy;" and Clever Little Trickster is about as perfect a name as Hlakanyana could bear. Many tricksters start out young; for example, the very first

---

[1] False friends are words in one language that sound similar to a word in another language but do not mean the same thing. The classic example is the English word "embarrassed" and the similar sounding Spanish word "embarazada" which actually means "pregnant." Mix those words up with a Spanish speaker and you may find yourself a bit desconcertado when they ask when the baby is due. False friends are not to be confused with false cognates which are words in different languages that mean something similar but don't share an etymological origin. Furthermore, false friends should not be confused with real friends, who are people that will give you a ride to the airport for a 5am flight or let you know when something is hanging out of your nose.

"Hlakanyana" by David Stokes

act of newborn Hermes was a sneaky cow-snatching, but Hlakanyana started stirring things up even before he was born. While still in utero, he called out to his mother to let her know when he wanted to be born. And doing so frightened his poor pregnant ma so badly that she promptly went into labor and gave birth to a tiny child with the face of an old, wizened man who then cut his own umbilical cord with a spear. A mythic being born fully formed is certainly not unique, but with Hlakanyana it wasn't that he was born as a full-sized adult, but that he simply never got any bigger. This became his greatest asset because it led others to dismiss and underestimate him. As the mongoose kills the more frightening looking snake, so too does Hlakanyana twist and dissemble to bring down his opponents. Again and again in his exploits, Hlakanyana exemplifies the idea that strength of mind can be far more powerful than hulking muscles.

He was credited with great wisdom, and yet, Hlakanyana's goals never became very lofty. In most of his adventures his goal was usually nothing more than hoping to (A) eat; or (B) not get eaten. Even before his birth, Hlakanyana was thinking of food, insisting that his mother let him out of the womb so he could get some meat before his father used it all up. For a small guy, Hlakanyana could pack away a lot of food, whether it was the meat rations for his entire village, numerous birds that he stole from other people's traps, or baby leopards that he stealthily ate while pretending to watch them for their mother.

Hlakanyana's full cleverness is on display during his frequent run-ins with cannibals or anthropophagous[1] ogres. In one tale, he is caught by two cannibalistic hunters who bring him home to be cooked by their mother. When her sons headed back out to do more hunting, Hlakanyana convinced the mother that they could play a fun game wherein they took turns cooking each other. He climbed into the pot first, which was just beginning to heat up. When it got too hot, he told the woman it was her turn and they swapped places. As the water boiled the woman screamed and Hlakanyana laughed. When the screaming stopped, Hlakanyana laughed even harder and dressed in the woman's discarded clothing. Unlike the Big Bad Wolf, Hlakanyana didn't use his trickery to try to eat the sons, but rather to get them to eat their own mother. He snuck out of the house as they were eating and when he had a sufficient head start, he called back to let them know that they were eating their own mother. The sons gave chase, but lost his trail at the bank of a wide river. Frustrated, one of them picked up a stick along the shore and tossed it to the other side of the river, never knowing that the stick was

---

[1] There it is again: people-eating.

Hlakanyana's disguise and they had just helped him make his final escape. In other stories, when ogres or leopards were trying to eat him, he used his diminutive stature to create exits too small for his pursuers to wriggle through.

Unlike some other tricksters, Hlakanyana doesn't offer much in the way of morality tales, at least not good ones. The Hero Twins of the Quiche Maya teach us that intelligence is a virtue, whereas excessive pride and arrogance are to be avoided. Many Coyote tales show that our reach ought not to exceed our grasp. Hlakanyana does not display any kind of moral code and rather than getting his comeuppance like Loki, Hlakanyana gets away with it. He eats babies in front of their mother and faces no consequences. He makes people eat their own mother and he walks away unscathed. If there is any moral to learn from Hlakanyana, it is nothing more than "if you're going to be an asshole, make sure you're smart enough (or small enough) to get away with it."

And, actually, if we're being honest, that may be one of the most useful or honest lessons to be learned from mythology.

Mbaba Mwana Waresa

a.k.a.: Nomkhubulwane, Lady Rainbow, "Mother of the Rains"
Pantheon: Zulu
Spouse/Lovers: Thandiwe
Parents: Umvelinqangi
Deity of: rain, agriculture, beer
Symbols: rainbow

There are numerous African myths of deities who keep their distance from humanity. Many times, they walk away from humanity after people prove to be wasteful, destructive, or disrespectful to the gods or to nature. There are variations on the distant god theme, including Imana of the Banyarwanda who has very long arms and keeps humanity at an arm's length or Leza, the Kaonde spin on Eshu, who rides around on people's backs, but is old and hard of hearing so he often doesn't hear or mishears prayer requests. Though many gods create walls of separation between Heaven and Earth, the goddess Mbaba Mwana Waresa is all about building bridges between the two.

As the rain goddess, Mbaba Mwana Waresa plays a vital role in the lives of the Zulu people in southern Africa. They are dependent on her life-giving rain

"Lady Rainbow Brewing Co." by Whitney Ruhlman

showers and hearing the thunderous drumming of her bongo was not cause for fear, but for rejoicing. After the rains, Mbaba Mwana Waresa's most important symbol, the rainbow, offers a beautiful link between land and sky.

Mbaba Mwana Waresa loved humanity so much that she married it. Or, at least, *a* human. Which did not sit well with the other gods at all. She was expected and even ordered to pick amongst the gods for a mate, but Mbaba Mwana Waresa wanted what she wanted and she refused to marry anyone but the person of her choosing. None of the gods suited her and so she defied Heaven and fell in love with a human man named Thandiwe. To prove his character and the sincerity of his love for her, she tried to pull a fast one on Thandiwe by having a different beautiful woman take her place while Mbaba Mwana Waresa disguised herself as an elderly woman. Thandiwe saw with the eyes of true love, though, and wasn't fooled for a moment[1]. The two married and lived happily ever after in her rainbow hut in the sky.

In choosing a mortal husband, Mbaba Mwana Waresa angered the gods and strained their relationship with humanity. To soothe the feelings of the butthurt gods, Mbaba Mwana Waresa gave what is regarded as her greatest gift to god and human alike: beer. Drunk on beer, humans and gods felt closer than ever, no doubt throwing their arms around one another and slurring: "I love you, man." As always, beer and drunkenness solved everyone's problems and nothing bad ever came from it.[2] By teaching humans to make beer, Mbaba Mwana Waresa made sure that they would be able to stay connected to the gods. To this day, beer drinking ceremonies[3] are observed by the Zulu, and as a nod to Lady Rainbow, women are the ones responsible for brewing it. Mbaba Mwana Waresa, like a nice cold drink, brings people together—or so the beer commercials would have us believe.

---

[1] Joan of Arc pulled off a similar feat when the French Dauphin put her abilities to the test.
[2] Being from "Beer City, USA" (a.k.a. Grand Rapids, Michigan) I am obliged to extol the virtues of beer and ignore the many dangers and tragedies resulting from the use and abuse of alcohol, even that which comes from craft microbrews.
[3] Part of which involves pouring some on the ground in honor of those who have died.

"Mwindo" by Cynthia Lynn Cooper

Mwindo

a.k.a.: "Little-One-Just-Born-He-Walked"
Pantheon: Nyanga
Parents: Nyamwindo and Shemwindo

Oral tradition often gets a bad rap. We often imagine it as a form of the telephone game wherein words are passed down from one person to another and quickly morph into something very different from what they had been originally. And that is absolutely the case. Sometimes.[1] When you play the telephone game and the information being passed from one person to another is something trivial or unimportant, the message can get garbled very quickly. But what if you are passing down vital information? What if what one person tells the next person is crucial, life-saving information? When we are talking about a culture's myths, the stories by which they attempt to understand themselves and the world around them, we are not talking about trivial information being passed down. We are talking about critical information. Add in the fact that people from pre-literate cultures, almost by necessity, must have keener memories and suddenly oral tradition is on much less shaky footing. And, in some ways, the fact that the story is not written down, not solidified in one specific form, can be a huge advantage. Rather than a fossilized relic of a particular era, such as what we have in the received version of *The Iliad*, a purely oral story remains alive, mutable, and adaptable. The African *Epic of Mwindo* may be the most significant example of the strength of oral tradition.

Mwindo's epic may be the most epic story to ever be called epic. If you watched all three *Lord of the Rings* movies and all three of the *Hobbit* movies back to back, it would take almost twenty hours. If you watched all eight *Harry Potter* movies, it'd be about the same. If you watched all four of the *Star Wars* movies[2] released prior to 2016, it would take just over eight hours. For the story of Mwindo? A full telling takes *twelve days*. Oh, and that's twelve days of story told by a single storyteller. That is binge-watching at its finest. One of the features of The Epic of Mwindo is that each storyteller is allowed and even encouraged to make it their own, infusing it with autobiographical pieces. In telling the story of Mwindo,

---

[1] Purple monkey dishwasher.
[2] I wonder if they'll ever get around to making Episodes I, II, and III. It'd be swell if they made a fourth *Indiana Jones* movie sometime, too.

they tell their own story and the larger story of their people. It is therefore always relevant, always relatable, and always unique.

The basic story of Mwindo hits a number of familiar Hero's Journey tropes. He was the son of Shemwindo who was the chief of his village. Shemwindo told all his wives to only have daughters, but wouldn't you know it? His favorite wife, Nyamwindo gave birth to a son, who rather than coming out the usual way, crawled through her body and emerged walking and talking from the palm of her hand. And he had with him a bag of magic rope, a scepter, and an ax because why not?

When Shemwindo got wind of the birth of a son (thanks to a nosey cricket who couldn't keep his business to himself), he attempted to kill mother and child by hurling spears at the birthing hut. All the spears missed, thanks to Mwindo reciting some magic words. So, then the boy was buried alive under dirt and banana trees. That evening a burst of light shot out from the grave and little Mwindo climbed out laughing. Shemwindo then had Mwindo put into a drum and the drum tossed into the sea. This third attempt on the newborn's life was as fruitless as the others. Mwindo escaped and decided to travel upstream to his aunt in another village.

Along the way he faced various traps laid out for him by his uncle. Mwindo, with the help of a spider, danced over the various pits of spikes and other dangerous snares, and then defeated his uncle and his uncle's servants. Being a merciful fellow, Mwindo brought them back to life when his aunt Iyangura asks him to.

Then, raising up an army, Mwindo headed back to his father's village to rain down holy terror on Shemwindo and his people. He received the help of Master Lightning, some of his uncles, and various other magical figures, and all but wiped out the village. But, Shemwindo escaped by uprooting a plant and slipping into the underworld. Mwindo followed, then helped out the princess of the underworld, and engaged in an over-the-top battle with her father Muisa. He and Muisa knocked the intestines out of each other. Mwindo was killed, and brought back to life by his own magical scepter. Eventually, Mwindo killed Muisa, but then his daughter implored him to bring Muisa back to life and so he did. The re-animated Muisa picked up right where he had left off and Mwindo eventually killed him a second time.

Various adventures in the underworld, including a helpful bird or two, gambling, and more, eventually led Mwindo to Shemwindo. Despite everything he had been through to find Shemwindo and despite the numerous times Shemwindo tried to kill him, when Mwindo finally met up with his father, they forgave each other and emerged from the underworld as a loving family. Mwindo restored Shemwindo's village, became co-chief along with his father, and eventually became the sole chief.

Years later, some of Mwindo's men were eaten by a dragon. Mwindo slew the dragon and released his men from its belly Little Red Riding Hood-style. Then, he cooked the dragon (there's some gross stuff about popping eye balls), and then Mwindo's old friend Master Lightning showed up. Master Lightning, as it happens, was also old friends with the dragon and so he punished Mwindo for killing it. Mwindo was exiled to the heavens for a year. We're not talking about Heaven, we're talking about the literal heavens. There, Mwindo did not have the protection normally provided by the sky and so he was beaten and burned and yes, even lectured, by the elements.

Returning from his exile, Mwindo brought with him a new perspective. Like Moses descending Mount Sinai, Mwindo returned to his people and gave them a series of laws. The law code of Mwindo included things like telling people they should live in nice houses, they should avoid arguing, and they should steer away from adultery. Most significantly, he tells them to be accepting of one another, regardless of gender, size, shape, or ability. Of all the law codes handed down by deities, Mwindo's may be the most positive.[1] And that, really, is what makes this story so important. It isn't just the stated rules that tell us how to live, but the story as a whole teaches tolerance and respect for all living beings. Mwindo himself says that being a hero is great and all, but it is just as great to be forgiving and kind. It is hard to find fault with a code of ethics built around acceptance, forgiveness, kindness and respect.

---

[1] In the interest of full disclosure, the punishment for breaking these laws was death, so it is not without its shortcomings.

"Anansi" by Allie Wass

Anansi

a.k.a.: Ananse, Kwaku Anansi, Mr. Nancy, Aunt Nancy, Kompa Nanzi, Hapanzi

Pantheon: Ashanti (also various other West African groups, and African diaspora in the Americas)

Spouse/Lovers: Aso, Shi Maria (Caribbean)

Parents: None; Asase Ye and Nyame

Offspring: various, Fat Charlie[1]

Deity of: creation, wisdom, stories

Symbols: spider, spider webs

Possibly the most well-known and most beloved figure of African mythology is the spider-man himself: Anansi. Ostensibly an Ashanti figure, belief in Anansi spread throughout western and central Africa and made the transatlantic voyage to become remarkably popular in the African diaspora in the Caribbean and the American south.[2]

Anansi is a trickster, which is about the only thing about Anansi that is consistent. He may be portrayed as a spider or as a human, or as a human with spider-like qualities, or a spider with human-like qualities. He is most often male, but is sometimes female.[3] He is malignant when he isn't benign. He is wise and generous or he is foolish and greedy. In some ways, he is the archetypal trickster. His schemes and scams are often driven by his appetites for food, sex, power, or knowledge and the results range from utter failure and humiliation to inadvertently or advertently structuring the cosmos as we know it today. A lot of the time he just ends up with a full belly and a good chuckle.

Whether he is scamming yams from a turtle or rewriting the art of the deal by up-trading a corncob to get his hands on the sun and moon, Anansi's stories are always entertaining. Without question, though, the most significant Anansi traditions are about the acquisition of knowledge, or of stories themselves.

One version gives a less than flattering view of the spider-man. Anansi, we are told, was not a wise man, though he was smart enough to recognize that fact and to want to change it. Traditional schooling was not for him and so he took

---

[1] See Neil Gaiman's *Anansi Boys*.

[2] Many of his stories stateside became the stories of Br'er Rabbit, one of the great folk figures of the southern U.S., who was in turn an inspiration for the even more iconic Bugs Bunny.

[3] Such as when he becomes "Aunt Nancy" in the Caribbean.

the road less traveled and began begging. He stood along the road holding a sign that read: "Need Wisdom. Anything Helps. Nyame Bless." As people walked by they'd toss loose bits of knowledge into the large gourd at his feet—the Pythagorean Theorem, how to diagram a sentence, ontology, all kinds of knowledge that no one has any use for. Then he started going door-to-door. "Spare some wisdom?" he'd ask and, eventually, his enormous hollow gourd became quite full indeed. He had acquired all the wisdom that there was in the world and he did so without a single dollar in student loan debt.

Once Anansi had his stockpile of knowledge, he decided he wanted to keep it all to himself. "Where can I put this where no one will be able to steal it?" he asked himself—which was an excellent choice because he himself knew everything and therefore very quickly pointed to a very tall tree nearby. If he were to hide it in the uppermost branches, no one would be able to find, let alone obtain, his precious gourd of wisdom. Being a spider-man, Anansi did whatever a spider can and he strapped the gourd to his belly and began to climb. But the gourd was so big and so heavy with knowledge that the climbing proved more difficult than anticipated.

He could barely get his hands on the tree with the gourd in front of him and so he struggled to progress up the tree.

Along came Anansi's youngest son, who was not even old enough for school, but was, apparently, old enough to wander alone through the west African wilderness. He saw his father's frustrated attempts to climb the tree and said to him: "Daddy, wouldn't it be easier if the gourd was on your back instead of your belly?" "Wouldn't it be easier if the gourd was on your back instead of your belly?" Anansi replied in a mocking tone. "Get lost kid, you bother me." But when his son was out of sight, Anansi spun the strap around so that the gourd hung against his back. The climbing came easy then and Anansi was soon at the top of the tree. Rather than celebrating, though, Anansi was angry. "What good is all the knowledge in the world if a stupid child is still smarter than me?" Anansi may not have been a great father, but he did have a point. And because he had the gourd of wisdom, he knew he had a point. This made him so infuriated that he took the gourd and from the top of the very tall tree he hurled it down to the ground. The gourd shattered, spilling out the entirety of the world's knowledge. People from all over came and scooped up bits of knowledge, some taking a lot, some a little and, in the case of Young Earth Creationists, none at all. But those who had taken the knowledge shared it and the wisdom grew and spread. No one person would have a monopoly on all knowledge, but it would be available to all who sought it.

316

Another version of the story tells us the story of stories. Long ago, we're told, the sky god Nyame owned all stories. One day, Anansi climbed his spider web up to the realm of the gods and asked to buy the stories from Nyame. Not wanting to part with his treasury of tales, Nyame gave a price that he assumed Anansi would never be able to pay: he asked Anansi to capture and bring up to heaven some of the most dangerous and elusive beings in the world. A leopard, a snake, killer wasps, and a fairy.[1] With guile and panache, Anansi tricked each and every one of the creatures and brought them up to Nyame. Nyame, true to his word, turned the stories over to Anansi. This Anansi was not the selfish, temperamental Anansi who tried to hide his gourd of knowledge; this Anansi was a benevolent trickster who willingly let loose the stories for all the world to enjoy.

Anansi made the trip across the Atlantic, as so many people did, in the bottom of a slave ship. His stories provided his people with entertainment and a connection to the world they had lost, as well as offering hope for a better world where any enemy, any challenge, could be defeated with cleverness. It may not be as easy as Anansi made it seem, but with knowledge, creativity, and persistence there is no obstacle that cannot be overcome.

---

[1] The particular creatures he's asked to collect vary somewhat from one version to another. In at least one, Anansi offers to throw in his own mother to sweeten the deal.

Afterword

Mythology Matters

We live in a paradoxical age. Fantastic technologies dreamed up by science fiction writers of yesteryear are now unremarkable commonplaces deeply integrated into the lives of those who can afford them. Notions of identity and self-definition have changed radically in a few short years, and once-immutable characteristics have become remarkably fluid. Cheek by jowl with this futurism, however, ancient mythologies continue to play a powerful role in all realms of human life throughout the world. The words of long-ago desert prophets are invoked by various factions in a variety of wars, and the worship of old gods continues to gain ground in the supposedly post-religious western world.

Mythology permeates our private and public discourse. When our friends, colleagues, and political leaders speak of praying for the victims of violent tragedy, of a deity granting a specific land to members of a single religion, and of the deceased going to a better place, they are forwarding ancient dialogues concerning supernatural figures that listen to our silent thoughts and grant wishes, contracts with otherworldly beings that trump political negotiations, and an invisible essence within human beings that separates from the body at death and travels to another world. In these and many other instances, the worldviews of today are not so different from those of ancient times.

Citizens of the western world are generally familiar with the mythologies of Christianity, Judaism, and Islam. At least, they believe themselves to be. Followers of the Abrahamic religions—the Big Three that share belief in the god of Abraham—often have detailed knowledge of the tales of their own tradition and general familiarity with the figures of the other two. These are the faith systems that are deeply woven into the fabric of our experience. Their intertwined histories and ongoing conflicts continue to affect life today, from the smallest personal interactions to the largest global conflicts. Even those who don't actively believe in the ultimate truth of the myths speak the language of these traditions.

Beside the Abrahamic mythologies stand those of the Greeks and Romans. As a child, my parents—who both long ago left religious orders to become philosophy professors—told me that I could believe whatever I wanted when I

318

grew up, but that I had to know the Abrahamic and Greco-Roman myths in order to be a citizen of the world. Art, music, theater, literature, politics, and popular culture have invoked the gods and heroes of classical antiquity for millennia, and they continue to do so today. These myths are all around us, from politicians who negotiate under the shadows of marble gods to readers who thrill to the latest young adult series featuring the Greek gods interacting with modern children.

Yet there is more to mythology than this. Other myths and other gods also play important roles in our cultural and political lives. From Wagner's operas to Marvel superheroes to Scandinavian metal to the modern religion of Ásatrú, Norse mythology has been and remains a deep well from which to draw wisdom and inspiration. Many roads lead northward, guiding generations or readers, writers, composers, and listeners to tales of Odin and Thor. The novels of J.R.R. Tolkien, the comics of Stan Lee and Jack Kirby, and now cable television programs centered on old Viking heroes and newly returned deities continue to generate interest in the gods, goddesses, giants, dwarves, elves, and dragons of the Norse myths. These myths are the remnants of a religion that was consciously eradicated over long centuries of Christian expansion, but a new version of the religious tradition has arisen that once again celebrates the myths in a spiritual context. Since its founding in Iceland in 1972, the Ásatrú religion has now spread to nearly one hundred countries and has approximately forty thousand followers worldwide.

Many other mythologies have similar stories of survival and revival. Like Norse mythology, the Celtic myths have experienced a notable resurgence since an explosion of interest during the Romantic Era. African mythology has long been embraced by African-Americans interested in reinforcing connections to the lands of their ancestors. Myths of ancient Egypt and Mesopotamia still percolate through human consciousness and manifest in unexpected artistic and literary forms. The indigenous mythologies of the Americas continue to thrill and inspire visitors to ancient sites of celebration and sacrifice. The myths of China and Japan continue to play powerful roles in the cultural and spiritual lives of millions of people around the world.

Engagement with the ancient myths enriches our experience of living. That may seem like an outsized statement, but mythology is an outsized category. The more we learn about the mythologies of the world, the more we both recognize commonality and understand difference. All of these myths arose from human experiences that we all share, but they also developed in specific historical and cultural settings. In our troubled modern world, anything that can help us to find

319

common ground while embracing true diversity is greatly welcome. Enjoy the myths, and be open to learning from them.

Dr. Karl E. H. Seigfried
The Norse Mythology Blog
norsemyth.org

Acknowledgements

Special thanks go out to all those who supported our fundraising campaigns so that we could include all the beautiful art found in this book. Thank you to Shawn Hunt, Matt Smith, Dian Dewi, Harry Guiremand, Sir David Stewart Harris, Taylor Grin, Dave Fernandes, Ryan Bradford, Andrew Gabry, Kaitlin Janecke, Carlos Galvan, Dave McVean, Simon Whitlock, Matthew McArthur, Maria Peak, David Moser, Steve Bloomfield, and Anna Harrison.

This book would not be what it is without the contributions from the many artists who put in a great deal of time and effort for not nearly enough compensation. Please, check out their contact information in the back of the book, follow their work on the various social media and hire them for all your artistic needs. And a very special thanks to Philip Mitri for the beautiful cover design.

The great joy of my professional life has been teaching courses on Mythology at Kendall College of Art and Design. I cannot thank the people at KCAD and Ferris State University enough for giving me the opportunity to teach and to learn from the hundreds of students I've had the pleasure to share a classroom with. Seeing artists (many whom contributed their work to this book) being inspired by mythological characters and stories gave me the inspiration to create this book.

Thanks to Jonathan Pearce and Onus Books for making this dream of mine into a reality. Johno patiently waded through my convoluted syntax and obscure references and helped massage *Myth Education* into what it is now. Which I mean as a compliment, not an accusation.

A multi-continental team of proof readers, Evan Heird and Matthew McArthur, meticulously combed through the text to make sure all the grammar and punctuation was real goodly did; they're work is mush appreciated.

Thanks also to Cas Tokarski for saving my computer, and with it, this book.

I would be remiss if I did not also thank Jeremy Beahan for being the one who got me my job teaching Mythology, because he didn't want it. Whether he wants to admit it or not, he has been a lifesaver and one of the most important influences on my professional, philosophical, and personal development.

Most importantly, I need to thank my wife and children. Not only would none of this be possible without them, it wouldn't be worth doing if not for them. Thank you to Shiloh, Cassidy, Peyton, Avi, Valkyrie, and Kris for absolutely everything.

Selected Bibliography

Ashkenazi, Michael. *Handbook of Japanese mythology.* Oxford: Oxford U Press, 2008.

Belcher, Stephen Paterson. *African Myths of Origin.* London: Penguin, 2005.

Bellows, Henry Adams. *The Poetic Edda: the Mythological Poems.* Mineola, NY: Dover Publications, 2004.

Birrell, Anne. *Chinese Mythology: an Introduction.* Baltimore: Johns Hopkins U Press, 1999.

Brown, Nancy Marie. *Song of the Vikings: Snorri and the making of Norse myths.* Basingstoke: Palgrave Macmillan, 2014.

Budge, E. A. Wallis. *The Egyptian Book of the Dead: the Papyrus of Ani.* New York: Barnes & Noble , 2005.

Callaway, Henry. *Nursery tales, traditions, and histories of the Zulus.* Springvale, Natal: J.A. Blair, 1868.

Chamberlain, Basil Hall. *The Kojiki: Records of Ancient Matters.* Rutland, VT: C. E. Tuttle, 1993.

Crawford, Jackson. *The Poetic Edda: Stories of the Norse Gods and Heroes.* Indianapolis: Hackett Publishing Company, Inc., 2015.

Dalley, Stephanie. *Myths from Mesopotamia: Creation, the Flood, Gilgamesh, and Others.* Oxford: Oxford U Press, 2008.

Davis, Kenneth C. *Don't Know Much About Mythology: Everything You Need to Know About the Greatest Stories in Human History but Never Learned.* New York: Harper, 2006.

The Epic of Gilgamesh. Harmondsworth, Middlesex: Penguin , 1972.

Faulkner, Raymond O., and James P. Allen. *The Ancient Egyptian Book of the Dead.* New York: Fall River Press, 2010.

Ford, Clyde F. *The Hero With an African Face.* New York: Bantam, 2000.

Frankel, Valerie Estelle. *From Girl to Goddess: the Heroine's Journey Through Myth and Legend.* Jefferson, NC: McFarland & Co., 2010.

Gantz, Jeffrey. *Early Irish Myths and Sagas.* Harmondsworth: Penguin, 1988.

Gómez-Cano, Grisel. *The Return to Coatlicue: Goddesses and Warladies in Mexican Folklore.* LaVergne, TN: Xlibris, 2010.

Hahn, Theophilus. *Tsuni-Goam: the Supreme Being to the Khoi-Khoi.* London: Trubner, 1881.

Hathaway, Nancy. *The Friendly Guide to Mythology: a Mortal's Companion to the Fantastical Realm of Gods, Goddesses, Monsters, and Heroes.* New York, NY: Viking, 2004.

Heidel, Alexander. *The Babylonian Genesis: the Story of Creation.* Chicago: U of Chicago Press, 1993.

Hyde, Lewis. *Trickster Makes This World: Mischief, Myth, and Art.* New York: Farrar, Straus and Giroux, 2010.

Kherdian, David. *Monkey: a Journey to the West: a Retelling of the Chinese Folk Novel by Wu Ch'eng-en.* Boston: Shambhala, 2005.

Kramer, Samuel Noah. *Sumerian Mythology: a Study of Spiritual and Literary Achievement in the Third Millennium B.C.* Philadelphia: U of Pennsylvania Press, 1998.

Larrington, Carolyne. *The Poetic Edda.* Oxford: Oxford U Press, 2014.

Leeming, David, and Jake Page. *Goddess: Myths of the Feminine Divine.* New York: Oxford, 1994.

Leeming, David Adams, and Jake Page. *The Mythology of Native North America.* Norman: U of Oklahoma Press, 1998.

Lindow, John. *Norse Mythology.* Oxford: Oxford U Press, 2005.

Pinch, Geraldine. *A Guide to the Gods, Goddesses and Traditions of Ancient Egypt.* Oxford: Oxford U Press, 2002.

Pinch, Geraldine. *Egyptian Myth: A Very Short Introduction (Very short introduction ; 106).* N.p.: Oxford U Press, 2004.

Rolleston, T. W. *Celtic Myths and Legends.* New York: Dover Publications, 1990.

Rosenberg, Donna. *World Mythology: an Anthology of the Great Myths and Epics.* 2nd ed. Lincolnwood, Ill. U.S.A.: National Textbook Co., 1994.

Saunders, Chas, and Peter J. Allen. *Book of the Gods: 600 Gods from 20 Pantheons Explained.* Stroud: History Press, 2010.

Simpson, William Kelly., and Robert Kriech Ritner. *The Literature of Ancient Egypt: an Anthology of Stories, Instructions, and Poetry.* New Haven CT: Yale U Press, 2003.

Sproul, Barbara C. *Primal Myths: Creation Myths the World.* San Francisco: HarperSanFrancisco, 1991.

"The Story of Hlakanyana." *Xhosa Folk-Lore: The Story Of Hlakanyana.* Retrieved January 12, 2017, from http://www.sacred-texts.com/afr/xft/xft11.htm

Sturluson, Snorri. *The Prose Edda: Norse Mythology.* Trans. Jesse L. Byock. London: Penguin , 2005.

Tedlock, Dennis. *Popol Vuh: the Mayan Book of the Dawn of Life.* New York: Touchstone, 1996.

Willis, Roy G., ed. *World Mythology.* New York: Metro, 2012.

Wu, Chengen. *Monkey.* Trans. Arthur Waley. New York: Grove Press, 2006.

Yang, Lihui, Deming An, and Jessica Anderson. Turner. *Handbook of Chinese Mythology.* Oxford: Oxford U Press, 2008.

Yoda, Hiroko, and Matt Alt. *Yokai Attack!: the Japanese Monster Survival Guide.* Tokyo: Tuttle, 2012.

Artist Contact Information

Jon Alderink (*Mawu*)
Website: alderinkart.com
Instagram: @jonalderink
Twitter: @JonAlderink

Adrianna Allen (*Panku*)
Website: photonillustration.com
Email: photonillustration@gmail.com
Instagram: @adriannaallen4space

Annamarie Borowiak (*Maat, Tuan Mac Starn, Mami Wata*)
Email: borovee.create@gmail.com
Instagram: @cosmic_creates

Tessa Brown (*Raiden, Celtic Intro*)
Website: tessabrownarts.weebly.com
Email: tessahbrown@gmail.com

Jerry Butler (*Jotun, Huitzilopochtli, Oya*)
Email: jbjab88@gmail.com

Ashley Campos (*Nu Gua, Finn McCool, Freyr, Hai-uri, Indigenous American Intro*)
Email: asheface.illustration@gmail.com
Twitter: @asheface
Tumblr: asheface-illustration.tumblr.com

Mandy Cantarella (*Mesopotamian Intro, Kappa, Valkyries, Windigo*)
Website: mandycantarellaart.com
Email: cantarella409@yahoo.com

Cynthia Lynn Cooper (*Xingtian, Mwindo*)
Website: DivergentDepictions.com
Email: divergentdaydreams@gmail.com

Madeleine Graumlich (*Ra, Amaterasu, the Morrigan*)
Email: mjgraumlich.illustrations@gmail.com
Instagram: @mjgraumlich_illustrations

Alayna Guza (*Xipe Totec*)
Website: photonillustration.com
Email: photonillustration@gmail.com
Instagram: @alaynaguza

Mallory Heiges (*Jade Emperor, Brigid*)
Email: msheiges@gmailcom

Naomi K Illustration (*Xiwangmu, Itherther*)
Website: naomikillustration.com
Email: naomik.illustration@gmail.com

Christian Jackson (*Bastet, Lugh*)
Email: jacksc53@ferris.edu

Rayne Karfonta (*Zao Jun*)
Instagram: @karfontafonta
Facebook: karfontaart

Christopher Kraklau (*Osiris*)
Email: ckraklauart@gmail.com
Facebook: ChrisKraklauArt

Aaron Kroodsma (*Susanoo*)
Instagram: @pykra

Sarah Lindstrom (*Yi, the Dagda, Sif*)
Website: sarahlindstromart.com
Email: sarahlindstromart@gmail.com

Emily Luyk (*Fomorians, White Buffalo Woman*)
Website: emilyluykart.com
Email: emilyluyk@gmail.com

David Manderville (*Gilgamesh, Yu, Cu Chulainn, Norse Intro, Balder*)
Twitter: @chromatic_gray

Taryn Marcinowski (*Gonggong*)
Email: tarynmarcinowski@gmail.com
Facebook: TarynIllustration

Ella Newman (*Izanami & Izanagi*)
Website: ellasillustrations.com

Matthew Olack (*Kuan Yin*)
Website: mattolack.com

Darian Papineau (*Egyptian Intro, Bes, Ea, Hero Twins, Eshu*)
Email: sugardogstudio@gmail.com
Facebook: sugardogstudio
Artstation: Darian Papineau

Trevor Plaggemeyer (*Quetzalcoatl*)
Email: trevorplag@gmail.com

Lindsay N. Poulos (*Hachiman, Tengu*)
Email: greekgoddess09@gmail.com
Instagram: @ladyrandombox
Facebook: LindsayPoulos
Twitter: @ladyrandombox
DeviantArt: lindsay-n-poulos.deviantart.com
Art Station: Lindsay Poulos
YouTube: Lady Random Box

Clayton Prell (*Aesir & Vanir, Thor*)
Website: claytonprell.com
Email: claytonprell@gmail.com
Instagram: @claytonprell

Caitlin Rausch (*Horus, Thoth, Waka*)
Website:caitsart.com
Email: caitlin@caitsart.com
Instagram: @cait.rausch
Facebook: caitsart

Matt Renneker (*Marduk, Cagn*)
Email: renneker.matt@gmail.com

Whitney Ruhlman (*Shichi Fukujin, Tlazolteotl, Mbaba Mwana Waresa*)
Email: whitneyruhlman@gmail.com
Instagram: @wild.rumpus

Malena Salinas (*Sekhmet, Chinese Intro, Lei Gong & Dien Mu, Monkey, Kitsune, Tanuki, Coyote, Blue Jay*)
Email: ABoxDino@gmail.com
DeviantArt: BoxDino

Ian Sedgwick (*Loki, Tyr*)
Email: ian.sedgwick99@gmail.com
Twitter: @IanSedgwick99
DeviantArt: Edoki
Tumblr: lord-bazil.tumblr.com

Christian Sitterlet (*Khepri, Ishtar, Fu Xi, Tsukumogami, Loki's Children, Tezcatlipoca, Heitsi-eibib*)
Email: cnsitterlet@gmail.com
Instagram: @cnsitterlet

Kyle Smith (*Japanese Intro*)
Website: torkirby.com

Tyler Space (*Anubis, Fudo Myo-o, Heimdall*)
Instagram: @tylerspace.art

Chloe Stewart (*Kishimojin, Coatlicue, African Intro*)
Website: chloe.stewart.myportfolio.com
Email: chloe.stewart05@gmail.com
Instagram: @stewy_art
Twitter: @stewy_art

David Stokes (*Seth, Hlakanyana*)
Email: d.mstokes.1993@gmail.com
Instagram: @davidms_93

Allie Wass (*Hathor, Sedna, Anansi*)
Website: alliewass.com
Email: allie.wass@gmail.com
Instagram: @alliewass_illustration

Andrew Zesiger (*Ragnarok*)
Website: andrewzesiger.artstation.com

Zhangrui Zhou (*Yggdrasil*)
Email: zhouz@ferris.edu

Qing Zhu *(Tsukiyomi, Oshun)*
Website: zhuquing1996.wixsite.com/cyan
Email: zhu.qing1996@hotmail.com

Amanda Zylstra *(Isis, Ereshkigal, Tuatha de Danann, Odin, Freyja)*
Email: amandaszylstra@gmail.com
Instagram: @ritualoffering

David Fletcher